T0386168

GENDER, NATION AND THE FORMATION OF THE
TWENTIETH-CENTURY MEXICAN LITERARY CANON

LEGENDA

LEGENDA, founded in 1995 by the European Humanities Research Centre of the University of Oxford, is now a joint imprint of the Modern Humanities Research Association and Routledge. Titles range from medieval texts to contemporary cinema and form a widely comparative view of the modern humanities, including works on Arabic, Catalan, English, French, German, Greek, Italian, Portuguese, Russian, Spanish, and Yiddish literature. An Editorial Board of distinguished academic specialists works in collaboration with leading scholarly bodies such as the Society for French Studies and the British Comparative Literature Association.

MHRA

The Modern Humanities Research Association (MHRA) encourages and promotes advanced study and research in the field of the modern humanities, especially modern European languages and literature, including English, and also cinema. It also aims to break down the barriers between scholars working in different disciplines and to maintain the unity of humanistic scholarship in the face of increasing specialization. The Association fulfils this purpose primarily through the publication of journals, bibliographies, monographs and other aids to research.

LONDON AND NEW YORK

Routledge is a global publisher of academic books, journals and online resources in the humanities and social sciences. Founded in 1836, it has published many of the greatest thinkers and scholars of the last hundred years, including Adorno, Einstein, Russell, Popper, Wittgenstein, Jung, Bohm, Hayek, McLuhan, Marcuse and Sartre. Today Routledge is one of the world's leading academic publishers in the Humanities and Social Sciences. It publishes thousands of books and journals each year, serving scholars, instructors, and professional communities worldwide.

www.routledge.com

Gender, Nation and the Formation of the Twentieth-Century Mexican Literary Canon

SARAH E. L. BOWSKILL

Modern Humanities Research Association and Routledge

2011

First published 2011

Published by the
Modern Humanities Research Association and Routledge
2 Park Square, Milton Park, Abingdon, Oxon OX14 4RN
711 Third Avenue, New York, NY 10017, USA

LEGENDA is an imprint of the
Modern Humanities Research Association and Routledge

Routledge is an imprint of the Taylor & Francis Group, an informa business

© Modern Humanities Research Association and Taylor & Francis 2011

ISBN 978-1-907975-05-9 (hbk)

CONTENTS

ACKNOWLEDGEMENTS

This book is a substantially revised version of my doctoral thesis completed at the University of Manchester in 2008. First and foremost, therefore, I would like to thank my supervisors Professor Hilary Owen and Dr Patience Schell for their invaluable help and encouragement, and for preparing me for life after my thesis. I would also like to thank my examiners Professor Nuala Finnegan and Dr Par Kumaraswami for their feedback and ongoing interest in my work.

Thank you also to Professor Catherine Davies for her contribution to the early stages of this project and her continuing support, to Dr Jon Beasley-Murray for his commitment to and enthusiasm for Latin American Cultural Studies and to Dr Susan Frenk for introducing me to Mexican literature as an undergraduate.

In writing my thesis and my book I was greatly facilitated by working in a supportive and stimulating environment first in the Department of Spanish, Portuguese and Latin American Studies at the University of Manchester and later in the Department of Modern Languages at Swansea University, and my thanks go to all my friends and colleagues at both institutions. This book has benefited considerably from the generous help and advice of Dr Graham Nelson and the editorial team at Legenda and the comments of anonymous readers — thank you all. I am deeply grateful to the Arts and Humanities Research Council (AHRC) for their financial support in the form of a doctoral award which enabled me to pursue my studies at doctoral level and undertake fieldwork in Mexico. During my fieldwork in Mexico City, I was assisted by staff who gave generously of their time and expertise to help my research. Thanks, in particular, to the staff at the Hemeroteca Nacional, the Archivo General de la Nación, the archive of the Secretaría de Educación Pública and the Centro Nacional de Información y Promoción de la Literatura.

Personal and heartfelt thanks to: my family — Mum, Dad, Edward and my grandparents, and, of course, to Rob. Thanks to you I believe I can achieve anything.

★ ★ ★ ★ ★

Part of Chapter 2 appeared in a different form in 'Yo también, Adelita: A National Allegory of the Mexican Revolution and a Call for Women's Suffrage', in *Revolucionarias: Conflict and Gender in Latin American Narratives by Women*, ed. by Par Kumaraswami and Niamh Thornton (Oxford: Peter Lang, 2007), pp. 139–64. I thank the editors for their advice in the writing of that paper and Peter Lang for permission to include the material in this book.

Part of Chapter 4 appeared in a different form in 'Women, Violence and the Mexican Cristero Wars as Represented in *Los recuerdos del porvenir* and *La ciudad y el viento*', *Modern Language Review*, 104.2 (2009), 438–52. I thank the editors of

MLR for their advice in the writing of that paper and for permission to include the material in this book.

The cover image depicting the central campus of Ciudad Universitaria, UNAM, including the Rectory and Central Library, was provided by IISUE/AHUNAM/ Colección Carlos Lazo-Saúl Molina and I am grateful for permission to use this image.

NOTE ON TRANSLATIONS

All translations in this book are by the author with the exception of the English translations of *El indio* in Chapter 1 which are taken from Gregorio López y Fuentes, *El indio*, trans. by Anita Brenner (New York: Frederick Ungar, 1937, repr. 1961).

LIST OF ABBREVIATIONS

AGN/LCR	Archivo General de la Nación. Galería 3, Presidentes: Fondo Lázaro Cárdenas
CNIPL	Centro Nacional de Información y Promoción de la Literatura
CNIPL/EXP.AM	Documento Hemerográfico perteneciente al Archivo Hemerográfico de Escritores del CNIPL del INBA. Expediente Ángeles Mastretta
CNIPL/EXP.DC	Documento Hemerográfico perteneciente al Archivo Hemerográfico de Escritores del CNIPL del INBA. Expediente Dolores Castro
CNIPL/EXP.SP	Documento Hemerográfico perteneciente al Archivo Hemerográfico de Escritores del CNIPL del INBA. Expediente Sergio Pitol
CNIPL/EXP.sXIX/1	Documento Hemerográfico perteneciente al Archivo Hemerográfico de Escritores del CNIPL del INBA. Expediente Escritores del siglo XIX Expediente 1
CONACULTA	Consejo Nacional para la Cultura y las Artes
CTM	Confederación de Trabajadores Mexicanos
FCE	Fondo de Cultura Económica
FR/CF	Biblioteca Nacional. Fondo Reservado. Fondo Silvino M. González. Fichero Bio-Bibliográfico: Carlos Fuentes
FR/DC	Biblioteca Nacional. Fondo Reservado. Fondo Silvino M. González. Fichero Bio-Bibliográfico: Dolores Castro
FR/GLF	Biblioteca Nacional. Fondo Reservado. Fondo Silvino M. González. Fichero Bio-Bibliográfico: Gregorio López y Fuentes
INBA	Instituto Nacional de Bellas Artes
PCM	Partido Comunista Mexicano
PLM	Partido Liberal Mexicano
PNR	Partido Nacional Revolucionario
PRI	Partido Revolucionario Institucional
PRM	Partido Revolucionario Mexicano
SEP	Secretaría de Educación Pública
Supl.	Suplemento de / Supplement of
UNAM	Universidad Nacional Autónoma de México

INTRODUCTION

This book examines the mechanisms, power structures and values that underpinned the formation of the twentieth-century Mexican literary canon. I ask why some novels became canonical while others were soon forgotten and why most canonical novels are male-authored. I challenge the still widespread assumption that if woman-authored texts were excluded it was because they were not good enough to be included in the literary canon. I argue that interpretive strategies played a decisive role in restricting women authors' access to the canon as it is represented in histories of Mexican literature.[1] Whilst this book addresses questions about how the Mexican novelistic canon was formed and how it might be re-formed it is my belief that the insights and approaches in this book may be usefully applied and tested in other contexts.

My focus on the creation of a Mexican national literature reflects the important role culture has played in post-revolutionary nation-building. The value of studying national literatures has been brought into question by approaches which emphasize broader spheres of influence and wider networks of exchange. However, in this case, a national focus is appropriate because it acknowledges the fact that the Mexican national canon is underpinned by different values to those which led to the creation of a canon of Latin American literature, which included Mexican literature, in the United States.[2] By emphasizing the national over the international or transnational I am able to highlight the circumstances in which most literature by Mexican authors was first produced and received whilst also drawing attention to the impact of international acclaim on Mexican author's status within Mexico. Whether or not literary canons should be tied to nation-building agendas will be discussed at a later point.

My analysis of six twentieth-century Mexican novels asks not only how value was produced and by whom but also what was valued and why. Following the recommendation of Pierre Bourdieu, to ascertain how value is produced and by whom, I locate each work in the context of the literary field in which it was produced and received.[3] I highlight the circumstances in which the novels were published and examine how they were received and interpreted by reviewers. I use contemporary reviews to identify how individual texts were read and what was valued and draw on historical circumstances to explain why. In addition, I show how new readings can be produced and how texts could be re-evaluated if we adopt alternative interpretive strategies. I thereby assume that meaning and value are not inherent in the text. Rather, as Stanley Fish has argued, meaning comes from the application of interpretive strategies which are produced and shared by interpretive communities so that 'there is no single way of reading that is correct or natural, only "ways of reading" that are extensions of community perspectives' (16). Bourdieu similarly suggests that the 'objective structures of the field of production' help to create 'categories of perception which structure the perception and appreciation of its products' which account for the alignment that exists between the critic, the newspaper and the reader (95). Inclusion in the Mexican national canon, therefore, is seen to depend on an interpretive community of similarly located, privileged readers who have learned the same way of reading and so agree on, or share, an interpretation of a text. This common interpretive strategy leads them to read texts in the same way and to value and reject texts according to shared criteria and assumptions. They are privileged because they have a platform from which to influence and shape the readings of others.

Debates about the canon, what constitutes the canon, how it is formed and what ought and ought not to be included have elicited passionate responses from academics of differing backgrounds and political persuasions. Some of the most recent contributions to the debate have come from the field of Cultural Studies, which questions the very desirability of a canon. Aiming to abolish the canon, however, is counter-productive, serving only to further conceal the mechanisms and power structures at work in selecting what is considered to be 'great literature'. Instead, we must look more closely at canon formation and consider ways in which the canon may be reformed as well as re-formed.

This study takes regular inclusion in histories, dictionaries and encyclopaedias of Mexican literature published in Mexico as evidence of a text being canonical. According to Verity Smith, writing about the canon in Latin America:

> anthologies and works of reference — such as dictionaries and encyclopaedias of literature — are quite reliable guides to the literary canon of a given period because it is not part of their remit to take risk by, say giving prominence to controversial or experimental works.[4]

Literary histories create value, publicize, and make the works they include more accessible (V. Smith, 46). Nonetheless, it should not be forgotten that writing literary history is a selective and subjective process in which texts are typically selected for a purpose, for example, to illustrate the development of a national conscience.[5] Beatriz González-Stephan notes that since they were first published, histories of literature in Latin America have been closely connected to processes of nation-building.[6] Histories of literature were first produced in Latin America between 1850 and 1860. At a time of growing political stability, the new nations aimed to differentiate themselves from Spain and from their new neighbours and foster nation-building by laying claim to a distinctive literary tradition (212, 220, 125–27). By representing the nation in a book it could be demonstrably shown to exist and to have a history (214).

According to González-Stephan, one cycle of literary histories ended in Mexico in 1910 with the publication of José María Vigil's *Historia de la literatura mexicana* (213). It is my assertion that a second cycle of literary histories began in Mexico in the 1920s. At this time, the post-revolutionary nation was stabilizing and new histories of Mexican literature were published that embodied and aimed to unify the new nation that had emerged from the revolution of 1910–17. Furthermore, the

1920s saw the intellectual elite trying to define national literature.[7] Just as González-Stephan claims that histories of literature in the nineteenth-century expressed the 'preferencias ideológicas del sector dominante' (212) [ideological preferences of the dominant sector] so too, twentieth-century histories of literature expressed the ideologies of the new elite.

Twentieth-century histories, dictionaries and encyclopaedia of Mexican literature show a remarkable degree of consensus over a significant period of time and they also reveal a clearly evident process for adding new texts and authors to the tradition. The reader of successive editions of histories of literature by Julio Jiménez Rueda, Emmanuel Carballo, Carlos González Peña and José Luis Martínez will soon notice how new authors and texts are simply added on to the list of authors included in the previous edition to create a Mexican canonical tradition.[8] In the case of Jiménez Rueda the process of adding authors to the pre-existing tradition was made particularly transparent by the subtitle 'edición puesta al día y aumentada con buen número de notas bibliográficas' [updated and expanded with a good number of bibliographical notes]. Women authors, with few exceptions, are not consistently included in these texts and so we can conclude that women have been largely excluded from the twentieth-century Mexican canon. All of the male authors in this study belong to the canonical tradition as it is embodied in histories of literature while the women authors are rarely named.

Given that I identify the canon with regular inclusion in histories of Mexican literature we may look to these texts to answer the question how is the canon formed. The prefaces and contents pages of these numerous volumes suggest that aesthetic quality was not the main criteria used by the authors and editors to select works to be included. The compilers of these volumes were more concerned with identifying texts and authors that, in the words of José Luis Martínez, were 'representativos de la época' [representative of the period] (*La expresión nacional*, p. 5). The nationalist intent behind the works is evident in Carlos González Peña's suggestion that it was one's patriotic duty to read these texts and that, through his work, he aimed to 'revivir una tradición espiritual de la que debemos gloriarnos y a la que insistentemente hay que conocer y amar' [revive a spiritual tradition of which we should be proud and which we must persistently know and love] (*Prefacio*). Furthermore, rather than being organized according to literary movements or trends, post-revolutionary histories of literature were usually presented in terms of historical periods, such as the Conquest, Independence, the *Porfiriato* and the present, which reflected the prevailing nationalist ideologies. Histories of twentieth-century Mexican literature thus presented a canon in which inclusion was based on national and political rather than aesthetic concerns.

As I have noted, few women authors are included in the Mexican canon as it is represented in histories of Mexican literature. The exclusion of women from the canon has been a central concern of feminist scholars, some of whom have attempted to address women's traditional exclusion from the canon by establishing a competing canon of 'women's writing'. This canon is well represented in Martha Robles' *La sombra fugitiva. Escritoras en la cultura nacional* and in the collection of essays by Fabienne Bradu, *Señas particulares: Escritora. Ensayos sobre escritoras mexicanas del siglo XX.*[9] Following the publication of these works, there has been a growing tendency to identify a *boom femenino* in writing by women in Mexico in the 1980s and 90s. However, the work of those authors most associated with the *boom femenino* is frequently dismissed as 'popular fiction' and omitted from histories of literature.[10] I resist placing women authors in a separate canon in which inclusion is primarily based on the author's gender because, in my view, this is not helpful. The separation of woman-authored texts from those by their male counterparts further marginalizes, if not excludes, novels by women from the category of 'literature'. One of the main aims of the present study, therefore, is to propose and test a new approach which judges male- and female-authored novels against the same criteria and according to the same standard as a means to produce a reformed national canon.

Although I take a different approach in rejecting the creation of a separate canon of women authors as means to challenge women's exclusion from the national canon, this study owes a considerable debt to the work of feminist scholars who paved the way by recognizing a tradition of writing by women in Mexico.[11] At the forefront of this tradition are Nellie Campobello, Rosario Castellanos, Elena Garro and Elena Poniatowska. These authors, who are now thought of as part of the canon and included, although by no means consistently, in histories of literature, seem to present a challenge to my assertion that women are excluded from the Mexican novelistic canon. However, it is important to recognize the effort that has been required to recover even these few women for literary history. As we become accustomed to their names appearing in histories of literature and reading academic articles about their work it is all too easy to forget that, when first published, their novels were often overlooked. Campobello's *Cartucho: relatos de la lucha en el Norte de México*, for example, is now considered a classic novel of the Mexican Revolution but, as Elena Poniatowska notes, when it was published in 1931: 'En un mundo de machismo, nadie la toma en cuenta, y — ¡por favor! — ¿qué hace una mujer en medio de la fiesta de las balas? ¡Sólo eso nos faltaba!' [In a world of *machismo*, no one paid her any attention, and — please — what's a woman doing in the middle of this party of bullets? That's just what we needed!][12]

Rosario Castellanos' novels *Balún Canán* (1957) and *Oficio de tinieblas* (1962) were likewise not well received when first published and José Joaquín Blanco notes that Castellanos was 'ninguneada en los medios culturales' [ignored in the cultural media].[13] Poniatowska explains: 'Por escribir sobre los indios y sus conflictos a Rosario se le consideró provinciana y caserita' (*Crónica literaria*, 136) [Rosario was considered provincial and homely for writing about the Indian and their conflicts]. This opinion is expressed in the appendix of the tenth edition of Carlos González Peña's *Historia de la literatura mexicana* in which *Balún canán* is described as

> un relato en que surge la vida social del pueblo de Chiapas, complicada y mal organizada, con sus prejuicios de clase, la explotación del indio, todo en torno y en el fondo de un dramático juego de sentimientos y pasiones en cuyo primer plano está siempre la sensibilidad de la niña, eje del relato (1975, 309).

> [a story in which the social life of Chiapas comes to the fore, complicated and badly organized, with its class prejudices and the exploitation of the Indian all

around and as the background to a dramatic game of feelings and passions in which the sensitivities of the little girl at the heart of the story are always at the forefront.]

Oficio de tinieblas was also seen as 'otra buena muestra de la devoción de la autora por su lugar de origen, y corona con gran éxito, la corriente de la llamada novela indigenista' (González Peña 1975, 309) [another good example of the author's devotion to her birthplace which crowns with great success the current of the so-called *indigenista* novel]. On the surface, the comments are positive, but by associating the novel with the provinces and with the *indigenista* tradition, which was at its height in the 1930s, there is an inference that the novel is somewhat *passé* and of minor interest as Poniatowska notes 'a Rosario se le tachó de "indigenista" (por lo tanto de menor)' (*Las siete cabritas*, 125) [they labelled Rosario 'indigenista' (and therefore minor)]. In order to be incorporated into the twentieth-century Mexican canon novels needed to be interpreted as addressing issues of national concern and, regardless of the acknowledged qualities of Castellanos' novel, *indigenismo* was no longer the pressing concern that it had been when Gregorio López y Fuentes won the *Premio Nacional de Literatura* [National Prize for Literature] in 1935 for his *indigenista* novel, *El indio*, making Castellanos' novels a curiosity at best for contemporary commentators whose attention had turned to Mexico City as the site for mid-twentieth-century Mexican literature.[14]

According to Catherine Grant, Castellanos was finally incorporated into the canon because she was championed by feminist critics in the 1970s and 1980s who successfully argued for her inclusion.[15] Grant notes that the task of recovering Castellanos' *oeuvre* required 'the work of several generations of academic critics in the 1970s and 1980s', alongside 'the interventions of a host of Mexican women writers who happily and, for the first time, noisily acknowledged their debt to Castellanos' (posthumously successful) struggle to be heard as a woman author' (vii). Blanco proposes an alternative explanation for the growth in interest in Castellanos' work following her death in 1974: 'Finalmente, con su nombramiento de embajadora y de ejemplo echeverrista de la mujer mexicana, y su muerte lamentable, pasó a encarnar un mito nacional' (*Crónica literaria*, 488) [Finally, when she was named ambassador and an example of President Echeverría's Mexican woman, followed by her pitiful death, she came to embody a national myth]. In the case of Elena Garro events in her life also contributed to her work being acknowledged when it might otherwise have gone unnoticed by the critical establishment.

A rather descriptive, but generally favourable, review of Garro's *Los recuerdos del porvenir* (1963) by Huberto Batis was published in *La Cultura en México*, the supplement of *Siempre* in February 1964.[16] The device of having the town of Ixtepec as the narrator was considered 'más eficaz que molesto' [more effective than irritating], Garro was said to have produced 'una hazaña en la literatura mexicana, pues consigue pensar el Tiempo junto con el Espacio' [an achievement in Mexican literature in managing to think about Time as well as Space] (Batis, 41–42). To conclude, Batis described Garro's first novel as 'pasmosa' (42) [breathtaking]. Emmanuel Carballo, however, recalls that, although *Los recuerdos del porvenir* is now a celebrated novel, when it was published: 'Según recuerdo no hubo muchas reseñas del libro. Elena siempre ha tenido sus *fans* y sus enemigos.' [As I recall there were not many reviews of the book. Elena has always had her fans and her enemies].[17] The case studies in this book suggest that the initial reception of a text is often decisive in determining whether or not it will be incorporated into the Mexican canon and so the critical silence Carballo remembers surrounding the publication of *Los recuerdos del porvenir* did not bode well. Carballo continued to explain that Garro's 'enemies' were

> todas las personas que atacaron a Rulfo en 1955 diciendo que *Pedro Páramo* era una novela reaccionaria. Del mismo modo, hubo toda una campaña para decir que Elena Garro era una escritora reaccionaria. Ahora, eso de reaccionaria podemos discutirlo, aunque yo creo que no son las cuestiones ideológicas el propósito fundamental de sus obras, sino más bien la desdicha, la dicha, el amor, la inteligencia, etc. Fue atacada muy duramente [...] (Batis, 77).

> [all those who attacked Rulfo in 1955 saying that *Pedro Páramo* was a reactionary novel. In the same way, there was a campaign to say that Elena Garro was a reactionary writer. Now, we could debate whether or not she was reactionary, but I do not think that ideological issues are fundamental to her work; rather, misfortune, luck, love, intelligence etc are. She was severely criticized.]

Carballo's comments reveal that Garro's novel was interpreted as being backwards looking, probably because of its rural setting or, as in his case, it was seen as being nothing to do with topical issues. The novel, therefore, was not in keeping with the prevailing mood of the time and so did not meet the requirements for canonical national literature.

The reception of Garro's later work was further complicated by a widespread tendency 'to conflate Garro's life and work' in criticism and journalism.[18] According to Rebecca E. Biron, the blending of 'sociocultural commentary' with 'individual history', which is characteristic of Garro's later work, presents a significant problem for the Mexican reception of her work (140). Garro's refusal to respect the private/public divide, Biron argues, has led to 'Mexico's current ambivalent reception of her' (150). This study suggests that woman-authored novels like Garro's which were seen as blurring the division between public and private did not fare well in the twentieth-century Mexican literary canon and that texts which were interpreted as prioritizing the public sphere were more likely to become canonical.

In Mexico, interpretation and evaluation of Garro's work was influenced by her private life which was perhaps also responsible for the interest of US academics in her work, which, Luis Enrique Ramírez suggests, also led to further attention in Mexico; he writes: 'Como suele ocurrir con los escritores mexicanos, la revaloración de la obra de Elena Garro partió no de aquí sino del extranjero, principalmente Estados Unidos, donde el interés en su obra a nivel académico resulta notable' (45) [As usually occurs with Mexican authors, the revalorization of the work of Elena Garro did not come from here but from abroad, principally from the United States, where there is notable interest in her work at an academic level].[19] For both Mexican and US critics interest in Garro frequently stems from the fact that, between 1937 and 1959, she was married to one of the most important figures in the Mexican cultural milieu of the second half of the twentieth-century and the 1990 Nobel laureate, Octavio Paz. As Poniatowska, writes:

Es difícil separar la obra de la vida de Elena Garro porque, más que la de otros escritores, su obra es autobiográfica y porque su vida — más que la de otros escritores — suscita el morbo y la curiosidad. Claro, el hecho de haber estado casada con Octavio Paz es primordial (*Las siete cabritas*, 124–25).

[It is difficult to separate the life of Elena Garro from her work because, more than in the case of other writers, her work is autobiographical and because her life — more than in the case of other writers — elicits morbid pleasure and curiosity.]

Garro's controversial involvement in the politics of 1968 and the Tlatelolco massacre, details of which began to emerge as government documents were declassified, combined with her subsequent exile and return to Mexico in 1991 only served to attract more attention to her work.[20] Clearly, not all of the lives of women authors will elicit the kind of interest Garro's attracted nor is it desirable that women authors receive attention because of their private lives even if it leads to their work being recognized. More effective mechanisms for incorporating women novelists into the canon are required.

This study focuses exclusively on the Mexican novelistic canon. It should be noted, however, that women have enjoyed greater recognition as poets, short story writers and authors of *testimonio* and *crónicas*, all of which, to a greater or lesser extent, have been accorded a different, if not always lesser, status to 'literature' in the context of twentieth-century Mexican national letters. Elena Poniatowska is a case in point of an author who has achieved significant national and international recognition for her journalism and for texts which entail, to use Blanco's word, 'inventar con grabadura' (*Crónica literaria*, 509) [inventing with a tape recorder]. The vast majority of Poniatowska's texts are not novels but fictionalized biographies and texts which document social and gender inequality and political corruption including, for example, *Hasta no verte Jesús mío* (1969), *La noche de Tlatelolco* (1971), *Querido Diego te abraza Quiela* (1978), *Fuerte es el silencio* (1980) and *Tinísima* (1992). Poniatowska's novel, *Flor de lis*, however, did not get the favourable response one might expect given her status as a respected journalist and chronicler. In his 1988 review, Blanco noted that the novel 'toca terrenos poco frecuentados en la literatura mexicana' (*Crónica literaria*, 373) [touches on areas seldom visited by Mexican literature]. He acknowledged the novel's qualities in reproducing the atmosphere and context in question but concluded that '*La flor de lis* no se propone reportajes o retratos de vastas situaciones o conjuntos sociales o intelectuales, sino la recuperación conmovida de la educación sentimental de una mujer — mexicana, católica, burguesa — de mediados de este siglo' (*Crónica literaria*, 373) [*La flor de lis* does not aim to provide reports or portraits of vast situations or social or intellectual groups but tries to sympathetically recover the sentimental education of a Catholic, bourgeois woman in mid-century Mexico]. Blanco is typical of many male reviewers in late twentieth-century Mexico who are not openly hostile to woman-authored novels but whose comments reveal that they continue to view novels by women only in the context of the marginalized category of 'women's writing' and not in the context of 'Mexican literature'.[21] More fundamental changes in attitudes are required if novels by women authors are to receive the recognition they deserve on equal terms with male-authored novels. Re-evaluating the interpretive strategies which underpin canon formation is one way to achieve this goal.

Nellie Campobello, Rosario Castellanos, Elena Garro and Elena Poniatowska are the exceptions that prove the rule of women's exclusion from the twentieth-century Mexican novelistic canon. It should not be forgotten, however, that, while feminist scholars have had some success in negotiating the inclusion of individual women authors into the canon, this ad hoc approach is ultimately inadequate. As the author and critic Brianda Domecq states:

> Lo que es importante señalar es que estas 'excepciones' no están de ninguna manera integradas al 'corpus' de la literatura escrita por hombres, sino que parecen pender como extraños colgajos prendidos apenas con los alfileres de la concesión paternalista a la epidermis de la impenetrable tradición masculina.[22]

> [It is important to note that these 'exceptions' are in no way integrated into the 'corpus' of literature written by men, instead they seem to hang like strange pieces of flesh barely hanging on by the clip of the paternalistic concession to the outer skin of the impenetrable masculine tradition.]

In order to effectively challenge women's exclusion from the canon and affect wider reaching, fundamental changes in attitudes to literature by women it is imperative that we identify and challenge the practices underpinning canon formation in Mexico.

We must guard against the assumption that because a few women have gained a foothold in the canon other women whose work is 'good enough' will be duly recognized. It is often argued that novels will be recognized and included in the canon if they are 'good enough' and that if women authors are excluded then it is because their work is of inferior quality, but the cases of Campobello, Castellanos, Garro and Poniatowska provide evidence to the contrary. Their experiences, and those of the other women authors in this study, suggest that 'being good' is not enough as their inclusion owes much to the extraordinary efforts of feminist scholars in Mexico and abroad or to interest in the author's private life. Even when women have been included they have often been kept at the margins of canonical literature because their work is identified as belonging to a particular genre or because of the 'unusual' content of their work. Indeed, this study suggests that woman-authored novels are often criticized for their 'unusual' or 'insignificant' content and highlights the fact that such readings are a product of dominant interpretive strategies which insist on evaluating literature according to whether or not it contributes to the public sphere, where issues of contemporary national importance are presented and discussed. I challenge the still widespread assumption that the woman-authored texts in this study, like so many other woman-authored novels, were omitted from the canon because they were not 'good enough' by examining whether these texts would be 'good enough' if they were judged according to the same criteria as those applied to male-authored texts and using interpretive strategies that are not gender-biased.

How texts were interpreted and received at the time they were published can be determined by an analysis of book reviews that appeared in national newspapers and magazines. Identifying the ways in which specific texts were read and why they were valued, or not, enables me to uncover how the twentieth-century Mexican novelistic canon was formed. To be included in Mexico's new, post-revolutionary canon a text had to be interpreted as furthering the goal of nation-building. In the aftermath of the revolution this was likely to mean that it was also State-building literature in that it furthered the political aims of the regime in power. Over time, this connection between State and nation-building literature was diluted and nation-building literature came to be that which was interpreted as addressing issues of public concern or capturing the spirit of the moment. A comparison of reviews of canonical male-authored texts with reviews of non-canonical woman-authored texts reveals that the latter were rarely interpreted as addressing issues of national concern and so these novels were largely excluded from the twentieth-century literary canon.

Reviewers and critics form a privileged community of readers whose opinions carry significant weight and influence, and their role in interpreting texts must be considered when looking at canon formation. Bourdieu has noted the crucial role they play in the literary field because 'discourse about a work is not a mere accompaniment, intended to assist its perception and appreciation, but a stage in the production of the work, of its meaning and value' (110). In Mexico throughout the twentieth-century there has been a clearly identifiable group of intellectuals, authors, reviewers and literary critics who, alongside the State's cultural institutions acting as agents of legitimation, have been responsible for the consecration of texts.[23] Between them, these intellectuals have written many canonical novels, much literary criticism, including reviews and histories of literature, and they have regularly sat on panels of judges awarding prizes for literature. The continuity within the group is remarkable; the same people reviewed several of the novels in this study and also wrote histories of literature. This group was responsible for starting the debate about the need for a national literature in the mid-1920s and continued to oversee the national literary tradition for the rest of the century. Notable names in this almost exclusively male group include: Ali Chumacero, Emmanuel Carballo, Adolfo Castañón, Jacobo Dalevuelta, Christopher Domínguez Michael, Carlos Fuentes, Octavio Paz, Carlos González Peña, José Luis Martínez, Carlos Monsiváis, Julio Jiménez Rueda, and Francisco Zendejas. By positioning themselves as the custodians and transmitters of literary knowledge and literary capital, this group of people has contributed more than any other to creating the twentieth-century Mexican literary canon. As much as the State, these men working with, or separate from, State institutions, but always with the State's tacit endorsement, have defined which texts will be read and how they will be read.[24]

This group, which I call the 'custodians of literary knowledge', should be understood as part of an imaginary tradition. Just as John Guillory suggests the canon itself is an 'imaginary tradition' to which texts can be added or (less frequently) removed but which is never completed, this group is also flexible enough to include new people over time as heirs to the tradition and its membership is not finite.[25] The members of this male-dominated group often know each other, or at least show a familiarity with one another's work and that of their predecessors. One way in which this group evolves is illustrated in a history of literature entitled *La literatura mexicana del siglo XX* which was published in 1995 and was a collaborative work by the established literary historian, José Luis Martínez, and relative newcomer, Christopher Domínguez Michael.[26] In the *Preliminar* [Preface], Martínez wrote:

> Cuando me propusieron, en abril de 1990, escribir, en el plazo de un año, una historia de la literatura mexicana de 1910 a nuestros días, hice cuentas alegres. En principio, indiqué que sólo me comprometía a llegar a 1960, porque conocía insuficiente la caudalosa literatura de las últimas décadas. Convivimos en encargar el período 1960–1990 a Christopher Domínguez Michael, quien aceptó la tarea' (14).

> [When they suggested in April 1990, that I write, in one year, a history of Mexican literature from 1910 to the present I was overly optimistic about how long it would take me. In principle, I agreed to write about the period up to 1960, because I did not know enough about the abundant literature of the last few decades. We decided to ask Christopher Domínguez Michael to write about the period 1960–1990 and he accepted.]

Martínez invited Domínguez's participation in the project as the expert on the second part of the twentieth-century and the man who would inherit a legacy and become part of the next generation of custodians of literary knowledge.

The tradition of the custodians is reinforced by the fact that they themselves are often included (and include themselves) in histories of literature as part of the Mexican canonical tradition. They are mentioned in these texts as essayists and critics as well as, in many cases, authors. In the aforementioned work by Martínez and Domínguez, for example, Martínez says that he chose to include

> los ensayistas y estudiosos a los que llamé 'organizadores de la cultura': humanistas, historiadores, críticos literarios, antropólogos, sociólogos, filósofos, críticos de arte, bibliógrafos, etcétera, en cuanto hubieran contribuido a la formación de nuestras ideas culturales (14).

> [the essayists and scholars who I called 'cultural organizers': humanists, historians, literary critics, anthropologists, sociologists, philosophers, art critics, bibliographers, etc. in so much as they had contributed to the formation of our ideas about culture.]

Martínez was by no means the first to transcribe such a tradition; Jiménez Rueda, for example, included religious writings, philosophy, history, oratory, journalism and 'obras varias' [miscellaneous works] in the many editions of his *Historia de la literatura mexicana.*[27] The inclusion of the custodians of literary knowledge in such works provides evidence that they see themselves as forming a tradition of their own as well as being responsible for creating the canonical tradition of Mexican literature.

A further example of the way in which this group perpetuates itself and its literary values involves one of the authors studied in this book, Sergio Pitol, and one of the foremost contemporary custodians of literary knowledge, Carlos Monsiváis. Monsiváis checked the first proofs of Pitol's early short stories and Pitol's novel, *El desfile del amor*, is dedicated to him and to Margo Glantz.[28] Monsiváis wrote a very favourable review of *El desfile del amor* for *La Jornada Semanal*.[29] Since the publication of *El desfile del amor*, both Pitol and Monsiváis have won the *Premio Juan Rulfo de*

Literatura, one of the most prestigious literature prizes in Mexico. In 1999, when Pitol won the prize, Monsiváis was on the panel of judges and, when Monsiváis won it in 2006, Pitol was one of the judges.[30] The example of Pitol and Monsiváis is typical and shows how a closed elite group has a considerable influence on which novels will come to be included in the canon. Members of this group write the first interpretations of a novel in reviews which are considered to be authoritative because of the status of their authors, they also judge prizes and mentor younger writers of their choosing. In addition, some of them contribute further to establishing the canon by producing anthologies, histories and dictionaries of literature. The members of this elite have often studied at the Universidad Nacional Autónoma de México (UNAM) and/or worked for government departments.[31] So few women are members of this group that one may conclude that women's exclusion from the twentieth-century Mexican literary canon is, at least in part, a consequence of the male dominated nature of the cultural elite.

The custodians of literary knowledge do not work alone, however, because, as Guillory suggests, canon formation requires institutional support 'to ensure the *reproduction* of the work, its continual reintroduction to generations of readers' (28). The Mexican State has provided the necessary institutional support and has been one of the major employers and supporters of Mexican intellectuals in the twentieth-century. As Graham Huggan has noted, one way in which the State can establish and exercise its authority to consecrate texts is through literary prizes.[32] In 1935, the Mexican State, through the Secretaría de Educación Pública (SEP) [Ministry of Education], created the *Premio Nacional de Literatura*.[33] The State has continued to sponsor numerous literary prizes and related activities through the Instituto Nacional de Bellas Artes (INBA) [National Institute of Fine Arts], created in 1946, and, more recently, through the Centro Nacional de la Información y Promoción de la Literatura (CNIPL) [National Centre for the Information and Promotion of Literature], an agency devoted to promoting Mexican literature. In the mid-1930s the State supported the creation of the publishing house, Fondo de Cultura Económica (FCE), and has even been involved in sponsoring the publication of histories of literature through the Consejo Nacional para la Cultura y las Artes (CONACULTA) [National Council for Culture and the Arts].[34] As the provider of institutional support 'by means of subsidies, commissions, promotion, honorific posts, even decorations, all of which are for speaking or keeping silent, for compromise or abstention' the state is also able to 'orient intellectual production' (Bourdieu, 124). The State's role in the cultural institutions of twentieth-century Mexico has often been instrumental and so, the relationship between canon formation, the custodians of literary knowledge, the State and nation-building will be explored in this book.

Nation-building was of primary concern in post-revolutionary Mexico and, as evidenced by histories of literature, literature was harnessed to support this project. Historians have shown, with reference to other spheres, that the State's nation-building project was heavily gendered and I aim to show how nation-building in the literary sphere was similarly founded on gendered assumptions. Nira Yuval-Davis has observed that 'nationalism and the nation have usually been discussed as part of the public political sphere' and that women are excluded from discourses about nationalism and the nation because they are excluded from the public sphere.[35] The association between men and the public sphere and women and the private sphere meant that reviewers of Mexican literature were more likely to interpret male-authored novels as being about the public sphere and as having national significance. Woman-authored novels were rarely interpreted as being about the nation. Furthermore, reviewers seeking nation-building literature were more likely to adopt interpretive strategies which looked for meaning in the public and not in the private sphere. As a result, they frequently overlooked woman-authored texts which appeared to them to only relate to the private sphere and also ignored the significance of the private narratives which could be identified within male-authored texts.

This study shows that if we use alternative interpretive strategies to those adopted by contemporary reviewers then Mexican woman-authored texts can also be read as being about the nation. Therefore, instead of privileging one interpretation of a novel based on a single interpretive strategy this book highlights the potential benefits of reading texts through an interpretive prism from which multiple readings emerge, based on different interpretive strategies.[36] Twentieth-century custodians of literary knowledge sought novels which addressed contemporary national issues but dominant interpretive strategies overlooked the potential national significance of woman-authored novels. I aim to show that national readings of woman-authored novels are facilitated by an interpretive strategy which reads the private sphere as commenting on the public situation and that this strategy also produces new readings when applied to male-authored texts. This interpretive strategy will be referred to as the private-national reading.[37]

Private-national readings see the private sphere as commenting on the public situation. The relationship between the public and the private in literature has been explored by Fredric Jameson who proposes that there is a different relationship between the public and private spheres in 'first-' and 'third-world' literature. He argues that 'first-world' literature maintains a 'split between the private and the public'. In contrast, 'third-world' literature employs national allegory which brings public and private together and uses the private sphere to comment on the public situation (Jameson, 69). The different relationships reviewers perceived between the public and private spheres in canonical and non-canonical literature is, I believe, fundamental to explaining how the Mexican canon was formed. Therefore, I substitute Jameson's terms 'first-world' and 'third-world' with 'canonical' and 'non-canonical' because the relationship of dominance and subordination Jameson describes as existing between 'first-' and 'third-world' texts maps onto that between 'canonical' and 'non-canonical' texts.

Jameson suggests that texts which bring together the public and the private are 'resistant to our conventional western habits of reading' and are, therefore, alienating to 'first-world' readers (69). Underlying Jameson's analysis of the difficulties faced by 'first-world' readers when confronted by a 'third-world' text appears to be an assumption that 'first-world' readers have a shared interpretive strategy; this parallels my own assertion that there was a shared interpretive practice among the custodians of literary knowledge in twentieth-century Mexico. Thus, in the same way that Jameson sees 'third-world' literature as being resistant to 'first-world' reading habits, so too, I propose that woman-authored novels were resistant to dominant interpretive strategies in post-revolutionary Mexico and were consequently excluded from the canon. Following Jameson, but incorporating Fish's emphasis on the role of the reader, I argue that, in order to become canonical, texts needed to be seen to be about the public sphere and maintain a 'split between the private and the public' (Jameson, 69). Literature which appeared to reviewers to be more about the private than the public sphere or blurred the distinction between public and private was not well received because dominant interpretive strategies meant that it could not readily be interpreted with reference to the nation and consequently these novels were excluded from the canon. National readings of those texts which were excluded from the canon are facilitated by interpretive strategies which read the private sphere as a reflection of the public situation. It is not essential to be able to read them as national allegories. The use of the private to comment on the public situation is not limited to national allegory and for this reason I have adopted the broader term private-national reading for my interpretive strategy.

While Jameson claims that all national allegory is a feature of 'third-world' literature, Aijaz Ahmad has noted that allegories are also produced in the 'first-world' by black and feminist authors.[38] Thus, the relationship Jameson identifies between public and private is not exclusive to 'third-world' texts but rather can be readily found in writing produced by authors who are marginalized or excluded from the public sphere. It is hoped, therefore, that private-national readings of other texts produced by those who are marginalized from the public sphere at a given time and place, be they black or feminist writers or people writing under a colonial power, may yield interesting results. These writers are excluded from the public sphere in which the nation is usually discussed and so their texts are more likely to benefit from ways of reading which are attentive to the possible use of the private to comment on the public situation. These potential public and national interpretations are, however, often overlooked by 'first-world' or dominant interpretive communities who must be encouraged to use an interpretive prism so as to consider a wider range of interpretive strategies.

Ahmad also disagrees with Jameson's statement that all 'third-world' literature is national allegory and cites early Urdu prose narrative as an example of 'third-world' literature which does not use national allegory. Jameson, however, qualifies his central thesis that all 'third-world' literature is national allegory by saying that this is 'particularly true when their forms develop out of predominantly western machineries of representation, such as the novel' (69). Urdu prose narratives did not 'develop out of predominantly western machineries of representation' and, therefore, Jameson may not expect them to be national allegory. The novel emerged during the colonial period more than half a century after these early Urdu narratives, suggesting that the emergence of national allegory was closely linked to the experience of colonization (Ahmad, 18–19). In light of Ahmad's observations about the emergence of the novel in colonial India and the existence of national allegory in 'first-world' texts by black and women authors, I suggest that interpretive strategies which allow national allegory to be identified in a text and which read the private as commenting on the public sphere are likely to be particularly useful when applied to texts produced at times when the category of the nation is brought into question. Such was the case at the time of Indian Independence when the nation became a contested category which needed to be defined and national allegories written by black and feminist writers can be seen as attempts by these authors to write themselves into the nation. By bringing public and private spheres together, these texts can be seen to challenge this dichotomy and to question who is included in the nation, and on what basis, as well as acting as a means to negotiate inclusion.

Turning our attention to Latin America, Doris Sommer has shown that, in the post-Independence period, national romances, which often incorporated national allegory, aimed 'literally to engender new nations' and to define who was included in them (18). National romances were used to 'promote communal imaginings' in which 'erotic passion' provided the 'opportunity (rhetorical and otherwise) to bind together heterodox constituencies: competing regions, economic interests, races, religions' (Sommer, 14). These romances did not 'distinguish between ethical politics and erotic passion, between epic nationalism and intimate sensibility. It collapses the distinctions' (Sommer, 24). Unlike Jameson's 'first-world' readers who struggle to understand the private as commenting on the public situation, Sommer's nineteenth-century 'writers and readers of Latin America's canon of national novels' readily assumed 'what amounts to an allegorical relationship between personal and political narratives' (Sommer, 41). We would therefore expect in post-revolutionary Mexico to see the continued use of national allegory and other forms which bring together the public and private spheres because the category of the nation and who was to be included in it was again the subject of constant negotiation. However, as will be seen, readers were no longer able (or were unwilling) to read the private in terms of the public situation and so novels which would have benefited from this interpretive strategy failed to become canonical, whereas those that did not rely on the application of such an interpretive strategy to highlight their national significance were more likely to become canonical. This study proposes that an interpretive strategy which is attentive to the possibility of understanding the public sphere through the lens of the private proves particularly effective in uncovering the perspective of those who were still trying to negotiate the terms for inclusion in the post-revolutionary nation.

The following chapters examine and interrogate the gendered process of nation-building through literature which led to the formation of the twentieth-century Mexican canon. The six case studies illustrate different aspects of post-revolutionary Mexican canon formation. Chapter 1 evaluates the impact of the *Premio Nacional de Literatura* on the formation of the Mexican canon by examining the government decree which created the prize and its first winner, *El indio* by Gregorio López y Fuentes.[39] Chapter 2 brings to light the long-forgotten novel *Yo también, Adelita* by Consuelo Delgado and shows that this woman-authored text could have been interpreted as being in keeping with official discourses and adopted as nation-building literature, had alternative interpretive strategies been applied.[40] Chapter 3 examines the circumstances surrounding the publication of *La región más transparente*

[*Where the Air is Clear*], the first novel by the renowned author Carlos Fuentes, and demonstrates how the criteria for inclusion in the canon had evolved by the mid-century. Nonetheless, reviewers only looked for national significance in the public sphere leading them to overlook the significance of the private sphere which is a key aspect of Fuentes' work.[41] Chapter 4 addresses some of the problems which arise from canon formation being tied to nation-building. The chapter focuses on the *cristero* novel *La ciudad y el viento* by Dolores Castro, which tried to negotiate inclusion in the nation for those Catholics who were excluded by the State as a result of the ongoing Church–State conflict.[42] Chapters 5 and 6 examine the relationship between gender, genre and canonicity. Initially, *El desfile del amor* [*Love Parade*] by Sergio Pitol appears to be the exception that proves the rule as reviewers were in this case able to interpret the private in terms of the public and to accept this novel into the Mexican canon.[43] However, I demonstrate that one of the main reasons for the novel's acceptance was that reviewers identified the novel as detective fiction and had already learned to adapt their interpretive strategies to accommodate this genre. When it came to identifying the genre of *Arráncame la vida* [*Tear this Heart Out / Mexican Bolero*] by Ángeles Mastretta, reviewers were unable to adapt their interpretive strategies and so did not, as I do, read Mastretta's novel as a novel of female adultery.[44] I suggest that a reviewer's choice of interpretive strategy is significantly influenced by the author's gender and the novel's perceived genre. The six case studies add to our understanding of canon formation in post-revolutionary Mexico and it is my belief that the insights and approaches developed here may be usefully applied and tested in other contexts.

The novels studied in this book were selected to be considered in pairs each made up of one male- and one female-authored novel published at approximately the same time (*El indio* and *Yo también, Adelita*, *La región más transparente* and *La ciudad y el viento*, and *El desfile del amor* and *Arráncame la vida*). The pairs were published at three distinctive moments in the history of twentieth-century Mexico when there were identifiable shifts in the zeitgeist as a result of historical circumstances. Using texts which together span the greater part of the twentieth-century, it can be seen that, while there are subtle changes, there is also a remarkable degree of continuity in the interpretive strategies adopted by the custodians of literary knowledge and the values which underpinned the canon remained consistent. Each chapter considers the circumstances in which the text was published and the extent to which they were a factor in whether or not the novel became canonical. Contemporary reviews are used to analyse historical ways of reading, to identify the dominant interpretive strategy of the period and to show how these strategies led to the dismissal of woman-authored texts. My analysis of the reviews provides what Janice Radway has termed an 'ethnography of reading' which shows 'how actual communities actually read particular texts'.[45] My 'ethnography of reading' shows how privileged reviewers, who had the authority to consecrate a text, read six novels in different ways with the result that three became canonical and three were omitted from the canon.

Radway recommends that 'ethnographies of reading' should sit alongside textual interpretation and so my discussion of the circumstances in which a text was published and my analysis of its reception by reviewers is followed by an analysis of each of the novels. My analysis incorporates relevant details of the historical context in order to highlight the ways in which the novels can be, and in the case of male-authored texts, were interpreted as responding to the key issues of their time. In the case of the woman-authored texts, I use a private-national reading to show how they could have been seen to have national significance even though this possibility was overlooked by the original reviewers. My approach to woman-authored novels suggests that by interpreting the private sphere in terms of the public situation we can appreciate the full extent to which woman-authored novels could be seen to address national issues. I am thus able to produce new interpretations of these novels which enable them to be evaluated on equal terms to their canonical male-authored counterparts, in other words, according to whether or not they contributed to the post-revolutionary nation-building agenda. In order to maintain my practice of applying the same interpretive strategy regardless of the gender of the author I also produce private-national readings of *El indio*, *La región más transparente*, and *El desfile del amor*. In so doing, I am able to provide new insights into these male-authored texts which were overlooked by dominant interpretive strategies which disregarded the private sphere. It is hoped that the approach outlined above and undertaken in the following analyses will be a first step towards unmasking the values subsuming the canon and reformulating the canon to include more woman-authored texts. In future, interpretive strategies should not depend on perceived genre or the author's gender and literary value need not be based on whether or not a novel contributed to post-revolutionary nation-building.

Notes to the Introduction

1. The term 'interpretive strategies' is taken from Stanley Fish, *Is there a text in this class? The Authority of Interpretive Communities* (Cambridge, MA: Harvard University Press, 1980). See in particular: Introduction, Chapter 7 'Interpreting the Variorum', and Part Two 'Interpretive Authority in the Classroom and in Literary Criticism'.
2. On the formation of a Latin American canon in the US see María Eugenia Mudrovcic, 'Reading Latin American Literature Abroad: Agency and Canon Formation in the Sixties and Seventies', in *Voice-Overs: Translation and Latin American Literature*, ed. by Daniel Balderston and Mary Schwartz (New York: State University of New York Press, 2002), pp. 129–43.
3. Pierre Bourdieu, *The Field of Cultural Production*, ed. and intro. by Randal Johnson (Cambridge: Polity Press, 1993), p. 32.
4. Verity Smith, 'Canon. The Literary Canon in Spanish America', in *The Encyclopedia of Latin American Literature*, ed. by Verity Smith (London: Fitzroy Dearborn Publishers, 1997), pp. 163–64 (p. 163).
5. David Perkins, *Is Literary History Possible?* (Baltimore, MD: Johns Hopkins University Press, 1992), pp. 4–5, p. 13, p. 19.
6. Beatriz González-Stephan, *Fundaciones: canon, historia y cultura nacional. La historiografía literaria del liberalismo hispanoamericano del siglo XIX* (Madrid: Iberoamericana, 2002), p. 127.
7. On 1920s debates which aimed to define a Mexican national literature see: Juan Bruce-Novoa, 'La novela de la Revolución Mexicana: la topología del final', *Hispania*, 74 (1991), 36–44; John Englekirk, 'The "Discovery" of Los de abajo', *Hispania*, 18 (1935), 53–62; Alfonso Reyes and Héctor Pérez Martínez, *A vuelta de correo. Una polémica sobre la literatura nacional*, ed. by Silvia Molina (Mexico: UNAM and Universidad de Colima, 1988).
8. Julio Jiménez Rueda, *Historia de la literatura mexicana* (Mexico: Editorial Cultura, 1928); Julio Jiménez Rueda, *Historia de la literatura mexicana*, 2nd–7th edn (Mexico: Ediciones Botas, 1934,

1942, 1946, 1953, 1957, 1960); Emmanuel Carballo, *Diecinueve protagonistas de la literatura mexicana del siglo XX* (Mexico: Empresas Editoriales, 1965); Emmanuel Carballo, *Protagonistas de la literatura mexicana*, 2nd edn (Mexico: Ediciones del Ermitaño/SEP, 1985); Emmanuel Carballo, *Protagonistas de la literatura mexicana*, 4th rev. edn (Mexico: Editorial Porrúa, 1994); Carlos González Peña, *Historia de la literatura mexicana. Desde los orígenes hasta nuestros días*, 5th edn (Mexico: Editorial Porrúa, 1954), first pub. 1928; Carlos González Peña, *Historia de la literatura mexicana. Desde los orígenes hasta nuestros días*, 8th–10th & 12th edn, ed. with an appendix by the Centro de Estudios Literarios de la UNAM (Mexico: Editorial Porrúa, 1963, 1966, 1969, 1975); José Luis Martínez, *Literatura mexicana siglo XX 1910–1949. Primera parte* (Mexico: Antigua Librería Robredo, 1949); José Luis Martínez, *Literatura mexicana siglo XX 1910–1949. Guías Bibliográficas. Segunda parte* (Mexico: Antigua Librería Robredo, 1950). José Luis Martínez and Emmanuel Carballo were also involved in (re-) creating a tradition of Mexican literature which went back to the nineteenth-century. José Luis Martínez, *La expresión nacional. Letras mexicanas del siglo XIX* (Mexico: Imprenta Universitaria, 1955); Emmanuel Carballo, *Historia de las letras mexicanas en el siglo XIX* (Mexico: Reloj de Sol, 1991); Emmanuel Carballo *Diccionario crítico de las letras mexicanas en el siglo XIX* (Mexico: Editorial Océano & CONACULTA, 2001).

9. Martha Robles, *La sombra fugitiva. Escritoras en la cultura nacional* (Mexico: UNAM, 1985); Fabienne Bradu, *Señas particulares: Escritora. Ensayos sobre escritoras mexicanas del siglo XX* (Mexico: FCE, 1987).

10. On the *boom femenino* in Mexico see *The boom femenino in Mexico: Reading Contemporary Women's Writing*, ed. by Nuala Finnegan and Jane Lavery (Newcastle: Cambridge Scholars, 2010). The dismissal of novels by women authors as 'popular' or 'light' literature will be discussed further in Chapter 6 with reference to Ángeles Mastretta's *Arráncame la vida*. See also Sarah E. L. Bowskill, 'The origins of the *boom femenino mexicano*', in *The boom femenino in Mexico: Reading Contemporary Women's Writing*, ed. by Nuala Finnegan and Jane Lavery (Newcastle: Cambridge Scholars, 2010), pp. 73–89.

11. See, for example, Susan Basnett, *Knives and Angels: Women Writers in Latin America* (London: Zed Books, 1990); Anny Brooksbank Jones and Catherine Davies, *Latin American Women's Writing: Feminist Readings in Theory and Crisis* (Oxford: Clarendon Press, 1996); Debra A. Castillo, *Talking Back: Toward a Latin American Feminist Literary Criticism* (Ithaca, NY: Cornell University Press, 1992); Debra A. Castillo, *Easy Women: Sex and Gender in Modern Mexican Fiction* (Minneapolis: University of Minnesota Press, 1998); Jean Franco, *Plotting Women: Gender and Representation in Mexico* (London: Verso, 1989); Kay S. García, *Broken Bars: New Perspectives from Mexican Women Writers* (Albuquerque: University of New Mexico Press, 1994); Kristine Ibsen, *The Other Mirror: Women's Narrative in Mexico, 1980–1995* (Westport, CT: Greenwood Press, 1997); Amy K. Kaminsky, *Reading the Body Politic: Feminist Criticism and Latin American Women Writers* (Minneapolis: University of Minnesota Press, 1993); Beth Miller, *Women in Hispanic Literature: Icons and Fallen Idols* (Berkeley: University of California Press, 1983); Claudia Schaefer, *Textured Lives: Women, Art and Representation in Modern Mexico* (Tucson: University of Arizona Press, 1992); Cynthia Steele, *Politics, Gender and the Mexican Novel, 1968–1988: Beyond the Pyramid* (Austin: University of Texas Press, 1992); María Elena de Valdés, *The Shattered Mirror: Representations of Women in Mexican Literature* (Austin: University of Texas Press, 1998).

12. Elena Poniatowska, *Las siete cabritas* (Mexico: Era, 2000), p. 169. Despite the subtitle of *Cartucho*, 'relatos de la lucha en el Norte de México', it is usually referred to as a novel.

13. José Joaquín Blanco, *Crónica literaria. Un siglo de escritores mexicanos* (Mexico: Cal y Arena, 1996), p. 488. Originally published in *Crónica de la poesía mexicana* (1977).

14. The circumstances in which *El indio* came to win the *Premio Nacional de Literatura* and in which Mexico city became the focus for mid-century literature are discussed in Chapters 1, 3 and 4 respectively.

15. Catherine Grant, 'Preface', in *Monstrous Projections of Femininity in the Fictions of Mexican Writer Rosario Castellanos*, by Nuala Finnegan (Lewiston, NY: Edwin Mellen Press, 2000), pp. xvii–xviii (p. xvii).

16. The review is reprinted in Huberto Batis, *Crítica bajo presión. Prosa Mexicana 1964–1985. Selección del autor* (Mexico: UNAM, 2004), pp. 41–42.

17. Transcript of a radio interview between Emmanuel Carballo and Huberto Batis in 1981 published in *Sábado*, supl. *Unomásuno* in 1989 and reprinted in Batis, pp. 69–86 (p. 77).

18. Rebecca E. Biron, '*Un hogar insólito*: Elena Garro and Mexican Literary Culture', in *The Effects of the Nation. Mexican Art in an Age of Globalization*, ed. by Carl Good and John V. Waldron (Philadelphia: Temple University Press, 2001), pp. 138–59 (p. 141).

19. Luis Enrique Ramírez, *La ingobernable. Encuentros y desencuentros con Elena Garro* (Mexico: Hoja Casa Editorial, 2000), p. 45.

20. On Garro's role in denouncing authors and intellectuals as behind the massacre at Tlatelolco see Christopher Domínguez Michael, *Diccionario crítico de la literatura mexicana (1955–2005)* (Mexico: FCE, 2007), pp. 181–82.

21. The marginalization of woman authored novels as 'women's writing' is discussed in more detail in Chapter 6.

22. Brianda Domecq, *Mujer que publica... Mujer pública. Ensayos sobre literatura femenina* (Mexico: Editorial Diana, 1994), pp. 76–77.

23. 'Agents of legitimation' is Bourdieu's term used to refer to those (usually to institutions rather than individuals) who have the authority to 'consecrate a certain type of work and a certain type of cultivated person' (121).

24. Barbara Herrnstein Smith has noted that it is not necessary for these intellectuals to work with or for State institutions in order for them to share the official ideology. It is this shared ideology which guarantees their privileged position. Barbara Herrnstein Smith, *Contingencies of Value: Alternative Perspectives for Critical Theory* (Cambridge, MA: Harvard University Press, 1988), p. 51.

25. John Guillory, *Cultural Capital: The Problem of Literary Canon Formation* (Chicago: University of Chicago Press, 1993), p. 30.

26. José Luis Martínez and Christopher Domínguez Michael, *La literatura mexicana del siglo XX* (Mexico: CONACULTA, 1995).

27. Editions of Rueda's *Historia de la literatura mexicana* were published in 1928, 1934, 1942, 1946, 1953, 1957 and 1960.

28. Eduardo C. Serrato, 'Pitol: la nueva picaresca', *El Nacional*, 8 June 1991, pp. 12–13.

29. Carlos Monsiváis, 'Sergio Pitol: Las mitologías del rencor y del humor', *La Jornada Semanal*, 16 July 1989, pp. 23–29.

30. Ericka Montaño Garfias, 'Confieren a Carlos Monsiváis el premio literario Juan Rulfo', *La Jornada*, 5 September 2006, online at <http://www.jornada.unam.mx/2006/09/05/index.php?section=cultura&article=a04n1cul> [accessed 11 February 2010].

31. On the relationship between the intellectual elite, UNAM and politics see Roderic A. Camp, *Intellectuals and the State in Twentieth Century Mexico* (Austin: University of Texas Press, 1985).

32. Graham Huggan, *The Post-colonial Exotic: Marketing the Margins* (London: Routledge, 2001), p. 118.

33. The creation of this prize and the precedents it established will be examined further in Chapter 1.

34. On the creation of the FCE see Camp, pp. 187–88.

35. Nira Yuval-Davis, *Gender and Nation* (London: Sage Publications, 1997), pp. 12–13.

36. In this analogy the novel is like white light which, when shone into the prism, reveals its constituent parts by splitting into its component colours. Out of the interpretive prism emerges a rainbow of readings each based on a different interpretive strategy.

37. Fredric Jameson and Doris Sommer have read the private as commenting on the public situation in national allegory and nineteenth-century national romances in Latin America respectively. However, they see meaning as intrinsic to the text and so do not identify this way of reading as a potential interpretive strategy which could be adopted systematically in order to identify national narratives in woman-authored texts. Fredric Jameson, 'Third-World Literature in the Era of Multinational Capitalism', *Social Text*, 15 (1986), 65–88; Doris Sommer, *Foundational Fictions: The National Romances of Latin America* (Berkeley: University of California Press, 1991).

38. Aijaz Ahmad, 'Jameson's Rhetoric of Otherness and the "National Allegory"', *Social Text*, 17 (1987), 3–25 (p. 15).

39. Gregorio López y Fuentes, *El indio*, 5th edn (Mexico: Editorial Porrúa, 1972), first pub. 1935.

40. Consuelo Delgado, *Yo también, Adelita* (Mexico: Ediciones del Grupo en Marcha, 1936).

41. Carlos Fuentes, *La región más transparente*, 7th edn, ed. and intro. by Georgina García Gutiérrez (Madrid: Cátedra, 1999), first pub. 1958.

42. Dolores Castro, *La ciudad y el viento* (Xalapa: Universidad Veracruzana, 1962).
43. Sergio Pitol, *El desfile del amor* (Mexico: Era, 1989), first pub. 1984.
44. Ángeles Mastretta, *Arráncame la vida* (Madrid: Suma de Letras, 2001), first pub. 1985.
45. Janice A. Radway, *Reading the Romance: Women, Patriarchy, and Popular Literature* (Chapel Hill: University of North Carolina Press, 1991), p. 4.

CHAPTER 1

Setting the Standard:
El indio and the
Premio Nacional de Literatura

In the mid-1930s the Mexican State set out to define 'Mexican literature' and form a national canon which would reflect and reinforce its nation-building agenda. To this end, in 1934 the interim government of Abelardo L. Rodríguez (1932–34) established a national prize for literature, the *Premio Nacional de Literatura*.[1] The competition was organized by the *Secretaría de Educación Pública* (SEP) through the *Departamento de Bellas Artes* and was judged by some of the most prominent figures on the Mexican literary scene: the journalist and critic José de J. Núñez Domínguez, Julio Jiménez Rueda, the author of several histories of Mexican literature, and the successful novelist Mauricio Magdaleno. In July 1935, a full-page announcement in the newspaper *El Universal Gráfico* invited Mexican nationals to enter the competition by submitting a work of published or unpublished prose or poetry.[2] The competition offered significant rewards to both the State and the prize-winner: the winner gained public recognition and the considerable sum of $2000 pesos prize money, while the State gained the authority to consecrate cultural products in keeping with its own agenda.

The State required a national literature which would consolidate post-revolutionary nationhood and promote its values. Article four of the decree which created the *Premio Nacional de Literatura* stated:

> Se adoptará el criterio más amplio para valorizar el mérito de cada obra, prefiriéndose aquellas henchidas de mayor sentido social, y de un espíritu moderno, tanto por los problemas en que se inspire, como por la técnica con que los realice.[3]

> [The broadest possible criteria will be adopted to evaluate the merit of each work, with preference for those works which demonstrate the greatest social awareness, and a modern spirit in the problems which inspire them and in the technique employed.]

Thus, the State decided that Mexican literature should have a social purpose and be modern in terms of subject matter, style and form. It was against this standard that twentieth-century Mexican literature would be measured, firstly by the judges of the *Premio Nacional de Literatura* and subsequently by the many reviewers and critics who adopted these criteria as their own. In so doing, reviewers acted as agents of legitimation for both the texts and the State's nation-building project. The result is a literary canon which consists of novels which were interpreted as addressing issues of national importance and, consequently, contributed to the creation of the post-revolutionary nation.

The decree may have provided a new model for literary production and criticism or it may have formally established pre-existing preferences and trends in literary criticism. Certainly, a similar preference for socially relevant, nation-building literature was evident in the post-independence period.[4] Either way, not everyone endorsed this approach to literature. Gonzalo de la Porra, writing in the newspaper *El Universal* in 1936, complained that writers deliberately pandered to the prize's criteria and judges were too bound by them.[5] Both judges and entrants, he wrote, were 'amalgamados en el contubernio del oportunismo político' (3) [mixed up in the conspiracy of political opportunism]. De la Porra also objected to the importance the *Premio Nacional de Literatura* attached to a novel's content claiming that 'todo lo subordinamos a la política y a las ideas en boga' (3) [we subordinate everything to politics and the ideas in vogue]. According to de la Porra, the prizes were not awarded to the best novel or poem, but to those which supported the government's position.

However valid de la Porra's objections may be, the State was successful in its project of nation-building through literature as can be seen from the selection and critical reception of the first winner of the *Premio Nacional de Literatura*, *El indio* by Gregorio López y Fuentes. Thus distinguished, *El indio* was well placed to be incorporated into the nascent post-revolutionary canon and Gregorio López y Fuentes' position was quickly consolidated by his inclusion in histories, dictionaries and encyclopaedias of Mexican literature, where he continues to feature to this day.[6]

When they evaluated the novel the judges and reviewers employed similar terms to those used in the decree that created the award. John Englekirk quoted the judges as saying that *El indio* 'suma "a su valor estético, un sentido humano y una tendencia social acordes con el espíritu mexicano moderno"' [combines 'aesthetic value, human feeling and a social awareness that is in keeping with the modern Mexican spirit'].[7] A similar vocabulary was used by Celestino Herrera Frimont in *El Nacional*, where he described *El indio* as an 'obra artística y de tendencia social mexicana' [a Mexican work of artistic merit possessing social awareness].[8] The fact that reviewers referred to the conditions of the prize underlines the importance they attached to them.

There was a clear consensus amongst the judges and reviewers in the national press that *El indio* combined aesthetic value with social purpose in its representation of Mexico's indigenous population.[9] For reviewers, the appeal of *El indio* lay in its subject matter, and they agreed that *El indio* was about one or more than one of the following: the indigenous way of life, the hardship suffered by Mexico's indigenous communities and the relationship between the indigenous and white / *mestizo* community. However, they could not agree as to whether the novel proposed a course of action or simply highlighted the problems faced by the indigenous population and those who aimed to help them. Nonetheless, a concerned exposition of the situation was sufficient to assure the novel a positive reception.

El indio's contribution to contemporary debate about how to integrate Mexico's indigenous communities was considered so significant that reviewers elevated the novel out of the realm of fiction and into that of fact. For them, the novel was more than a work of fiction; it was an anthropological, sociological and historical document. In *El Universal*, Salomón de la Selva stated that *El indio* was 'un volumen indispensable para todos los estudiosos de la sociología o de la política o de la historia, así como de la literatura de Hispano América' (3) [an indispensable text for all students of sociology, politics and history as well as students of Spanish American literature]. Furthermore, Ernesto Higuera (151), Salvador Cordero (2), A. Pereira Alves (4), and an anonymous reviewer in the *Revista de México de Cultura* (7 August 1955, 9) all commented on the accuracy of the novel's portrayal of indigenous communities. At a time when the State was promoting anthropological study as a way of creating a more unified *mestizo* nation, it seems that reviewers envisaged *El indio* as fulfilling a similar role. A novel which was interpreted as addressing such pressing social issues and contributing to nation-building projects could not help but become canonical.

Reviewers also compared *El indio* to Mexican art as a way of praising López y Fuentes' novel and its achievement as socially committed literature. De la Selva compared *El indio* to Mexican art and claimed that the novel would put Mexican literature on an equal footing with Mexican painting making the country a leader in both fields (3). De la Selva's comments highlight the value reviewers placed on international recognition, and the comparison to art is flattering to the novel. Mauricio Magdaleno similarly wrote that the novel was 'hondo y ancho y soberbio [...] como un lienzo mural' (1) [profound, broad and magnificent [...] like a mural]. As we shall see in later chapters, reviewers of *La región más transparente* and *El desfile del amor* also compared these novels to murals; an analogy which associates these canonical novels with the canonical tradition of didactic, socially aware, public art in Mexico.

The criteria for awarding the *Premio Nacional de Literatura* stated that, in addition to having social value, the winning entry should be modern in subject matter, style and form.[10] *El indio*'s first critics agreed on both counts; as well as praising the contemporary relevance of the novel's message about the plight of the indigenous communities, they appreciated its simple and effective style. De la Selva wrote that the style was 'vívido y sencillo. Es directo. Clásico puro' (3) [vivid and straightforward. It is direct. Purely classical]. Like De la Selva, Jacobo Dalevuelta praised López y Fuentes' minimalist style saying: 'No hay un renglón de más ni una línea de menos' (June 1935, 3) [There is neither one line too many nor one line too few].[11] For Dalevuelta, this style resulted in a 'lectura fácil' [easy reading] which 'mantiene constante y vivo el interés' (June 1935, 3) [keeps one's interest constant and alive]. Dalevuelta's comments are particularly interesting when compared to remarks about style in reviews of *La región más transparente* and *Arráncame la vida*.[12] The style of *La región más transparente* and other *boom* novels was acclaimed by critics because of its complexity while that of *Arráncame la vida* was criticized for being too easy to read. In contrast, the simple, easy to read style of *El indio* was considered a positive attribute. The changing attitudes towards style demonstrate that a canonical aesthetic which is universal and unchanging does not exist. Nonetheless, the criteria for judging the *Premio Nacional de Literatura* and the reviewers' comments about *El indio* suggest that a novel was often credited with being well written in order to explain or justify canonical status which was awarded primarily on the grounds of content.

Undoubtedly, winning the *Premio Nacional de Literatura* facilitated López y Fuentes' entry into the canon but other factors also worked to the advantage of *El indio*, including the author's status in the literary community. When *El indio* was published, López y Fuentes had already been included in Julio Jiménez Rueda's *Historia de la literatura mexicana* as the author of poetry, short stories and three novels: *Campamento* (1931), *Tierra* (1933), and *Mi General* (1934) (Rueda 1934, 247). According to Celestino Herrera Frimont, when *Mi General* was published López y Fuentes was already considered to be 'uno de los grandes autores de Ibero-América' (3) [one of the major authors of Latin America]. As well as being an established author, López y Fuentes was a long-standing journalist for the daily newspaper *El Universal*. His earlier work revealed a keen interest in social issues and his reputation in this area probably encouraged reviewers to highlight the social message of *El indio*.

El indio also benefited from being published and well marketed by the reputable Ediciones Botas. As Bourdieu has noted, a publisher recommends the books and authors they publish and the more consecrated publishers provide stronger consecration (76–77). Ediciones Botas had its own bookshop, the Librería Andrés Botas, and a magazine, *Letras Publicación Literaria y Bibliográfica*, in which it promoted its publications. *Letras* primarily consisted of lists of books and *El indio* was included several times and featured in a larger advertisement in the June 1935 edition.[13] In addition to appearing in *Letras*, on four occasions extracts of *El indio* were printed in a regular column in *El Universal Gráfico* called 'Enciclopedia Mínima'.[14] *El indio* cost $2 pesos and such prohibitive pricing meant that extracts in a newspaper allowed parts of the novel to reach a much wider audience than would otherwise have been the case. Featuring in 'Enciclopedia Mínima' may have conferred prestige on the novel and, since it was unusual for one text to feature more than twice, the fact that *El indio* appeared four times may indicate its popularity, or the desire of the column's author, F. González Guerrero, or the newspaper's editor to promote the novel.

Success abroad, or the potential to be recognized outside Mexico, also influenced whether a novel became canonical, as the State and the custodians of literary knowledge wanted to establish a unique national literature which would show the world that Mexico was a 'civilized' and independent nation. Reviewers proudly announced that an edition of the novel was forthcoming in Chile and an English translation by Anita Brenner, with illustrations by Diego Rivera, was under way.[15] They also insisted that *El indio* deserved a place alongside the 'classics' of Latin American literature and in the continent-wide canonical tradition of *indigenista* literature (De la Selva, 3; Salazar Mallén, 3; Englekirk, 'El indio', 8). Thus, *El indio* was praised because it served a national and international purpose.

We cannot know whether the reviewers adopted the criteria established for the *Premio Nacional de Literatura* as their own or whether the judges took into account reviewer opinion when making their decision. We do, however, know that in post-revolutionary Mexico the custodians of literary knowledge adopted an interpretive strategy which prioritized social value and national significance, both of which they associated with the public sphere, and it was against this standard that canonical literature would be measured for the remainder of the twentieth century. Reviewers identified both of these qualities in *El indio* which they interpreted as addressing the pressing matter of the relationship of Mexico's indigenous communities to the new nation and justified their praise with reference to aesthetic value. As a result, the novel was immediately incorporated into the national canon.

Reviewers saw López y Fuentes' novel as tackling the key issue of how to incorporate the indigenous population into the post-revolutionary nation. When *El indio* was published government discourses and projects aimed to consolidate the nation by tackling the marginalization of indigenous communities. The government advocated a multi-faceted approach to achieving integration through education, economic improvements, and by reducing the influence of the Catholic Church. Although it is possible, as Cynthia Steele has done, to read the novel as an account of the failure and undesirability of integration, this was not the interpretation which attracted the attention of reviewers and the judges of the *Premio Nacional de Literatura*.[16] Thus, my reading highlights how each instance of unsuccessful integration is presented as having had the potential to succeed if *cardenista* policies had been implemented. In so doing I aim to show the full extent to which *El indio* can be, and indeed was, interpreted as being perfectly attuned to the very latest government thinking and so was an ideal example of the nation-building literature the *Premio Nacional de Literatura* aimed to foster.[17]

In keeping with the *indigenismo* of the post-revolutionary period, *El indio* called for the sensitive integration of indigenous communities into the nation. Whereas Porfirian nation-building projects had advocated, where necessary, the 'forcible assimilation' of indigenous groups, after the revolution it was thought that integration was best achieved by improving the social conditions of indigenous communities.[18] Furthermore, under President Lázaro Cárdenas (1934–40), the dominant Porfirian stereotype of the 'lazy Indian' was replaced, as advocates of *indigenismo* and educators 'saw in indigenous peoples many of the behavioural traits that they sought to promote in Mexican society, including honesty, nobility, cooperativism, and a solid work ethic'.[19] This change in attitude complemented the earlier trend, which had emerged in the 1920s, of recognizing the country's indigenous past as part of Mexico's new *mestizo* identity.

In the 1920s and '30s, to be Mexican was to be *mestizo*. According to the 'nationalist rhetoric' of Manuel Gamio and others, 'to be truly Mexican one had to be "part indigenous or at least to embrace the idea that indigenousness was vital to the national consciousness"'.[20] Thus, the State advocated the integration of indigenous communities and urged the non-indigenous population to incorporate selected elements of indigenous culture and identity. *Indigenismo* facilitated both the valorization of the indigenous part of the mixture and the mestizoization of indigenous communities through greater integration and so was an important adjunct to the ideology of *mestizaje*.

In *El indio*, as Jeannette Kattar has proposed, each member of the group who goes to the *ranchería* to get revenge for the attack on the white prospectors can be said to represent one of the official attitudes that had been adopted toward the indigenous communities at different times in Mexican history.[21] The municipal president's secretary represents the *científicos* of the Porfirian era who thought that indigenous people were racially inferior (76). The schoolteacher, who suggests that the indigenous people should be incorporated into the nation without destroying their way of life, is the spokesperson for *indigenista* beliefs (Kattar, 76; Steele, *Narrativa indigenista*, 65). The teacher persuades the municipal president not to seek revenge and so the group of white men leave without attacking the *ranchería*; their departure symbolizes the novel's rejection of Porfirian beliefs and its acceptance of the *indigenista* point of view.[22]

As well as adopting an *indigenista* standpoint, *El indio* rejects the stereotype of the 'lazy Indian'; instead it values positive indigenous character traits and advocates the need to understand and preserve Mexico's indigenous heritage. Far from being lazy, the indigenous characters in the novel are intelligent and astute in their battle with the whites. They work hard on the *hacienda* and for their community, show skill and strength in fishing, precision when sowing crops, and agility when crossing difficult terrain. The indigenous community's harmonious relationship with nature is presented as positive and its way of life as one that should be emulated. The novel also expresses regret that the indigenous population has not valued its own heritage, in that they no longer understand the significance of the stones that were uncovered when the road was built. Through its positive portrayal of the indigenous way of life and by lamenting the erosion of this culture, *El indio* can be seen to participate in the process of 'ethnicizing' the nation.

One of the main ways in which post-revolutionary governments envisaged incorporating and mestizoizing indigenous populations was through education. Discourses about education abounded in Mexico in the 1920s and '30s, as it was believed that education would lead to greater national cohesion. It was thought that there could be no such cohesion without a common language and so one of the major challenges which national discourses and policy aimed to address was the education of indigenous people who did not speak Spanish.[23] Before 1934, the debate focused on the merits of monolingual versus bilingual education. Under Cárdenas, however, teachers became increasingly concerned with the broader social, economic and political circumstances of their students. This change of emphasis led to the *cardenistas* adopting a more integrated approach between 1920 and 1940, when the SEP's education project also began to address economic improvements. It became clear that this approach would be more effective in incorporating indigenous communities into the nation.

El indio can be interpreted, as Steele and Kattar have suggested, as supporting the socialist education project which, in the Cárdenas era, envisaged the rural schoolteacher as someone who, in addition to providing basic education, would try to improve the social, economic and political circumstances of the community in which he or she worked (Steele, *Narrativa indigenista*, 66–67; Kattar, 81). In the words of Joseph de Anda, the character of the teacher-leader illustrates that 'the true role of the rural teacher is as a community leader who will reorganize the community for a better life'.[24] By contrasting the approaches of different teachers, the novel illustrates that language has an important role to play in integrating the indigenous population into the nation and clearly endorses government initiatives that promoted bilingual education in rural schools. Thus the monolingual Spanish-speaking teacher cannot teach the indigenous people because he does not speak their language; he is aware of the need for language training for teachers, but the authorities ignore his requests for help. The lack of official support leads him to become disillusioned and return to the town. The bilingual teacher-leader, on the other hand, can teach the children of the *ranchería*, but he also becomes discouraged because the *mestizo* parents can afford to send their children to school whereas the indigenous parents cannot and have to send their children to work because they need the money. *El indio* thus acknowledges the importance of bilingual education but recognizes that it alone is not sufficient to overcome the marginalization of the indigenous population, and it follows *cardenista* discourses in advocating an integrated approach that addresses the economic as well as educational needs of indigenous communities.

One of the economic measures favoured by the *indigenistas* to facilitate integration was to build roads which connected indigenous communities to non-indigenous towns and villages. Road construction, which began under President Plutarco Elías Calles (1924–28), expanded under Cárdenas to include the building of roads to connect small communities. Wendy Waters' case study of a community in Veracruz, López y Fuentes' home state, shows that, once a road was built in a town, school enrolments often increased as greater contact with the outside world made apparent the benefits to be derived from education.[25] In particular, the roads encouraged the people to learn Spanish so that they could communicate with people who did not speak their language and with whom they now had more regular contact (Waters, 239). The cost and the large numbers of people required to build a road meant that local people had to work voluntarily on its construction (225). The people's labour was supposed to benefit the community. Frequently, however, the system, known as the *faena* system, was abused causing it to be outlawed by the 1917 Constitution. Nonetheless, such practices persisted. Waters' research shows the potential benefits and pitfalls associated with post-revolutionary road building. If successful, the roads would integrate the indigenous community and pave the way for other nation-building projects. However, road-building projects could further alienate indigenous communities if the abuses connected with the *faena* system continued.

Ultimately, *El indio* can be seen to endorse the view expressed by the first teacher, that the quickest way to integrate the indigenous communities is through the building of roads between *rancherías*. Roads, he believes, are key to establishing communication and restoring the trust of the indigenous population:

> 'Mi teoría radica en eso precisamente, en reintegrarles la confianza. ¿Cómo? A fuerza de obras benéficas... atrayéndolos con una protección efectiva... y, para ello, nada como las vías de comunicación, pero no las que van de ciudad a ciudad, por el valle, sino las que enlacen las rancherías; las carreteras enseñan el idioma, mejor que el escuela...' (31).[26]

> ['My theory rests precisely on that, on restoring confidence. How? By kindness.... We should treat them in a different way, attract them by giving them some real help... And for all this, there is nothing like roads. But not those that go through the valley to connect the cities; link the Rancherias instead. Highways teach language better than schools' (77).]

However, the road built in the novel does not go to the *ranchería* and the community's labour is exploited by the local politician and so an integrated approach is not adopted and, as a result, the indigenous community remains isolated. Overall, the novel argues in favour of the wide-ranging reforms promised by post-revolutionary governments, but highlights the need for these reforms to be integrated if they are to be effective, otherwise partial or incorrect implementation will lead to alienation rather than conciliation.

Through roads, education and the valorization of indigenous culture, the governments of the 1920s and '30s aimed to make indigenous people members of the national family. The government's rival in this mission was the Catholic Church. Post-revolutionary governments, especially that of Plutarco Elías Calles (1924–28), saw religious 'fanaticism' as an obstacle to progress and a threat to national unity. Thus, through a series of measures, they sought to limit the influence of the Catholic Church and clergy over the people. In the field of education, in particular, the Church opposed government efforts to remove the clergy from schools and opposed Cárdenas' socialist education plan. As a result of the Church's resistance to key national projects, anticlerical discourses became a feature of post-revolutionary political life.

El indio can be seen to follow the example of official discourses in presenting the Catholic Church as one of the major obstacles to revolutionary progress. The novel's anticlericalism is evident in the portrayal of the priest who uses the indigenous community to obstruct government projects to build a road and a school. The priest is not interested in the *ranchería* until he can use it as a battleground on which to fight the State. Competing with the State for the loyalty of the indigenous community, the priest asks them to build a church and to go on a pilgrimage. However, the narrator says that the church and the pilgrimage are only pretexts to prevent the community from working for the government:

> Pero lo más curioso era que el señor cura, una vez que dejó tirados los hilos para la construcción, se marchó sin ocuparse más de la obra, como si tan solo hubiera querido distraerlos de los trabajos encomendados por la autoridad (105).

> [But the most curious part of it all was that the reverend father, having left the cords stretched to mark the plan of the building, went off without paying any more attention to it; as if all he had wanted was to take them away from the work ordered by the authorities (220).]

The novel suggests that government projects, if properly realized, have a much greater potential for improving the circumstances of the indigenous people than those proposed by the priest.

While the government aims to educate the indigenous population, the priest tries to maintain control over them by fostering ignorance and making them believe that their survival depends on their obedience to the church. He tells them that the recent smallpox epidemics were a punishment from God and that if they do not build a church quickly 'quien sabe qué otra desgracia llovería sobre los naturales' (101) ['who knows what further misfortunes might rain down on the villages' (211)]. The indigenous community builds the church and goes on the pilgrimage but the narrator says that they do so out of fear not devotion and at the expense of their livelihood: 'Sólo el temor les hizo terminar la carretera y proseguir la iglesia: los campos estaban llenos de hierba y entre ésta se ahogaban las matas de maíz' (105) [It was only fear that made them finish the highway and continue with the church. The fields were full of weeds, choking the maize (220)]. Thus, the Church is portrayed as an obstacle to revolutionary progress because it abuses its position in its power struggle with the State.

As this discussion has shown, *El indio* readily sustains an interpretive strategy which focuses on the novel's social value and national significance at the time it was published. It can be interpreted as a resounding endorsement of numerous national discourses and nation-building projects of the Cárdenas era, some of which had only recently gained currency when the novel was published. Although no successful model of integration is presented, the first teacher, acting as the mouthpiece for *indigenista* discourses, clearly sets out how government aims can be achieved and the novel presents no reason to doubt his word. We can justifiably classify *El indio* as an *indigenista* novel which recognizes the value of Mexico's indigenous heritage, advocates bilingual education and argues, just as the SEP was doing, that education needs to be accompanied by social and economic reform. *El indio* can also be interpreted as being in keeping with official hostility towards the Church in a period when Church–State relations were strained. At a time when the State wanted to reward literature which shared its social values with national recognition and financial reward, *El indio* was an ideal candidate for the *Premio Nacional de Literatura*, which was awarded by a government seeking to replicate its success in producing nation-building art in literature by founding a new post-revolutionary literary canon.

Up to this point, I have followed the example of reviewers who looked for national significance in the public sphere and adopted an ethnographic view which saw the indigenous peoples as a collective and not as individuals. As a result of this perspective, reviewers showed little interest in the story about the guide and his fiancée which is based in the private sphere. I will now diverge from the reviewers' approach in order to show how, by adopting a private-national reading, these characters can be seen as forming the basis of a national allegory which uses the private sphere to comment on the public situation and convey a social message.

In *El indio*, the guide's experience can be interpreted as standing in for that of Mexico's indigenous population, so that, in accordance with Jameson's definition of national allegory, 'the telling of the individual story and the individual experience cannot but ultimately involve the whole laborious telling of the experience of the collectivity itself' (85–86). Written at a time when it was believed that the indigenous population could be integrated into the nation through increased contact between indigenous and non-indigenous peoples, the novel uses the guide's story to highlight the negative effects of past contact between these groups. Following his first contact with the white visitors to the *ranchería*, the guide is literally and figuratively crippled. His future father-in-law says that before he was appointed as the guide he was 'sano, hermoso y trabajador' (48) ['healthy, handsome and a good worker' (109)], but following the attack he is 'reducido a la mitad de su tamaño con las piernas torcidas como unas raíces quemadas y secas, encogido como una araña: ¡él que era tan bello y fuerte' (49) ['He has shrunk to half his size, with his legs as twisted as dry, burned roots, shrivelled like a spider: he who was so strong and beautiful' (110)]. When the smallpox epidemic breaks out no one comes to the village and the guide is unable or unwilling to seek outside help. His fiancée and her son die from the disease and he buries them in the hut, as he cannot even carry them to the burial ground. At the end of the novel, the guide keeps watch from his hiding place intent on avoiding further damaging encounters with the white population, suggesting that, thus far, attempts to integrate the indigenous population have failed because the trust of the indigenous population has been repeatedly abused. Given that the experiences of the young man represent those of the whole community, his failure to form a foundational couple with his fiancée or reproduce a next generation produces a cautionary ending which warns of what will happen if government policies aimed at sympathetically integrating the indigenous population are not fully adopted. The fact that such alternatives now exist, and we are shown that failures could so easily have been turned into successes, means that the ending is not as pessimistic as has been suggested.[27] Nonetheless, in *El indio*, as in the nineteenth-century national romances discussed by Sommer, the reader's emotional involvement with the foundational couple is also an emotional investment in the creation of the ideal nation and so the novel's unhappy ending leaves the reader longing for the new post-revolutionary nation in which the alternative approaches posited in the novel and by government policy are implemented and where the couple can live happily ever after (48). *El indio* uses the private narrative about the guide and his fiancée to comment on the public situation of Mexico's indigenous population and reinforce the call to promptly and efficiently implement government strategy. It is not essential, however, for readers to interpret *El indio* as a national allegory in order to identify the novel as being in keeping with the post-revolutionary government's nation-building agenda. Indeed, as illustrated by my previous discussion of the novel, it is possible to adopt an interpretive strategy whereby the story of the guide can be disregarded without entailing a loss in terms of the novel's perceived social value.

In the Introduction I suggested that interpretive strategies which allow national allegory to be identified in a text and which read the private as commenting on the public sphere are likely to be particularly useful when applied to texts produced by marginalized groups whose access to the public sphere is restricted. *El indio* can be seen to advocate the integration of the marginalized indigenous community into the nation and to use national allegory to do so. In this case, however, the national allegory does not threaten the status quo by trying to include those who the State aimed to exclude from the nation. Instead, it advocates the integration of indigenous communities along the same lines as the post-revolutionary government of Lázaro Cárdenas. Even in this case, in which the private narrative could be seen as reinforcing the novel's nation-building credentials, the story of the guide and his fiancée went unnoticed, suggesting that twentieth-century Mexican readers found it difficult to see the national reflected through the private rather than public sphere.

The *Premio Nacional de Literatura*, of which *El indio* was the first winner, established an expectation, or even a requirement, that national literature would contribute to the State's nation-building agenda. Dominant interpretive strategies employed by reviewers were apt to identify ways in which *El indio* could be seen to contribute to fostering a positive and constructive attitude towards the indigenous population, even without taking into account the private narrative of the guide and his fiancée. In this case, the interpretive strategy adopted by contemporary reviewers enabled them to see the novel's social purpose and they assessed its value accordingly. The only cost was that they overlooked the interest in the story of the guide, which a private-national reading revealed. In other cases, as will be seen, the limitations of using only one interpretive strategy had more serious consequences as novels whose potential national significance could only be identified with reference to the private sphere were often overlooked. In particular, we will see that woman-authored novels which could have been interpreted as contributing to post-revolutionary nation-building were excluded from the literary canon, when the adoption of alternative interpretive strategies which allow the private sphere to be seen as commenting on the public situation might have led to them being valued more highly. This chapter has taken an important first step towards uncovering the process by which the post-revolutionary canon was formed, starting with the *Premio Nacional de Literatura*, and has unmasked some of the core values subsuming the canon as they were established in the decree which created the prize. These values are now ripe to be challenged and new interpretive strategies will enable us to better acknowledge women's contributions to literature and national political debate.

Notes to Chapter 1

1. SEP Archive 1934–1936 Depto. de Bellas Artes Concursos y Certámenes 17–11–218 196. Referencia VII/357.2/3. Concurso de literatura, periodismo, obras científicas, etc. Asunto — Documentación relativa.
2. 'No lo olvide. Los premios nacionales sobre literatura, teatro, contribución científica y labor periodística', *El Universal Gráfico*, 9 July 1935.
3. SEP Archive 1934–1936 Depto. de Bellas Artes Concursos y Certámenes 17–11–218 196. Referencia VII/357.2/3. Concurso de literatura, periodismo, obras científicas, etc. Asunto — Documentación relativa.
4. Erica Segre, *Intersected Identities: Strategies of Visualization in Nineteenth and Twentieth-Century Mexican Culture* (New York: Berghahn Books, 2007), p. 11.
5. Gonzalo de la Porra, 'Puntos de Vista. Los "Premios Nacionales"', *El Universal*, 27 March 1936, 1st section, p. 3.
6. Gregorio López y Fuentes is included in the following histories of Mexican literature: María Edmée Alvarez Z., *Literatura mexicana e hispanoamericana. Manual para uso de los alumnos de las escuelas preparatorias*, 6th edn (Mexico: Porrúa, 1966), pp. 480–84; Emmanuel Carballo, *Bibliografía de la novela mexicana del siglo XX* (Mexico: UNAM, 1988), p. 181; Carlos González Peña, *Historia de la literatura mexicana. Desde los orígenes hasta nuestros días*, 5th edn (Mexico: Porrúa, 1954), pp. 404–06; Sergio Howland Bustamente, *Historia de la literatura mexicana. Con algunas notas sobre literatura de Hispanoamérica* (Mexico: Editorial F. Trillas, 1961), Chapter 16; Martínez, *Literatura mexicana. Primera parte*, p. 45; José Luis Martínez and Christopher Domínguez Michael, p. 90; María del Carmen Millán, *Diccionario de escritores mexicanos* (Mexico: UNAM, 1967); Aurora M. Ocampo, 'Gregorio López y Fuentes', in *Diccionario de escritores mexicanos siglo XX. Desde las generaciones del ateneo y novelistas de la revolución hasta nuestros días*, Tomo IV (H-LL), ed. by Aurora M. Ocampo (Mexico: UNAM, 1997), pp. 462–65; Alberto Valenzuela Rodarte, *Historia de la literatura en México* (Mexico: Editorial Jus, 1961), pp. 476–82.
7. John Englekirk, 'El indio. Novela mexicana, por Gregorio López y Fuentes', *Letras*, December 1937, p. 8.

8. Celestino Herrera Frimont, 'Gregorio López y Fuentes y el premio nacional de literatura', *El Nacional*, 9 August 1936, Suplemento, p. 3.

9. Eleven reviews of *El indio* were published: [Untitled review of *El indio*], *Revista de México de Cultura*, supl. *El Nacional*, 7 August 1955, pp. 8–9; Salvador Cordero, 'Un libro y un escritor', *Letras*, May 1936, p. 2; Jacobo Dalevuelta, 'Libros Nuevos', *El Universal*, 27 June 1935, p. 3; Jacobo Dalevuelta, 'Libros nuevos', *El Universal*, 27 December 1935, 1st section, p. 3; Englekirk, '*El indio*', p. 8; Herrera Frimont, p. 3; Ernesto Higuera, 'Una novela social de Gregorio López y Fuentes', *Cuadrante rojo*, 1939, pp. 149–52; Mauricio Magdaleno, 'Escaparate', *El Nacional*, 30 June 1935, 2nd section, p. 1; A. Pereira Alves, '*El indio*. Novela de Gregorio López y Fuentes', *Letras*, June 1938, p. 4; Rubén Salazar Mallén, 'En torno a la novela. *El indio*, de Gregorio López y Fuentes', *El Universal*, 19 December 1935, 1st section, p. 3; Salomón de la Selva, 'Un gran libro mexicano. *El indio* de Gregorio López y Fuentes', *El Universal*, 24 October 1935, 1st section, pp. 3, 10.

10. SEP Archive 1934–1936 Depto. de Bellas Artes Concursos y Certámenes 17–11–218 196. Referencia VII/357.2/3. Concurso de literatura, periodismo, obras científicas, etc. Asunto — Documentación relativa.

11. Jacobo Dalevuelta was the *nom de plume* of Fernando Ramírez de Aguilar.

12. For a detailed discussion of reviewers' comments on style in *La región más transparente* and *Arráncame la vida* see Chapters 3 and 6.

13. [Advertisement], *Letras. Publicación Literaria y Bibliográfica*, June 1935, p. 12.

14. F. González Guerrero, 'Enciclopedia Mínima. Aguila que cae', *El Universal Gráfico*, 14 June 1935, p .7, 13; F. González Guerrero, 'Enciclopedia Mínima. El volador', *El Universal Gráfico*, 17 July 1935, p. 6; F. González Guerrero, 'Enciclopedia Mínima. El Nahual', *El Universal Gráfico*, 22 August 1935, pp. 7, 11; F. González Guerrero, 'Enciclopedia Mínima. Superstición', *El Universal Gráfico*, 23 August 1935, pp. 7, 11.

15. De la Selva, p. 10; 'En busca de la identidad perdida', *El Excélsior*, 24 June 1983. CNIPL/ EXP.s. XIX/1.

16. Steele argues that the novel repeatedly shows the *cardenista* project to be impractical, unrealizable and full of contradictions (71). Steele claims that the novel supports national discourses through the speeches of the first teacher, but that these discourses are undermined on the level of plot and characterization (66–67). For her, the novel ultimately validates the indigenous rather than the *mestizo* way of life and undermines the thesis that integration is desirable (70). Cynthia Steele, *Narrativa indigenista en los Estados Unidos y México*, trans. by Manuel Fernández Perera (Mexico: Instituto Nacional Indigenista, 1985).

17. For a plot summary of the novel *El indio* see Appendix.

18. Alan Knight, 'Racism, Revolution, and Indigenismo: Mexico, 1910–1940', in *The Idea of Race in Latin America, 1870–1940*, ed. by Richard Graham (Austin: University of Texas Press, 1990), pp. 71–113 (p. 79).

19. Stephen E. Lewis, 'The Nation, Education and the "Indian Problem" in Mexico, 1920–1940', in *The Eagle and the Virgin: Nation and Cultural Revolution in Mexico, 1920–1940*, ed. by Mary K. Vaughan and Stephen E. Lewis (Durham, NC: Duke University Press, 2006), pp. 176–95 (p. 186).

20. Rick A. López, 'The Noche Mexicana and the Exhibition of Popular Arts: Two Ways of Exalting Indigenousness', in *The Eagle and the Virgin: Nation and Cultural Revolution in Mexico, 1920–1940*, ed. by Mary K. Vaughan and Stephen E. Lewis (Durham, N.C.: Duke University Press, 2006), pp. 23–42 (p. 36).

21. Jeannette Kattar,'Gregorio López y Fuentes et son roman: *El indio*' (unpublished doctoral thesis, Centre de Hautes Études Afro-Ibero-Americaines de l'Université de Dakar, 1969), pp. 75–76.

22. José Antonio Portuondo and Loló de la Torriente have also argued that the novel supports the *indigenista* project. José Antonio Portuondo, 'La concreción de un mito', in *Recopilación de textos sobre la novela de la Revolución Mexicana*, ed. by Rogelio Rodríguez Coronel (Havana: Casa de las Américas, 1975), pp. 283–87 (p. 285); Loló de la Torriente, '*El indio* y Huasteca en su tiempo', in ibid, pp. 308–15 (p. 309).

23. On the challenges of indigenous education and the solutions proposed in the post-revolutionary period see Lewis, 'The Nation, Education and the 'Indian Problem' in Mexico, 1920–1940'.

24. Joseph de Anda, 'The Indian in the Works of Gregorio López y Fuentes' (unpublished doctoral thesis, University of Southern California, 1969), pp. 149–49.
25. Wendy Waters, 'Remapping Identities: Road Construction and Nation Building in Post-revolutionary Mexico', in *The Eagle and the Virgin: Nation and Cultural Revolution in Mexico, 1920–1940*, ed. by Mary K. Vaughan and Stephen E. Lewis (Durham, NC: Duke University Press, 2006), pp. 221–42 (p. 238).
26. All references in this chapter are to Gregorio López y Fuentes, *El indio*, 5th edn (Mexico: Porrúa, 1972) unless otherwise stated. First published 1935. English translations of the novel are taken from Gregorio López y Fuentes, *El indio*, trans. by Anita Brenner (New York: Frederick Ungar, 1937; repr. 1961). All other translations are by the author.
27. Cynthia Steele, for example, argues that the novel reaches a pessimistic conclusion about the possibilities of future contact between the two groups because it shows that 'lo admirable de la sociedad indígena no puede sobrevivir al contacto con el mundo exterior' (*Narrativa indigenista*, 68) [that which is admirable in indigenous society cannot survive contact with the outside world]. See also: Anda, p. 267; Kattar, p. 81, p. 95; Fernando Alegría, 'López y Fuentes: trayectoria y temas' in Rodríguez Coronel, ed., *Recopilación de textos*, pp. 288–94 (p. 293).

CHAPTER 2

Yo también, Adelita:
An Unheard Call for Women's Suffrage

Written only a year after *El indio*, the reception of schoolteacher Consuelo Delgado's first novel, *Yo también, Adelita*, could not have been more different. While *El indio* achieved national recognition through the *Premio Nacional de Literatura*, *Yo también, Adelita* went virtually unnoticed. Reviewers did not interpret Delgado's novel as having social purpose, nor did they see it as contributing to post-revolutionary nation-building. As a result, *Yo también, Adelita* was quickly forgotten, omitted from all but two histories of Mexican literature, and excluded from the Mexican novelistic canon.[1] The discussion that follows, the first re-evaluation of the text in over half a century, shows how *Yo también, Adelita* could have been interpreted as responding to some of the key issues of the day, including women's suffrage, socialist education and defanaticization, as well as supporting official myths about the unified and ongoing Revolution, had alternative interpretive strategies been adopted.[2] However, reviewers made assumptions about the book based on the author's gender and, decisively for the fate of the novel, interpretations which would have identified the novel's national significance went unnoticed by contemporary reviewers.

Yo también, Adelita was published by Ediciones del Grupo en Marcha. The Grupo en Marcha was a left-wing organization of which Delgado was a valued member.[3] Founded by Enrique Othón Díaz in 1931, the group had political as well as literary interests.[4] They carried out social work in several states, including the Federal District, and published books which were 'de interés colectivo' [of general interest].[5] In a letter to Lázaro Cárdenas, Díaz reminded the new President that the Grupo en Marcha 'ha estado plenamente identificada en todos los momentos con el Gobierno de la Revolución' [has always identified with the Government of the Revolution].[6] Although Delgado was a member of this group which had some contact with President Cárdenas, this connection did not assist her literary career. Furthermore, *Yo también, Adelita* was Delgado's first novel and so, unlike Gregorio López y Fuentes, she was not an established author and, as a schoolteacher, she did not have a national, public profile. This situation was compounded by the fact that her novel was published by a small publisher that was largely funded by Othón Díaz himself and he is the only other author known to have books published with Ediciones del Grupo en Marcha.[7] It is unlikely that more than one thousand copies of *Yo también, Adelita* were printed and the book may have had limited commercial distribution. *Yo también, Adelita* was advertised only once in a small listing in *Letras* and was not awarded any literary prizes.[8] Clearly, Delgado's novel did not enjoy the same benefits *El indio* did in terms of being endorsed and promoted by a prestigious publisher who had an established place in the literary field, and these differences go some way to explaining why *Yo también, Adelita* struggled to find a place in the national literary canon.

Reviews had significant potential to boost a novel's profile. If a publisher wanted their book to be reviewed they had to send a sample copy to the newspaper.[9] The Grupo en Marcha is unlikely to have been able to send many free sample copies to reviewers, and books sent by more established publishers were likely to have taken priority over Delgado's novel. Consequently, *Yo también, Adelita* was reviewed fewer times than *El indio*. Only three contemporary reviews of *Yo también, Adelita* were written, all of which appeared in national newspapers in August 1936.[10] Two were published in weekly columns, 'Libros Nuevos' by Jacobo Dalevuelta in *El Universal* and 'Por el mundo de los libros' by Pedro Gringoire in *El Excélsior*, and the third was on the regular 'Página Femenina' page of *El Nacional*.[11] These reviews were written by influential custodians of literary knowledge and were likely to attract a loyal readership which valued the columnists' opinions. *Yo también, Adelita* should have benefited from being included in such articles; however, these reviews were somewhat critical of the novel and were brief in comparison to those of *El indio*.

All of the reviews noted that *Yo también, Adelita* drew attention to the role played by middle-class women during the revolution. Enriqueta de Parodi, for example, described Delgado's novel as 'Reminiscencia del heroísmo anónimo de las mujeres que en espíritu, en amor y resignación, aportaron su valioso contingente en la magna epopeya de nuestra lucha social' (6) [A reminiscence on the anonymous heroism of women who with spirit, love and resignation made a valuable contribution to the great epic of our social struggle]. The reviews commended the novel for shedding light on this hitherto neglected subject but it was not seen to warrant great praise. Indeed, all of the reviews identified shortcomings in the novel. Gringoire in particular complained that the novel dealt too briefly with the different stages of the revolution and took issue with the novel's ending, albeit, he admitted, because of a difference of opinion rather than for literary reasons. Gringoire did not think that the ending was in keeping with the rest of the novel. The conclusion, he said, was 'un toque final doctrinario en que parece que domina el deseo de ajustarse a la "ortodoxia" que está de moda' (2) [a final doctrinaire touch in which the desire to fit in with the current 'orthodoxy' dominates]. Gringoire's concern about the novel's politics and the reviewers' observations about the unusual focus of *Yo también, Adelita* confirm that, when evaluating a novel, the principal consideration was whether or not it had social purpose. In the Cárdenas era, to have social purpose meant contributing to nation-building by supporting official national discourses. Reviewers who had the authority to consecrate texts deemed that *Yo también, Adelita* did not engage with the key issues of the day or possess sufficient social value and, as a result, Delgado's novel was excluded from the canon.

In addition to noting the unusual subject matter of the novel, reviewers also commented on the aesthetic qualities of *Yo también, Adelita*. Dalevuelta said that the novel had many defects 'especialmente en la forma' (3) [particularly in form]. Gringoire criticized the novel for being too brief and lacking description. Parodi, on the other hand, praised the novel for being concise:

La habilidad de la autora, que en medio de la sencillez de su obra ha sabido hacerla interesante, consiste en que no ha tratado de engalanar los capítulos de inútil literatura, sino que abriendo horizontes en los que la vida de provincia se desarrolla serenamente, corta a veces en forma magistral el relato, que dejando de ser bucólico se torna casi epopéyico' (6).

[The skill of the author, who in the simplicity of her work has kept it interesting, lies in the fact that she has not tried to adorn the chapters with useless literature. Instead she opens up scenes in which provincial life unfolds serenely but then at times the story is masterfully interrupted and, ceasing to be pastoral, becomes almost epic.]

The discrepancy in the views about the novel's aesthetic value shows that aesthetic judgements were highly subjective and that content was the decisive factor in determining canonicity.

The critics did not wholly dislike *Yo también, Adelita*, but a comparison of comments made by reviewers about *El indio* and *Yo también, Adelita* reveals how they saw one as a 'classic' and the other as a curious novelty. Parodi welcomed *Yo también, Adelita*'s realistic portrayal of people and places, as did Gringoire who noted: 'la vida de aquellos días está [...] bien reflejada en conjunto' (2) [daily life of that time is [...] on the whole accurately represented]. Reviewers of *El indio* also attached great importance to accuracy in the novel, suggesting that realism was a requirement for literature at the time. However, while Parodi and Gringoire thought *Yo también, Adelita* was a true reflection of life, their praise was not as generous as that given to *El indio*. Likewise, Gringoire's comments comparing *Yo también, Adelita* to a 'cuadro' [painting] which 'tiene, a las veces, pinceladas maestras' (2) [has some masterful brushstrokes] fade in comparison to those made by reviewers of *El indio* who said that López y Fuentes' novel was like a mural. Gringoire saw *Yo también, Adelita* as being on a smaller scale than *El indio*; a novel which was able to show an often forgotten aspect of Mexican life rather than capturing the whole nation as murals did. Delgado's novel may have contained some masterstrokes, but its scope was not broad enough to be the equivalent in literature of the public murals which had clear social value and nation-building potential.

Overall, the reviews of *Yo también, Adelita* were lukewarm and reviewers neither loved nor hated Delgado's first novel. Crucially for its prospects of being included in the post-revolutionary canon, however, their interpretive strategies reflected their assumptions that a novel by a woman and with a female protagonist would not address the 'big picture' of the nation and caused them to overlook its potential social purpose. The first stage of my analysis of *Yo también, Adelita* shows how Delgado's novel could have been seen to engage with a range of contemporary debates surrounding women's suffrage, the role of the Catholic Church in society, and socialist education.[12] This interpretation, which highlights the novel's potential national significance, is facilitated by a private-national reading.

Women were central to many of the key issues of the day in the Cárdenas era, such as the campaign for women's suffrage. Women were seen as allies of the Catholic Church against the State, and most teachers were women at a time when the government was trying to introduce major reforms in education. In the national discourses of the period, therefore, women occupied a contradictory position as both the primary implementers of, and the major obstacle to, the revolutionary project and the nation's progress. At stake in these debates was the relationship of women to the public and private spheres as well as the nature of the division between public and private.

In the 1930s, the State wanted and needed women to participate in the revolutionary project in ways which extended their traditional, private roles. Through discourses on education and public health the State instilled in women an understanding of the rights and responsibilities of revolutionary citizenship. The State could be said to have succeeded beyond its own expectations in involving women in the public sphere as suffragists took these arguments to what they saw as their logical conclusion in campaigning for one of the fundamental rights of citizenship. Historian Jocelyn Olcott has noted that when staking claim to citizenship and the right to be enfranchised some women 'tapped into the masculinized rhetoric linking citizenship to military service, paid labor, and civic engagement' while 'others mobilized distinctly feminine assertions of citizenship rights based on unpaid reproductive labor, motherhood, and claims to morality'.[13] In the latter case in particular, the women blurred traditional distinctions between public and private spheres by drawing attention to the national significance of their 'private' roles. For a time women espousing each point of view formed two distinctive groups, but under Cárdenas and the Popular Front, formed in 1935, the distinction between the two groups became less pronounced (Olcott, 160).[14]

Women in favour of suffrage, including members of the Popular Front women's organization, and those opposed to suffrage, such as the Unión Femenina Católica Mexicana, invoked the ideal of the selfless and self-sacrificing *mujer abnegada* in order to win support for their cause (Olcott, 16). Opponents of women's suffrage used the stereotype of the *mujer abnegada* to suggest that women's passivity made them unsuited to the public realm, thus reaffirming the public–private divide (Olcott, 16). On the other hand, claiming to be self-sacrificing was one way in which suffragists challenged accusations that they were unfeminine and would neglect their roles as wives and mothers if granted suffrage. In so doing, they tried to demonstrate that they would be able to perform their private duties alongside their public role as citizens.

Yo también, Adelita can be interpreted as following the example of contemporary suffragists in breaking down the division between public and private spheres by claiming revolutionary citizenship, and therefore the right to vote, for women who contributed to the revolution via the public and private domains. Through the protagonist, Rosina, the novel highlights the public contributions made by women schoolteachers, whose role was to educate the country's future citizens and to continue the work of the revolution. In the private sphere, women's roles as wives and mothers are recast as part of their civic duties which entitle them to the rights associated with citizenship. Significantly, the narrator presents women's sacrifices and contributions as equal but different to those of men when s/he states: 'Así fue fecundada la Revolución con la sangre y la vida de los hombres y el dolor y sacrificio de las mujeres' (126–27) [Thus the Revolution was nourished with the blood and lives of men and the pain and sacrifice of women].[15] In this way, the sacrifices made by, for example Concha, whose husband and sons die in the revolution leaving her to endure emotional pain and financial hardship, are to be read as evidence that they are model *mujeres abnegadas* and full revolutionary citizens who deserve recognition in the form of the vote.

A major obstacle to women's suffrage under Cárdenas was the fear within the ruling party that it would lead to an electoral defeat. To allay such fears some of the interested parties proposed restrictions on women's suffrage. The Feminist Revolutionary Party, for example, proposed to limit suffrage to women who were '21 years old, not a member of any religious congregation, not collaborating in any occult activities, and economically independent and autonomous' (Olcott, 161). Such stipulations were designed to restrict the right to vote to those women who would vote for the PNR (Olcott, 168). These women were likely to be middle-class and liberal. Indeed, there is some evidence to suggest that there was a common, though not necessarily accurate, perception in the 1930s and '40s that whether or not women supported the institutionalized Revolution depended on their social class.[16]

If we interpret events in the private sphere as commenting on the public situation, *Yo también, Adelita* can be seen to share, or to have internalized, the belief of many in the PNR that upper-class women were anti-revolutionary. The narrator feels no sympathy towards the upper-class women in the novel, who are the main opponents of the revolution and usually Catholic. On the other hand, the novel strategically aligns middle-class women, and above all the protagonist Rosina, with the revolution, the State's policy on education and its attitudes to religion as a means to endorse their right to suffrage. At school, Rosina is bullied by an upper-class girl called Sara Romero and at the *Escuela Normal para Maestras* by Elodia who still supports Porfirio Díaz, even after he has been overthrown by Madero. Other elite women hold a *fiesta* for charity which the narrator claims aimed to 'adormecer la conciencia de los desheredados con el sueño de la dádiva' (57) [to dull the consciousness of the dispossessed with the promise of free gifts], thus preventing them from rebelling. These women are accused of actively opposing the revolution just as their middle-class counterparts are portrayed as active supporters of the revolution.

In its representation of upper-class women, *Yo también, Adelita* can be seen to suggest, as did official discourse, that not all women were supporters of the revolution. The novel may be interpreted as reflecting the view of those who proposed that only some women should be enfranchised. However, anti-revolutionary women are clearly in the minority, suggesting that the novel endorses the PCM's view that universal women's suffrage would not pose a threat to the Left or the PNR's electoral chances. This is a persuasive argument because, even if she was not directly involved with the PCM (which at this time was part of the Popular Front alliance with the PNR), as a teacher, it is highly likely that Delgado would have been aware of PCM policies and ideas.[17] Regardless of whether it adopts the PCM position or not, to some extent the novel can be seen to confirm the State's fears that some women were not ready to be 'good citizens' but it does so only to challenge the view that the majority of women were anti-revolutionary.

Of all the characters in the novel, Rosina's upper-class, Catholic aunt, Herlinda, is portrayed most unfavourably. Herlinda opposes the revolution because she fears changes which would threaten her own privileged position in society. She is the only one of the main female characters who does not behave as the ideal *mujer abnegada* [self-sacrificing woman]. Rather, Herlinda is a religious fanatic who abdicates her parental responsibilities and would rather leave her son Paco with her parents than curtail her Church activities. Her tendency to spend most of her time in church is described by the narrator as 'su debilidad principal' (16) [her principal weakness] and, in clear breach of the requirements to be a good, self-sacrificing *mujer abnegada*, she says that she would disobey her husband if he tried to stop her attending church. The portrayal of Herlinda thus suggests that the Church undermines rather than supports motherhood and the family. Furthermore, by interpreting the private narrative about Herlinda as shedding light on public circumstances the reader is led to conclude that the Church undermines the national family.

At the time *Yo también, Adelita* was published Catholic women were perceived as a particular threat because of the recent second *cristero* wars (*c.* 1934–37) which were fought to oppose the government's cornerstone education policy. In 1934, the SEP reiterated its commitment to banning religious education and incoming president, Lázaro Cárdenas, announced his intention to introduce the *Plan de Acción de la Escuela Socialista* (commonly referred to as 'socialist education'). In many ways, Cárdenas' education initiatives were designed to replace the Church as the centre of community life, with teachers as the new, secular missionaries. Thus, from 1934 to 1940, education was the major battleground on which the conflict between Church and State was fought.

In *Yo también, Adelita*, the Church is unfavourably compared with its revolutionary equivalent, the school. When Rosina does not want to pray, the priest tries to scare her into so doing. He says: 'Pues te va a llevar al Diablo! Un día de estos se te aparece' (41) ['Well the Devil is going to get you. He'll appear to you one of these days']. The narrator further reports that Rosina finds the atmosphere of the church oppressive: 'un gran temor la invade y le aprieta la garganta viéndose rodeada del mujerío ceñudo y amenazante' (41) [a great fear takes hold of her and her throat tightens on finding herself surrounded by all those scowling and threatening women]. When she explores the church Rosina finds incomprehensible writing, dark rooms, books covered in dust and blurred pictures. Her experience in the church is in marked contrast to that of the happy children that she can see through the window who have left school and are either playing in the garden or buying sweets. By contrasting the schoolchildren's experience with Rosina's, the novel can be interpreted as advocating school and education as replacements for the church and religion. The novel's potential social value as an endorsement of socialist education was, however, overlooked by contemporary interpretive strategies which did not allow for a private-national reading.

In *Yo también, Adelita*, as in nation-building discourses of the period, education is presented as a way of continuing the work of the revolution and removing social inequality. The Porfirian school is portrayed as fostering class division because the teachers give preferential treatment to children from upper-class backgrounds. The novel also expresses criticisms which historian Mary K. Vaughan suggests were common among 'middle-class thinkers' who thought that Porfirian education was 'verbalist, authoritarian, and divorced from everyday life'.[18] Thus, the narrator rejects Porfirian education methods, which involved reciting responses that had been learned by heart, as 'escuela carente del sentido de razón y llena de un rabioso sello individualista' (68) [education lacking in reason and filled by a fervent hallmark of self-interest]. However, education ultimately enables Rosina to triumph over her upper-class rival, Sara Romero, who bullies her at school. In the end-of-year exams, Rosina is more successful than Sara because she has worked hard, and she is even able to humiliate her rival by answering questions that Sara cannot. Rosina's academic success enables her to erase the troubling memory of her humiliation and go on to attend the *Escuela Normal para Maestras* in Mexico City. Rosina will be part of the new cadre of revolutionary teachers who, like the protagonist of *Yo también, Adelita*, were typically from the 'modest middle class, predominantly rural but sometimes urban' and 'had been weaned in the incipient liberal civic culture of the prerevolutionary period' (Vaughan, 12). In its portrayal of Rosina's educational career, the novel could be seen to have significant social value, as it endorsed the official view that education could overcome social inequality and continue the work of the revolution. However, the novel's potential social and national significance was overlooked by contemporary reviewers.

As this discussion makes clear, it is possible to interpret *Yo también, Adelita* as very much in tune with the contemporary political climate and broadly in line with the national discourses of its day with perhaps only minor divergence on the issue of women's suffrage. We may consider that *Yo también, Adelita* was excluded from the post-revolutionary canon because it was too far to the left of the PNR's position on suffrage, or that the issue was so contentious that reviewers preferred not to acknowledge its presence in the novel. This explanation is, however, insufficient. Reviewers assumed that a woman-authored novel about women's role in the revolution was a curiosity of limited significance and not, therefore, worthy of serious consideration. At the very time that suffragists were trying to break down the division between public and private which excluded women from citizenship, *Yo también, Adelita* broke down the barrier in literature and used the private sphere to comment on the public situation. Nonetheless, reviewers were unable or unwilling to understand the public significance of women's 'private' contributions in life or in literature and so the novel's call for women's suffrage went unheard.

In the Introduction I suggested that private-national readings of woman-authored texts are particularly fruitful in enabling their potential national significance to be identified and my reading thus far has shown this statement to be true of *Yo también, Adelita*. By reading Delgado's novel as a national allegory which challenges women's exclusion from the nation, as I will proceed to do, I am able to further underscore the novel's potential national significance which was overlooked by contemporary reviewers. As Jameson has suggested, in national allegory events in the private sphere are to be read as commenting on the public situation. National allegory is the ideal medium for those marginalized from the public sphere to challenge their exclusion, precisely because it breaks down the public and private to enable the excluded party to write themselves into the nation. Through the protagonist

Rosina, *Yo también, Adelita* places women at the centre of national allegory and the nation so that, in accordance with Jameson's definition of national allegory, Rosina's 'private individual destiny' is 'an allegory of the embattled situation of the public [...] culture and society' (69). In other words, Rosina's story is also that of Mexico.

An interpretation of *Yo también, Adelita* as a national allegory further shows that the novel can be seen to present the revolution as ongoing and unified just as it was in the official discourses of the Cárdenas era. Thomas Benjamin has demonstrated that one of the main concerns of post-revolutionary governments was to reconstruct the revolution, which consisted of different factions, as unified and ongoing in order to consolidate power and legitimize their rule.[19] Benjamin gives this myth of the Revolution as unified and ongoing the label '*la Revolución*', and notes that 'the Cárdenas administration reaffirmed the ideals of *la Revolución* more than any previous, or subsequent, Mexican government' (94). *Yo también, Adelita* can be seen to endorse the myth of *la Revolución* by using national allegory in order to (re)produce the same Revolutionary Family of Benito Juárez, the Flores Magón brothers, Francisco Madero, Venustiano Carranza, Francisco (Pancho) Villa, and Emiliano Zapata (though not Victoriano Huerta) that was favoured in official discourses of the 1930s. Rosina's grandfather, Estanislao, can be interpreted as representing an idealized version of Porfirio Díaz or as representing the liberal forefather of the Revolution, Juárez.[20] Estanislao's brother, Pedro, represents the *Magonistas* (supporters of the Flores Magón brothers) who were adopted as the 'official' precursors to the revolution and his sons the different factions who fought in the revolution.[21]

Pedro can be identified with the *Magonistas* because he fights and dies in the Viesca uprising, which was a forerunner of the revolution. Viesca and other similar revolts were organized by the Partido Liberal Mexicano (PLM) which was founded by Ricardo Flores Magón while he was in exile in 1905.[22] Estanislao is an influential character in Rosina's early life and he enables her future participation in the post-revolutionary nation by supporting her education when her father is unable to do so. If we equate Estanisalo with Juárez, the novel can be seen to recognize Juárez's role in Mexico's development as an independent nation and his significance as the (imagined) forefather of the institutionalized Revolution. Estanislao's cautious support of Carranza points to the latter as being Juárez's heir and the next generation in the Revolutionary Family. He says to Rosina: 'Tenemos gran fe en don Venustiano; sólo él es capaz de hacer un hecho las aspiraciones de las gentes del campo, de los trabajadores carne de explotación' (95–96) [We have great faith in Venustiano; only he is capable of fulfilling the aspirations of people in the countryside and the exploited workers]. However, the reader, with the benefit of hindsight, knows that Carranza was assassinated in 1920 and a conversation between Rosina and Estanislao introduces a note of caution:

> — ¿Crees, papalito que la situación ya se arregló? ¿Les darán sus tierras a los campesinos?
> — Te repito que hay gran fe en don Venustiano.
> — ¿Y si se olvidara?
> — No habría más remedio que volver a empezar (96).

['Do you think, grandfather, that the situation has been resolved? Will the
peasants get their land?'
    'I say again that there is much faith in Venustiano.'
    'And if he forgets?'
    'There will be no alternative but to start again.']

The novel, like President Calles in the 1920s, may be suggesting that Carranza
strayed from the true path of the revolution and consequently the struggle to fulfil
the goals of the revolution is ongoing.[23]

Madero and the *convencionista* cause are incorporated into the national allegory
through the characters of Pablo and Alberto, Pedro's sons, who are involved in
romantic relationships with Aurora and Rosina respectively. As is characteristic of
national allegories as defined by Jameson, libidinal investment in *Yo también, Adelita*
is to be read primarily in political terms (72). According to official discourses of
the ongoing Revolution, Madero was well intentioned but unable to establish
democracy (Benjamin, 51, 60). Pablo dies fighting Huerta and the description of
his untimely death is the key to interpreting the novel's portrayal of the revolution.
The narrator says that 'la adversidad tronchó en flor aquella magnífica vida,
prodigada, íntegra' (94) [adversity cut down that magnificent, full, upright life in
bloom]. Adversity prematurely ended Pablo's life in its prime ('en flor'), his life was
magnificent and whole, honest and complete, but was squandered. The verb used to
describe the beginning of Pablo and Aurora's love was 'florecer' (90) [to blossom] so
the cutting down of Pablo's life 'en flor' [in bloom] not only points to his physical
death but also to the death of the love between Pablo and Aurora. Pablo supported
Madero, who had the potential to 'blossom', but he failed to effect real change,
as Pablo notes: 'Con esta alma buena de don Panchito no hemos visto en realidad
mejoría alguna' (80) [With Madero's good intentions we have not really seen any
improvement]. As a result, Madero was defeated. Madero's valiant but doomed
effort to create a new nation out of the revolution is represented in the novel by the
failed union between Pablo and Aurora

Alberto is identified with the *convencionista* cause formed from the alliance
between Villa and Zapata at the Convention of Aguascalientes in 1914. He dies
fighting against Carranza and it seems that Alberto, like his brother, has failed
to provide a permanent father figure for Mexico. Following his death, however,
his wife, Rosina, discovers that she is pregnant with his child suggesting that the
convencionista cause, while unsuccessful in the short term, may prosper in the future.
The child represents hope for the future; its generation will continue the legacy
of the revolution. Reading the personal narrative as a comment of the political
situation, we are led to understand that there is hope in the long term although the
revolution has not been successful in the short term.

The novel is ambiguous in terms of which side it supports in the revolution.
All sides (with the exception of Huerta) are presented as having potential, though
it is never realized. The novel thus upholds the official myths of a unified and
ongoing Revolution and follows the example of post-revolutionary governments
who regularly claimed that their predecessors had strayed from the true path of the
revolution, which they now represented. Notably, the ending, whereby Rosina is
left alone to raise her child, can be seen to underline the importance of women's

contribution to this continuing project and the significant role women have in securing the future of the nation.

Yo también, Adelita's view of the Revolution as unified and ongoing was the same as that expressed in official discourses but, because reviewers did not read the private in terms of the public, this interpretation of the novel was ignored, potentially costing it a place in the canon. Influenced by the gender of the author and the protagonists, reviewers did not notice that *Yo también, Adelita* supported socialist education and shared the State's anticlericalism. Nor did they see how Delgado's novel can be seen to use the arguments of suffragists, which aimed to remove the traditional distinction between public and private, to argue that women were entitled to be enfranchised because of the important contributions they had made to the revolution and to the post-revolutionary nation as long-suffering wives and mothers, as supporters of the revolution in their own right, and as teachers. In particular, *Yo también, Adelita* can be read as highlighting and demanding recognition in the form of citizenship for the role played by middle-class women whose participation, as reviewers acknowledged, had been largely ignored in other narratives about the revolution, including the famous *corrido* from which the novel takes its title. According to my reading, it is these women that *Yo también, Adelita* suggests are particularly worthy of enfranchisement.

To appreciate the full extent to which woman-authored novels such as *Yo también, Adelita* can be interpreted as addressing issues of national concern, we have to put aside assumptions that novels by and about women will not address issues of national significance. We must be open to developing and adopting new interpretive strategies, including ones, such as that employed in this book, which allow the private sphere to be understood in terms of the public situation. Reviewers of *Yo también, Adelita* did not adopt this way of reading and so Delgado's first novel was dismissed as a curiosity that was not suitable for inclusion in the mainstream of canonical post-revolutionary literature. In the case of *El indio*, interpreting the private in terms of the public reinforced the novel's social message, but its social value was apparent without adopting such an approach. In contrast, in *Yo también, Adelita* it is essential to read in a way which does not enforce a binary division between public and private but, rather, interprets the private in terms of the public, otherwise our understanding of the text as possessing national significance is seriously limited and its potential social value is obscured.

In the 1930s, inclusion in the canon depended on a novel being interpreted as having social purpose which meant supporting official nation-building discourses and projects. Reviewers employed interpretive strategies which looked for social value in the public and not the private sphere. As a result, woman-authored novels, such as *Yo también, Adelita*, whose public significance emerges largely from a private-national reading, were frequently disregarded as irrelevant and consequently excluded from the national literary canon. Adopting an interpretive strategy which is attentive to the relationship between public and private while still maintaining the same criteria of social value that was established by the *Premio Nacional de Literatura* enables new interpretations and a revalorization of woman-authored texts such as *Yo también, Adelita*. Indeed, when the results of this new interpretive strategy are evaluated, *Yo también, Adelita* emerges in many ways as a more interesting text than *El indio*, albeit one that would still probably have been excluded from the canon at a time when texts were required to conform to the official party line. As will be seen in the following chapters, this requirement was relaxed somewhat over the twentieth-century. Ultimately, however, it may not be enough to adopt alternative interpretive strategies, new criteria for inclusion in the canon may be required.

Notes to Chapter 2

1. Delgado is included in Ernest Moore's *Bibliografía de novelistas de la Revolución Mexicana* [first pub. 1941] (New York: Burt Franklin, 1972), p. 30. According to the entry, Delgado was author of only one book. Delgado is also included in the section entitled 'Novelistas sin historia literaria (Anónimos y desconocidos)' in Xorge del Campo, *Cuentistas y Novelistas de la Revolución Mexicana, tomo VI*, 2nd edn (Mexico: Ediciones Luzbel, 1985), p. 255. All of the information provided by del Campo is taken from the novel's 'Presentación'.
2. To date, the only critical study of *Yo también, Adelita* is Sarah E. L. Bowskill, 'Yo también, Adelita: A National Allegory of the Mexican Revolution and a Call for Women's Suffrage', in *Revolucionarias: Conflict and Gender in Latin American Narratives by Women*, ed. by Par Kumaraswami and Niamh Thornton (Oxford: Peter Lang, 2007), pp. 139–64. Parts of this chapter are based and expand on material in the earlier publication.
3. 'Presentación', *Yo también, Adelita* by Consuelo Delgado (Mexico: Ediciones del Grupo en Marcha, 1936), pp. 7–9 (p. 9); Enriqueta de Parodi, 'Yo también... Adelita por Consuelo Salgado', *El Nacional*, 25 August 1936, 2nd section, p. 6.
4. Letter, 6 November 1934, Enrique Othón Díaz to Lázaro Cárdenas. AGN/LCR vol. 1306 Exp. 705.1/6.
5. Ibid.
6. Ibid.
7. Ibid.
8. [Advertisement] 'Andres Botas Librería y Papelería', *Letras. Publicación Literaria y Bibliográfica*, October 1936, p. 13.
9. Francisco Zendejas, 'Multilibros', *El Excélsior*, 1 October 1962, pp. 1B, 3B.
10. Jacobo Dalevuelta, 'Libros Nuevos', *El Universal*, 7 August 1936, 1st section, p. 3; Pedro Gringoire, 'Por el mundo de los libros', *El Excélsior*, 16 August 1936, 3rd section, p. 2; Parodi, p. 6.
11. Pedro Gringoire was the *nom de plume* of Gonzalo Báez Camargo.
12. For a plot summary of the novel see Appendix.
13. Jocelyn Olcott, *Revolutionary Women in Postrevolutionary Mexico* (Durham, NC: Duke University Press, 2006), p. 160.
14. The Popular Front was a coalition of the ruling Partido Nacional Revolucionario (PNR) and the Partido Comunista Mexicano (PCM).
15. All references in this chapter are to Consuelo Delgado, *Yo también, Adelita* (Mexico: Ediciones del Grupo en Marcha, 1936) unless otherwise stated.
16. See, for example, Lillian Estelle Fisher who, writing in 1942, suggested that upper-class girls joined Catholic philanthropic organizations while middle-class girls became teachers (212). Lillian Estelle Fisher, 'The Influence of the Present Mexican Revolution upon the Status of Mexican Women', *Hispanic American Historical Review*, 22 (1942), 211–28.
17. On the influence of the PCM among teachers see Olcott, p. 106.
18. Mary K. Vaughan, *Cultural Politics in Revolution: Teachers, Peasants, and Schools in Mexico, 1930–1940* (Tucson: University of Arizona Press, 1997), p. 27.
19. Thomas Benjamin, *La Revolución: Mexico's Great Revolution as Memory, Myth and History* (Austin: University of Texas Press, 2000), pp. 20–21. I follow Benjamin in using 'revolution' to refer to events of 1910–17 and 'Revolution' to refer to the institutionalized Revolution.
20. For an interpretation of Estanislao as representing Díaz see Bowskill, 'Yo también, Adelita, pp. 146–48.

21. On the incorporation of the *Magonistas* into the Revolutionary Family see Benjamin, p. 70.
22. On the Flores Magón brothers and the Viesca uprising see: James D. Cockcroft, *Intellectual Precursors of the Mexican Revolution (1900–1913)* (Austin: University of Texas Press, 1968), p. 152; Alan Knight, *The Mexican Revolution: Porfirians, Liberals and Peasants*, 2 vols (Lincoln: University of Nebraska Press, 1990), I, 45–47.
23. On the relationship between Calles and Carranza see Benjamin, p. 69.

CHAPTER 3

La región más transparente: Right Place, Right Time

No study of the Mexican canon would be complete without Carlos Fuentes. Since the publication of his first novel, *La región más transparente* (1958), Fuentes has been a cornerstone of the national canon, rarely, if ever, omitted from histories of Mexican or Latin American literature. The circumstances in which *La región más transparente* was published were especially propitious. In addition, reviewers saw in the novel a reflection of what post-revolutionary Mexico had become; its ambitious portrayal of the nation's capital, its critique of the betrayed revolution and its musings on the Mexican national character, or, as it was more commonly referred to, *lo mexicano*, were all features they identified and which spoke to them and of their time. Such resounding critical and commercial success propelled Fuentes to the forefront of Mexican literature. Nonetheless, this chapter demonstrates that reviewers adopted interpretive strategies which caused them to overlook important aspects of the novel which can be brought to light by a private-national reading.

Although *La región más transparente* was Fuentes' first novel he was already well established in Mexico City's social and literary communities, both as the son of a diplomat and as the author of two collections of short stories. Fuentes' pre-existing status meant that his fellow authors and peers were quick to respond to the novel's publication. More than forty reviews of *La región más transparente* were published, most of which were favourable. Emmanuel Carballo, with whom Fuentes co-founded and co-edited the *Revista Mexicana de Literatura*, wrote a positive review for *México en la Cultura*, the supplement of *Novedades*, and José Emilio Pacheco, editor of the literary magazine *Estaciones*, claimed that *La región más transparente* placed Fuentes 'en uno de los primeros sitios de nuestra actual literatura' [in one of the foremost ranks of our contemporary literature].[1]

Critical acclaim was accompanied by commercial success as the first edition of *La región más transparente* sold out within days, an event which Alfonso Rangel Guerra described as 'algo insólito en la historia de las letras mexicanas' [somewhat unusual in the history of Mexican literature].[2] Within months, a second edition was printed and a total of nine thousand copies had been sold (Carballo, '1958: el año de la novela', 1). A typical print run of the time was around one thousand copies, so *La región más transparente* was exceptional (Camp, 187). Furthermore, despite the novel costing well above average at $25.00 pesos per copy, readers rushed to buy Fuentes' first novel.[3]

Sales of the novel would have been boosted by positive reviews but even more so by the controversy which surrounded the novel. Prior to publication, extracts of *La región más transparente* appeared in *México en la Cultura* and other literary magazines. These previews caused controversy and fuelled interest because they included profanities and, according to Elena Poniatowska, the editor of *México en la Cultura* 'tuvo que explicar ante un severo tribunal por qué había admitido en el Suplemento a este muchacho tan indecente' [had to explain in front of a stern board why he had allowed such an indecent young man into the Supplement].[4]

Once published, *La región más transparente* continued to elicit lively debate. In May 1958 three reviews of the novel occupied almost the whole front page of *México en la Cultura* as well as large parts of its inside pages.[5] These reviews reflected on whether the novel's defects were greater than its achievements — a debate which was taken up in the many other reviews published in the Spring, Summer and early Autumn of 1958. Another controversy emerged three years later when an article in *El Excélsior* accused Fuentes of plagiarism.[6] These controversies certainly contributed to the novel's sales and may have played a part in the novel becoming canonical because, according to Bourdieu, value can be generated by a struggle over consecration (79). Commercial success does not guarantee that a novel will become canonical and indeed, can be a hindrance, as will be seen in Chapter 6 with reference to *Arráncame la vida*. However, in 1950s Mexico it seems that the custodians of literary knowledge had less reason to see their position as being potentially threatened by the interference of the general public; fewer books were published and in smaller quantities, literacy levels were low and only a minority of people could afford to buy novels. As a result, there was a closer correlation between commercial success and canonicity, and Fuentes' sales figures were unprecedented.

La región más transparente also enjoyed all the benefits associated with being published by one of the country's leading publishers, the Fondo de Cultura Económica (FCE). 1958 was a particularly good year for the FCE; that year it was the second most prolific publisher in Mexico and the company was expanding nationally and internationally.[7] The size of the FCE enabled it to distribute its books widely and one review claimed that *La región más transparente* was available in every bookshop in Mexico City.[8] The FCE promoted its authors through its own magazine, *La Gaceta*, which featured a lengthy interview with Fuentes on the front page of the March 1958 issue.[9] *La región más transparente* was also part of the FCE's Letras Mexicanas series, which Deborah Cohn suggests was influential in the formation of the twentieth-century canon.[10] Being part of this series was indicative of prestige and would have attracted readers and made it more likely to catch the attention of reviewers who, as previously noted, are privileged readers who have the authority to consecrate a text and the potential to shape other reader's opinions.

Perhaps the fact that *La región más transparente* was a *cause célèbre* written by an up-and-coming young writer from a privileged social background with a prestigious publisher was enough to assure it not only of sales but also of a place in the canon. Contemporary reviews of the novel, however, point to other factors which worked in the novel's favour and helped to assure *La región más transparente* a place in the national canon. Reviewers were convinced that *La región más transparente* spoke to and of its time capturing that particular moment in the development of post-revolutionary Mexico as it spoke of the betrayal of the revolution, the social stratification of society, and life in contemporary Mexico City. Recent criticism has diverged little from focusing on these aspects of the novel, suggesting that reviews shape how texts are read and that dominant interpretive strategies have changed little over the last fifty years.

The review by Ali Chumacero, an established custodian of literary knowledge, referred to each of these elements in the novel and this review probably played a particularly important role in shaping readers' expectations and their understanding of the novel as it was published (anonymously) on the cover of the first edition.[11] Manuel Lerín's review, published in the supplement of the newspaper *El Nacional, Revista de México de Cultura*, similarly emphasized the novel's representation of the city and stressed the importance of addressing contemporary issues of national concern.[12] Lerín claimed that 'uno de los elementos para que una novela despierte el interés descansa en el tema, sin éste aquélla puede caer en el olvido' (11) [one of the elements required in order that a novel may arouse one's interest lies in its subject matter, without which it will fall into oblivion]. He further noted that whilst novels about rural life and 'lo revolucionario' [to do with the revolution] used to be popular when 'tales motivos ocupaban la vida nacional' (11) [such topics filled national life] now the city was of primary interest. Lerín's comments indicate that a novel's subject matter was of primary importance in shaping a reader's opinion and only novels which were relevant to 'la vida nacional' [national life] would be included in the canon. Fortunately for *La región más transparente* reviewers were convinced that it was topical in both its representation of the city and its critique of the betrayed revolution.

Some reviewers, including *El Excélsior's* literary critic, Francisco Zendejas, commented on the novel's contribution to the debate about *lo mexicano*, in which there was renewed interest in the 1950s following the publication and popularization of Octavio Paz's essay 'The Labyrinth of Solitude'.[13] According to Zendejas, this connection to Paz's work was an attribute and, overall, Fuentes' indebtedness to Paz's work enhanced its prestige and contemporary significance.[14] Daniel Dueñas similarly commented on Paz's influence on Fuentes' novel.[15] Eulogio Cervantes believed that Paz's theories were so central to Fuentes' novel that he accused Fuentes of plagiarizing Paz's work: 'va exponiendo la tesis — sin perdonar ni una sola — de 'El laberinto de la soledad' como si fueran suyas' (FR/CF) [he sets out the thesis — without any apology — found in 'The Labyrinth of Solitude' as if it were his own]. As Richard M. Reeve points out, however, the name is a pseudonym and the article needs to be understood in the context of an ongoing argument in which Fuentes was involved ('The Making of *La región*', 53; 'Octavio Paz and Hiperión in *La región*', 14).

As well as having his work compared to that of Paz, reviewers also compared Fuentes to other well-known Mexican authors. Pacheco claimed that Fuentes 'se ha creado una obra digna de integrar con *La sombra del caudillo, El resplandor, Al filo del agua* y *Pedro Páramo* el pentágono de nuestra mejor ficción post-revolucionaria' (195) [has created a work worthy of inclusion alongside *La sombra del caudillo, El resplandor,*

Al filo del agua and *Pedro Páramo* in the pentagon of the best post-revolutionary fiction]. This imagined relationship between Fuentes and his predecessors can be usefully thought of in terms of a family tree of canonical texts where inheritance is through a male-line which excluded women authors. Anne McClintock has noted that the family tree

> represents evolutionary time as a *time without women*. The family image is an image of disavowal, for it contains only men, arranged as a linear frieze of solo males ascending towards the apogee of the individual *Homo sapiens*. Each epoch is represented by a single male type, who is characterized in turn by visible anatomical stigmata.[16]

In the family tree of Mexican literature, each novel referenced by Pacheco represents an 'epoch' in which there is only room for one man in each generation: in 1958 Fuentes became the heir to this canonical tradition.

Favourable comparisons with foreign authors further cemented Fuentes' place in the Mexican canon. Several reviews compared Fuentes to John Dos Passos, William Faulkner, Virginia Woolf and James Joyce.[17] With the exception of the reviews by Cervantes and Arturo Martínez Caceres, all were pleased that Fuentes had been influenced by these authors. At a time when Mexico was struggling to come to terms with the growing influence of the United States, it may have been comforting to the intellectual elite to find a Mexican novelist who stood comparison to the likes of Faulkner.

Perceived similarities to 'classics' of US and European literature raised expectations among reviewers that *La región más transparente* would be well received beyond national borders. E. S. Speratti Piñero, for example, wrote that the novel 'sobrepasará cómodamente las fronteras de México para ocupar un sitio destacado en todos los países de habla español' (28) [will easily travel beyond Mexico's borders to occupy a distinguished place in all Spanish-speaking countries]. The critics were right (if anything they underestimated *La región más transparente* in limiting its success to the Spanish-speaking world). *La región más transparente* was an international success and a source of great pride in Mexico where newspapers readily reproduced reviews from the US including one which reported that *La región más transparente* was the most successful Mexican novel ever translated into English.[18] As with *El indio*, international success helped to cement Fuentes' place in the canon.

Several reviews of *El indio* compared the novel to a mural and no fewer than five reviews of *La región más transparente* also likened Fuentes' novel to a mural.[19] To be considered an example of great national literature a novel had to 'measure up' to the scale of a mural and, according to contemporary reviewers, Fuentes' novel did. Rafael Solana specifically compared *La región más transparente* to Diego Rivera's mural in the Palacio Nacional: 'pinta la vida en México, en todas las clases sociales, en todos los ambientes, en un amplio período de la historia, como Diego Rivera pintó su mural del Palacio Nacional, sin dejar nada fuera' (FR/CF) [He paints life in Mexico, among all social classes, in all milieus and over a long period of time, like Diego Rivera painted his mural in the National Palace, without leaving anything out]. Pacheco was likewise struck by similarities between the content of the novel and the murals of Rivera, José Clemente Orozco and Juan Soriano: 'Por momento, las páginas de *La región más transparente* adquieren tal fuerza y tonalidad cromática, que parecen la transposición literaria de las mejores obras de nuestra pintura; Rivera, Orozco, Soriano, están presentes en el desarrollo de la novela' (194) [At times, the pages of *La región más transparente* acquire such strong and vivid tones that they seem to be the literary transposition of the best works of Mexican art; Rivera, Orozco and Soriano are present as the novel develops]. The murals were valued in post-revolutionary society for their ability to represent and (re-)imagine the new nation, because of their scope and content and specifically because of their (supposedly) realistic portrayal of the whole of Mexican life and society and these same qualities were demanded of canonical literature. The comparisons of *La región más transparente* to murals indicate that the novel was thought to hold similar nation-building potential and for this reason Fuentes' first novel was quickly incorporated into the Mexican literary canon by an intellectual elite which sought to replicate in literature the achievements of the mural movement.

Again in terms reminiscent of reviews of *El indio*, reviewers saw *La región más transparente* as being more than a work of fiction. Patricio Gilbert claimed: 'Fuentes no hace literatura. Hace vida. Se propuso contar la realidad a través de una novela social y lo logró' [Fuentes does not produce literature he produces life. He set out to describe reality in a novel and he succeeded].[20] The introduction to extracts of Chumacero's review which were reprinted in *El Excélsior* also stated that the novel possessed 'valores literarios y sociológicos' ('Gran éxito', 1) [literary and sociological value]. The perception that *El indio* and *La región más transparente* were 'more than' novels and, therefore, had social as well as literary value contributed to their being included in a post-revolutionary canon founded with a view to nation-building.

Although Fuentes' first novel was compared to the best Mexican and foreign authors and to Mexico's great muralists, reviewers were not unreserved in their praise. The criticisms bear out Bourdieu's assertion that value can be generated by a struggle over consecration and show that a novel did not need to be judged as flawless in order to be included in the Mexican canon (79). Two reviews were wholly critical of the novel; the review by Cervantes which accused Fuentes of plagiarism and one by Elena Garro who wrote the 'Contra' [Cons] side of the article 'El pro y el contra de una escandalosa novela' [The Pros and Cons of a Scandalous Novel] published in *México en la Cultura*. In this scathing critique Garro suggested that *La región más transparente* was 'un libro' [a book] rather than 'una novela' [a novel] because too much happened too quickly and remained unconnected and underdeveloped (10). Garro attributed the failings of the book to Fuentes' immaturity describing, for example, the representation of the revolution as 'una alegoría infantil, que pierde validez, por obvia' (10) [a childish allegory which loses its validity because it is too obvious]. Garro did not rule out the possibility that Fuentes may mature as a writer, but she was not as generous as Martínez Caceres was in his review in *El Nacional*. Despite writing an almost entirely negative review, Martínez was confident that Fuentes' work would improve in the future. This was an opinion commonly used to excuse shortcomings in Fuentes' first novel and, as the critic Oscar J. Montero notes, in many reviews 'the praise is given with the understanding that *La región más transparente* is a promising first novel'.[21]

   Apart from those by Cervantes and Garro, the other reviews were generally good but a significant number, including those by Solana and Zendejas, criticized the novel's style and form but ultimately agreed that content was more important. These reviews and histories of literature provide important evidence that aesthetic concerns were secondary when it came to forming the Mexican canon. In *El Universal* Solana claimed that the novel was 'un caos' [chaotic], a 'libro amorfo salido de madre, selvático [...] cuyo conjunto no tiene más sentido que una bola de fuego que viniera dando tumbos por el espacio' (FR/CF) [an amorphous book, out of control, wild [...] which as a whole does not have more sense than a fireball which travels with difficulty through space]. He conceded, however, that 'es, a pesar de todos sus defectos formales, un gran libro' (FR/CF) [in spite of all its formal defects, a great book]. Zendejas wrote that the main problem with *La región más transparente* was its 'afán puramente técnico' [purely technical obsession], but noted that this was compensated for by the 'tema y los acontecimientos' [subject and events] which 'dan, por ellos mismos, una novela excelente' [alone create an excellent novel] (9 April, 5). Solana and Zendejas' comments suggest that the novel's content more than compensated for its supposed technical shortcomings and so *La región más transparente* received the necessary endorsement of these prominent custodians of literary knowledge.
   The reviews of *La región más transparente* show that content was the deciding factor in whether a novel would become canonical or not and confirm that the criteria established by the *Premio Nacional de Literatura* that a novel needed to be interpreted as possessing social purpose and addressing contemporary national concerns were still in force. The first stage in my analysis of *La región más transparente*, therefore, aims to show the full extent to which Fuentes' novel could be interpreted as being perfectly attuned to the mood of the times.[22]
   In July 1958, shortly after the publication of *La región más transparente*, Adolfo López Mateos assumed the Presidency having campaigned as the official candidate of the ruling Partido Revolucionario Institucional (PRI) since November 1957.[23] López Mateos' election marked the beginning of a new direction in Mexican politics as he distanced himself from the pro-business administrations of Presidents Manuel Avila Camacho (1940–46) and Miguel Alemán (1946–52). Under Alemán, in particular, businessmen had 'considerable influence in the administration'.[24] On the other hand, the peasants and workers, who according to revolutionary discourse were the 'heirs of the Mexican Revolution', lost out.[25] To conceal the fact that he had betrayed the revolution Alemán paid lip service to the goals and ideals of the revolution but his words were no more than empty rhetoric.[26] Institutionalization of the ruling party in the form of the PRI in 1946 should have ensured that the State would maintain the social pact between capital and labour, but this balance was never achieved under Alemán who sided almost exclusively with the private sector.
   By 1951, the year in which most of the action of *La región más transparente* takes place, widespread corruption and the pursuit of rapid development at all costs had, as Frank Brandenburg puts it, 'alienated the masses'.[27] As a result, former Presidents Calles and Cárdenas wrested power from Alemán and did not allow him to choose his successor, as was customary, but instead forged an agreement between all of the

groups within the PRI whereby Adolfo Ruiz Cortines, 'a noncontroversial career civil servant', would be elected in July 1952 (Brandenburg, 106–07). As Peter Smith notes, Ruiz Cortines seemed to offer an alternative: he announced, but never fully implemented, counter-corruption measures and promised to keep the cost of living under control.[28] Ruiz Cortines reduced the price of staple foods but these measures alarmed businesses to the extent that some left the country, which led to a slowing down of economic growth (P. Smith, 347). In early 1953, faced with business flight, Ruiz Cortines changed policy in favour of the business sector, thereby reverting to the model favoured by his predecessor. By 1958, therefore, there was widespread discontent with Ruiz Cortines. The time had come for the PRI to move in a different direction.

Published at this moment of transition, Fuentes' novel is perfectly attuned to the new direction of the PRI. The novel can be interpreted as suggesting that the revolution was betrayed by Alemán's business-oriented policies which installed a new elite in power, exacerbating social inequality rather than removing it as the revolution had promised.[29] The character of Federico Robles is representative of the new elite and of the businessmen who prospered under, and with the help of, Alemán. Attention is drawn to the physical and ideological similarities between him and Presidents Díaz and Alemán to indicate that, far from affecting the radical change promised by the revolution, post-revolutionary elites, and especially those during Alemán's regime, betrayed the revolution by reverting to the Porfirian model.[30] Ixca comments on Robles' likeness to Díaz (249) and Robles claims to have joined the revolution without any clear motivation, even though his memories of his cousin, Froilán Reyero, and the strike at Río Blanco may lead the reader to question whether he has simply chosen to ignore his reasons because he knows he has betrayed his original intentions and his cousin's memory (234).[31] It is only later, he says, that the victors found a justification which was that they fought to bring order and progress to Mexico to 'defender los postulados de la Revolución y hacerlos trabajar en beneficio del progreso y orden del país' (246) [defend the goals of the Revolution and make them work to bring progress and order to the country]. Robles' stance calls to mind the Porfirian motto of 'order and progress'. Robles is also shown to be willing to compromise revolutionary goals and ideals for economic gain as he tries, as Alemán was doing, to establish 'una economía capitalista' (233). He says:

> Ahí nos tocó entrarle al torito y darnos cuenta de la única verdad política, el compromiso. Aquello fue el momento de crisis de la Revolución. El momento de decidirse a construir, incluso machacándonos las conciencias. De sacrificar algunos ideales para que algo tangible se lograra (246).

> [It fell to us to take the bull by the horns and accept that the only political truth is compromise. That was the moment of crisis for the Revolution, the moment we had to decide to build, even if it meant suppressing our consciences and sacrificing some ideals in order to achieve something tangible.]

Robles realizes that the goals of the revolution have been sacrificed for profit and personal gain but refuses to admit he was wrong and that there may be an alternative path.

Not only is the new post-revolutionary business elite able to improve its social and economic position but, as a result of the betrayal of the revolution, the Porfirian elite is also able to regain land, property and status which had been confiscated by the revolution. In 1951, the De Ovando family, members of the Porfirian aristocracy, are gradually recovering their lost wealth and status as they join forces with the new elite in a mutually beneficial arrangement. Ixca's thoughts on the new relationship between these two groups are cuttingly ironic: 'Norma y Pimpinela del brazo. Dame clase y te doy lana. Dame lana y te doy clase. No hay pierde. Te petateaste demasiado pronto, Porfirio' (178) [Norma and Pimpinela arm in arm. Give me class and I'll give you cash. Give me cash and I'll give you class. No one loses. You kicked the bucket too soon, Porfirio]. At the end of the novel, Pimpinela de Ovando evaluates the outcome of the revolution: 'la Revolución fue un choque tan espantoso, pero ya ve usted. No todo se perdió' (500) [The revolution was a terrible shock, but as you can see not all was lost]. In fact, life for the De Ovandos is returning to the way it was before the revolution indicating that the revolution was betrayed.

While the Porfirian elite, represented by the De Ovandos, is able to regain their former privileged positions, those characters who pursued revolutionary goals and ideals and should have benefited from the revolution, do not. Unlike Robles, Librado Ibarra refuses to abandon the ideals and goals for which the revolution was fought whereby 'iban a tener las mismas oportunidades el obrero y el campesino y el abogado y el banquero' (304–05) [workers, peasants, lawyers and bankers were going to have the same opportunities]. This promise was never kept. Ibarra pursues careers in agrarian law, the trade union movement and education, areas which should have been reformed in accordance with revolutionary ideals but were not. Ibarra never benefits from the revolution, rather he witnesses the failure of land reform because the caciques, who should have been removed by the revolution, retain their influence. Working in the trade unions, Ibarra sees the leaders attending parties with the Porfirian elite. While promoting education in rural schools Ibarra sees teachers killed and again observes the influence of caciques and the Church on rural life, influences which the revolution had aimed to curb. Many of Ibarra's friends who also remained faithful to the goals of the revolution are imprisoned on Islas Marías. As Lanin Gyurko summarizes, Ibarra's experiences reveal 'the rapacious exploitation, corruption and violence in the three major areas of supposed revolutionary advancement' ('Identity and the Mask', 92). Ibarra should have prospered in post-revolutionary society but, because men like Robles accepted compromise, the revolution was betrayed and only those willing to sacrifice their ideals gained.

The relentless and uncompromising pursuit of economic progress transformed Mexico City in the 1940s and '50s and led to an increase in migration to towns and cities. Between 1940 and 1970, four million people moved from the countryside to Mexico City.[32] In national discourses, the public imagination, and cultural products of the time, the city, and especially Mexico City, was transformed into the epitome of modern life and a symbol of the nation's progress, as well as a dangerous, corrupt and corrupting place full of crime and vice. As Anne Rubenstein notes:

A new national culture did develop after the Revolution, but it had two faces; one might even say it was comprised of two discourses. One was the set of ideas, arguments, attitudes and metaphors related to modernity, progress, industrialization, and urbanity. The other was a discourse of tradition, conservatism, rural life and Catholicism [...]. Both were deployed by representatives of the government, and their opponents, at various times and for various purposes.[33]

Rubenstein, with reference to comic books in the post-revolutionary period, and Rafael Hernández Rodríguez, with reference to cinema, have shown that these cultural products expressed contradictory attitudes to the urban environment and, I suggest, the same could be said of *La región más transparente* in literature.[34]

According to Octavio Paz, *La región más transparente* provided the 'primera visión moderna de la ciudad de México' [first modern vision of Mexico City].[35] In the novel, progress and modernity are represented by the skyscrapers, apartment blocks, motor vehicles, cinemas, bars, department stores and advertisements in neon lights. This urban landscape provides an exciting playground for the likes of Junior, Bobó, Charlotte and the international jet-setters, but there is another side to the city which is revealed when Gladys finishes her shift at the cabaret and has to walk through the filthy streets, and when Gabriel sees the small coffins in the funeral parlour and is reminded how four of his siblings died in childhood. In the modern city, it is every man for himself as the greed of the individual takes precedence over the needs of the collective. Ixca's mother, Teódula, says that in her hometown the beauty of her jewellery was to be enjoyed by everyone, and it was only when she moved to the city that she became aware that the jewellery actually belonged to her and that it could be stolen from her: 'Aquí en México es donde se me ocurrió que podrían robármelas, o que las joyas ya no eran de todos, sino sólo mías' (336) [Here in Mexico City is where I realized that they could be stolen, that the jewellery no longer belonged to everyone but only to me]. The city is represented as both the home of glamour and cosmopolitanism and of individualism and crime.

The city also exacerbates problems of social segregation and isolation. The narrator describes Robles' car journey from his gated house to his ninth-floor office, during which he studiously avoids contact with others, as 'Un vaso comunicante perfecto, aislado, individual' (192) [a vessel of communication, perfect, isolated and his alone]. Robles' wife, Norma, seems so different to Gladys that she appears like a goddess to her. Even during a national celebration like Independence Day, the rich and poor do not mix as the wealthy celebrate in Cuernavaca and the poor in the Zócalo. By showing how the people living in Mexico City are able to ignore one another's existence and, consequently, neglect their mutual responsibilities, *La región más transparente* posits a connection between the breakdown of social cohesion and the growth of the city, a topical concern that was also expressed in Luis Buñuel's classic film *Los olvidados* (1950) and comic strips such as *El viejo nido*.[36] Ultimately, however, *La región más transparente* also insists on the (frequently unacknowledged) interconnections between the city's inhabitants, as all of the character's paths cross at some point in the novel.

In an era of increasing centralization and rapid change in the urban environment, *La región más transparente* can be interpreted as capturing the contradictory attitudes of fascination and repulsion towards the city which were a feature of equally contradictory national discourses and were also expressed in other cultural products of the time. As John Brushwood states, the novel 'provided a definition of what Mexico City had become, and indicated, at the very beginning of the López Mateos presidency, the emphasis on the metropolis that was to mark the era'.[37] The interpretive strategies of reviewers who looked for social purpose and national significance in the public sphere were probably attuned to the contemporary concerns about the city in which they lived and worked, and saw in Fuentes' novel an expression of their shared anxieties about and aspirations for the nation's capital.

For the second stage of my analysis, I now use a private-national reading to show how *La región más transparente* can further be read as embodying the zeitgeist of the late 1950s through its contribution to the debate over *lo mexicano* which Joseph Sommers has described as 'la obsesión de ese período' [the obsession of this period].[38] Many critics of *La región más transparente* have commented on the novel's relationship to contemporary debates about the Mexican national character.[39] To date, however, analysis has focused on the male characters Ixca, Robles, Manuel Zamacona and Rodrigo Pola and ignored the significance of the female characters Mercedes Zamazona, Norma Larragoiti and Hortensia Chacón. All of these women are significant because of their relationships with Robles. The following private-national reading of *La región más transparente*, which draws on the same interpretive strategies I applied to *El indio* and *Yo también, Adelita*, accounts for the significance of these female characters and enables me to reveal more fully the extent to which Fuentes' first novel engaged with contemporary national debates about *lo mexicano*.

Roger Bartra and Claudio Lomnitz have identified the limitations of Paz's observations on the Mexican national character.[40] However, when Fuentes wrote *La región más transparente* he drew on 'The Labyrinth of Solitude' which represented the latest thinking on *lo mexicano*. In his essay Paz suggested that solitude was the defining characteristic of the Mexican who 'shuts himself away to protect himself' ('The Labyrinth', 29). Paz further connected the Mexican's solitude with his denial of his origins and past noting that when he denies his parentage and heritage 'the Mexican breaks his ties with the past, renounces his origins, and lives in isolation and solitude' ('The Labyrinth', 87). Therefore, according to Paz, although 'the history of Mexico is the history of a man seeking his parentage, his origins', the Mexican's tendency to deny his past meant that the country could 'conceive of itself only as a negation of its origins' ('The Labyrinth', 20 and 87). During the 'revolutionary movement', Paz believed that the Mexican searched for and briefly found himself ('The Labyrinth', 175). However, the revolution ultimately failed to create a 'community [...] a world in which men recognize themselves in each other' (Paz, 'The Labyrinth', 175). In order to escape the damaging effects solitude has on the individual and country and redefine *lo mexicano*, the Mexican must reconcile himself with his past, find his own identity and join together with others. It is this scenario that Ixca tries to bring about in *La región más transparente* when he encourages the inhabitants of Mexico City to tell him about their past in order to remember their origins and to transcend their solitude by acknowledging their connections to others.

Initially, Robles is reluctant to recall the past: 'Hay que olvidar todo aquello' (228) [All that must be forgotten], but eventually he gives in to Ixca's request. Before his conversation with Ixca, Robles had epitomized the Mexican *macho* whom Paz describes as 'power isolated in his own potency, without relationship or compromise with the outside world. He is pure incommunication, a solitude that devours itself and everything it touches' ('The Labyrinth', 82). In speaking to Ixca, Robles opens up and acknowledges his past which, following Paz's essay, is represented in the novel as a step towards renouncing his solitude. Subsequently, however, Robles debates whether or not to pursue the alternative path which Ixca has presented to him or to return to his old ways. Allegorically, this decision is presented as a choice between his wife Norma and his mistress Hortensia.

True to Jameson's definition of national allegory, the story of the 'private individual destiny' of Robles stands in for that of Mexico and 'libidinal investment is to be read primarily in political and social terms' (69, 72). Furthermore, in keeping with what I identified in the Introduction as the fundamental characteristic of national allegory, the storyline in *La región más transparente* involving Robles, Norma and Hortensia brings together the public and the private and uses the private sphere to comment on the national situation. Thus, Robles' dilemma over whether to stay with his wife, Norma, or go to his mistress, Hortensia, is a dramatization of Mexico's dilemma. Both Mexico and Robles have to choose either solitude and individualism or a path which accepts responsibility for the past and promises to move forward with greater concern for the collective.

Robles' choice between Norma and Hortensia maps onto a choice between remaining in solitude or acknowledging his origins and recognizing his shared responsibilities and connection to others. Robles, after his first meeting with Ixca, decides to stay with Norma indicating a temporary choice to remain in solitude in the 'esquema cerrado del mundo que sólo con Norma [...] podía compartir' (286) [closed world he could only share with Norma]. The narrator describes how Robles, having begun to open up to Ixca, once again mentally closes himself off from his past and the rest of the world: 'Federico canceló automáticamente, todos los momentos anteriores' (287) [Federico automatically erased all these memories of his past]. Norma's association with a life of closed isolation is confirmed by the fact that, unlike her husband, she never gives in to Ixca's request to reveal her past and consequently does not transcend her solitude. She tries to ignore her shared past with Rodrigo and dodges Ixca's questions about people from her past. She persistently refuses to remember her past or to acknowledge her connection to the people in it. As the narrator says: 'Es que siempre había rogado que la recordaran a ella, y nunca había deseado recordar a nadie (194) [She always wanted others to remember her and she had never wanted to remember anyone]. Norma's refusal to renounce her solitude by remembering her past ultimately causes her to lose her husband when he chooses to acknowledge his past and become part of the collective. Having chosen to reconnect with the rest of society, Robles leaves Norma and she dies in a fire shortly afterwards. Everything associated with Robles' life of selfish individualism is symbolically destroyed in that fire, indicating that this is not the future for Mexico.

The right path, and the one which Robles chooses, is the one represented by Hortensia, which recognizes his connections to others and enables him to transcend his solitude. As Hortensia explains to Ixca: 'Cuando Federico reconozca que yo existo, señor, que una persona exista fuera de él, de lo que ha sido, de su vida, entonces será lo que debió ser, sí' (457) [When Federico acknowledges that I exist, Sir, that someone other than himself exists, what he has been, his life, then he will be who he should be, yes]. At the end of the novel, Robles does acknowledge Hortensia and when he sees her for the first time after he has left his wife the narrator says: 'Robles se veía con otros, nunca más solo, y el rostro que mojaba los bigotes en la jícara de barro le decía que no es la soledad lo terrible, que estar con otros es el único dolor' (529) [Robles saw himself with others, alone no longer, and heard Reyero telling him that solitude is not so terrible, rather being with others is the only suffering]. Reyero had told Robles that when he was at Río Blanco and saw the suffering of the striking workers he knew he was not alone because not being alone meant sharing the suffering of others. Now, Robles understands Reyero's words and, as he climbs the stairs to be with Hortensia, he acknowledges and shares the suffering of others. To reinforce the importance of Hortensia as Robles' connection to others the narrator notes 'en ella viese al mundo' [in her he saw the world] (529). Thus, at the end of the novel Robles has rejected the selfish and individualistic life he shared with Norma and accepted collective responsibility, signified by his new life with Hortensia.

Hortensia also reconnects Robles to his past. He can thus be seen to take another step towards transcending his solitude, one which Paz saw as being vital to the future of Mexico. Unlike Norma, Hortensia willingly tells Ixca about her life and once Robles chooses to be with her, he too starts to remember more clearly. As he climbs the stairs to Hortensia's apartment he remembers more with each step he ascends: 'sentía que cada peldaño era un recuerdo' (527) [He felt that each tread of the staircase was a memory]. While in the past his memories were 'confusos, sin coyuntura, inexplicables a la luz de la razón inmediata' [confused, unconnected, inexplicable in light of present circumstances] now 'los recuerdos se detendrían y caerían en su verdadero orden, en su explicación original y ambigua' [memories stopped and fell into the correct order with their original and ambiguous explanations] (527). With a new understanding of his past, Robles, like Mexico, will be able to move forward.

In choosing Hortensia over Norma, Robles can also be seen to follow Paz's call to the Mexican to return to his origins. When he married Norma, Robles tried to assume the identity of successful businessman for which she was the perfect accessory. His true origins and identity, however, lie in his first sexual encounter with Mercedes. It is to this moment that the novel traces the source of Robles' power and success, but also the root of his downfall because, enraged at being abandoned, Mercedes cursed Robles and condemned him 'a vivir a ciegas y a sólo encontrar en lo oscuro su verdad y su satisfacción y su origin [...] lo condenó a recobrar en la oscuridad su poder y gastarlo en la luz' (521) [to live blind and only to find his truth, satisfaction and his origins in the dark [...] she condemned him to recover his power in the darkness and to spend it in the light]. As Ixca realizes, for Robles, being with Hortensia is a way of reliving this original encounter with Mercedes: 'la vida oscura y marginal que Hortensia Chacón le ofrecía era un sustituto, a lo sumo un reflejo intermedio de ese encuentro original' (459) [the dark and marginalized life that Hortensia offered was a substitute, in sum an intermediate reflection of this original encounter]. By marrying Hortensia, Robles is finally reconciled to his origins and no longer leads the cursed double existence to which he had been condemned.

'At the exit from the labyrinth of solitude', Paz wrote, 'we will find reunion (which is repose and happiness), and plenitude, and harmony with the world' ('The Labyrinth', 196). If we evaluate Robles' choice of Hortensia over Norma in terms of Paz's analysis we see that he makes the right decision and finds his way out of the labyrinth of solitude. Following Paz's recommendation for a better Mexico, Robles embraces his past, acknowledges his origins and recaptures the moment of collectivism the revolution had created. Thus, the ending of *La región más transparente* is, at least in part, optimistic: Robles has transcended his solitude and he and Hortensia have a son together who, in terms of the national allegory, represents a future for the nation. This son, who will know his father, replaces Robles' illegitimate son, Manuel Zamacona, who died not knowing who is father was. A future is now envisaged which did not exist when Robles was with Norma because their selfish attitudes were not conducive to fostering a family, just as Alemán's behaviour had a negative impact on the national family.

At a time of transition, when Mexico was trying to understand what had happened since the revolution and why while simultaneously searching for a way forward, the custodians of literary knowledge looked to literature for the answers. Answers were found in the form of Paz's essay 'The Labyrinth of Solitude' and in Fuentes' *La región más transparente*. The solutions presented were similar, as contemporary reviewers of Fuentes' novel observed, but the lack of references to Robles' choice to leave Norma and marry Hortensia suggests that they were not aware of the full extent to which Fuentes could be seen to have dramatized the dilemma Paz had presented. Through a private-national reading I have shown that *La región más transparente* can be seen to put forward the same arguments as those found in 'The Labyrinth of Solitude'. This interpretive strategy helps to position solitude and the search for Mexican national identity as one of the major themes in the novel to a greater extent than has been previously acknowledged.

My private-national reading has, I hope, shed new light on this hitherto overlooked aspect of the novel. However, it should be noted that the transformation of Robles from isolated *macho* to member of the community is first enacted in the public sphere as, on his way to Hortensia's apartment, Robles walks thorough the city; instead of going from his home to his office avoiding contact with the outside world Robles now wanders the streets and comes into contact with the outside world. As he passes Gabriel's funeral he is drawn inside and eventually he falls to his knees and places his hand on Gabriel's forehead, signifying his new-found connection to the lives of others (527). Furthermore, the novel's relationship to the contemporary debate over *lo mexicano* can be, and has been, identified in the novel without interpreting Robles' choice of Hortensia over Norma as a choice between collective responsibility and isolation. As in the case of *El indio*, even without a private-national reading, reviewers were able to see *La región más transparente* as relating to issues of contemporary national concern and so Fuentes' first novel was easily incorporated into the twentieth-century Mexican literary canon. Nonetheless, we have seen that new interpretive strategies can still yield new readings of the work of even the most studied Mexican author.

In Chapter 1, we saw a very close correlation between the ideas presented in *El indio* and official national discourses. It would be an oversimplification to suggest that *La región más transparente* was included in the canon because it was interpreted as being in line with official national discourses at a time when the PRI was in crisis and negotiating a period of transition and a new direction. What we can say is that privileged readers continued to evaluate texts primarily on the basis of their content, which had to be of national significance in order to receive their approval, and novels were still expected to have social, even nation-building purpose. The interpretive strategies they adopted continued to have no regard for the possibility of understanding the public sphere through the lens of the private.

Overall, it was probably the portrayal of the city, in which many of the reviewers lived and worked, which truly captured the imagination of the novel's first readers and this mural-like view of the nation's capital, combined with all the benefits of a good publisher, assured Fuentes a place at the forefront of Mexican letters. Fuentes was seen to place the new, modern city, with all of its social classes and contradictions, at the heart of his novel and the fact that he was one of the first, if not the first as some reviews claimed, to do so undoubtedly contributed to earning the novel a place in the twentieth-century Mexican literary canon. At a time when social, political and economic life became increasingly centred on Mexico City, *La región más transparente* was in the right place at the right time and there was no going back — as Dolores Castro, the author of *La ciudad y el viento*, discovered to her cost.

Notes to Chapter 3

1. Emmanuel Carballo, '1958: el año de la novela', *México en la Cultura*, supl. *Novedades*, 28 December 1958, pp. 1, 11; José Emilio Pacheco, 'Notas bibliográficas', *Estaciones. Revista literaria de México*, summer 1958, no. 10, pp. 193–96 (p. 195).

2. Alfonso Rangel Guerra, 'La novela de Carlos Fuentes', *Armas y Letras*, 1958, pp. 76–80 (p. 76).

3. [Advertisement] 'Nueva bibliografía Mexicana', *Boletín Bibliográfico Mexicano*, May–June 1958, p. 28. *La ciudad y el viento*, the other book I study from this period, cost only $14.00 pesos. [Advertisement] *La Palabra y el Hombre. Revista de la Universidad Veracruzana*, July–September, 1966, back page.

4. Elena Poniatowska, 'Carlos Fuentes, un tropel de caballos desbocados', *Novedades*, April 1958, pp. 1–2. See also: Richard M. Reeve, 'The Making of *La región más transparente*: 1949–1974', in *Carlos Fuentes: A Critical View*, ed. by Robert Brody and Charles Rossman (Austin: University of Texas Press, 1982), pp. 34–63 (p. 34; 47–51); Richard M. Reeve, 'Octavio Paz and Hiperión in *La región más transparente*: Plagiarism, Caricature Or...?', *Chasqui*, 3 (1974), 13–25 (p. 13); E. S. Speratti Piñero, 'Carta abierta a Carlos Fuentes a propósito de su primera novela', *Universidad de Mexico*, April 1958, p. 28.

5. Luis Cardoza y Aragon, 'El pro y el contra de una escandalosa novela. El pro', *México en la Cultura*, supl. *Novedades*, 11 May 1958, pp. 1, 2; Benjamín Carrión, 'El escritor ecuatoriano

Benjamín Carrión le entra al juega–jueguito de los críticos y juzga como una gran novela *La región más transparente*', *México en la Cultura*, supl. *Novedades*, 25 May 1958, pp. 2, 7; Elena Garro, 'El pro y el contra de una escandalosa novela. El contra', *México en la Cultura*, supl. *Novedades*, 11 May 1958, pp. 1, 10.

6. Eulogio Cervantes, 'Carlos Fuentes y el plagiarismo', *El Excélsior*, FR/CF. Reeve suggests that these accusations should not be taken too seriously as the article was published three years after *La región más transparente* first appeared as a result of an argument between Fuentes and other colleagues working at the UNAM radio station ('The Making of *La región*', p. 53; 'Octavio Paz and Hiperión in *La región*', p. 14).

7. Carballo, '1958', p. 1; Francisco Zendejas, 'Multilibros', *El Excélsior*, 4 April 1958, section B, pp. 1, 3.

8. 'Su mesa de redacción. Uno de los buenos éxitos', *Diorama de la Cultura*, supl. *El Excélsior*, 13 April 1958, p. 2.

9. Mario Calleros, 'Enjuicia el México de los últimos años', *La Gaceta*, March 1958, p. 1.

10. Deborah Cohn, 'The Mexican Intelligentsia, 1950–1968: Cosmopolitanism, National Identity, and the State', *Mexican Studies/ Estudios Mexicanos*, 21.1 (2005), 141–92 (p. 157).

11. Chumacero's review was also quoted at length in *El Excélsior* and appeared in its entirety in *Novedades*. Ali Chumacero, 'Primera novela de Carlos Fuentes', FR/CF; 'Gran Exito de la Obra de Carlos Fuentes', *El Excélsior*, 9 April 1958, 1st section, p. 7. FR/CF.

12. Manuel Lerín, 'Una novela sobre el destino urbano', *Revista de México de Cultura*, supl. *El Nacional*, 4 May 1958, p. 11.

13. Octavio Paz, 'The Labyrinth of Solitude', in *The Labyrinth of Solitude*, trans. by Lysander Kemp, Yara Milos, Rachel Phillips Belash (London: Penguin, 1990).

14. Francisco Zendejas, 'Multilibros' *El Excélsior*, 9 April 1958, 1st section, p. 5.

15. Daniel Dueñas, 'Repertorio', *El Sol de México en la Cultura*, supl. *El Sol de México*, 14 August 1977, p. 2.

16. Anne McClintock, *Imperial Leather: Race, Gender and Sexuality in the Colonial Contest* (London: Routledge, 1995), p. 39.

17. Rafael Solana, [Untitled], *El Universal*, 14 September 1958, FR/CF; Zendejas, 9 April, p. 1; Edmundo Meouchi, 'Buñuelosis galopante...', FR/CF; Cervantes, FR/CF; Pacheco, p. 195; José Alvarado, 'Correo menor', *Diorama de la Cultura*, supl. *El Excélsior*, 22 June 1958, p. 2; Cardoza y Aragon, p. 2; J. M. García Ascot, '*La región más transparente*: un libro de gran importancia que crece con la ferocidad de ciertas oposiciones', *México en la Cultura*, supl. *Novedades*, 11 May 1958, pp. 2, 10 (p. 2); Ali Chumacero, 'La revolución y sus descendientes', FR/CF; Arturo Martínez Caceres, 'Carlos Fuentes escándalo y literatura', *Revista de México de Cultura*, supl. *El Nacional*, 5 October 1958, p. 2.

18. 'Estados Unidos aclama la novela de Carlos Fuentes como una de las mejores de 1960', *México en la Cultura*, supl. *Novedades*, 19 December 1960, p. 3; Anthony West, 'El New Yorker comenta la obra de Carlos Fuentes', *México en la Cultura*, supl. *Novedades* 12 March 1961, p. 4.

19. Solana, FR/CF; Salvador Novo, 'Carlos Fuentes, una revelación', *El Sol de México en la Cultura*, supl. *El Sol de México*, 14 August 1977, p. 2; María Luisa Mendoza, 'Carlos Fuentes. El Mexicano', *El Excélsior*, 6 December 1959, FR/CF; Carlos Monsiváis, 'Carlos Fuentes visto por Carlos Monsiváis', FR/CF; Pacheco, p. 194; 'Libros', *Cuadernos Americanos*, July–October, 1958, pp. 581–83 (p. 581).

20. Patricio Gilbert, 'Carlos Fuentes. En la ruta de la buena novela', FR/CF.

21. Oscar J. Montero, 'The Role of Ixca Cienfuegos in the Thematic Fabric of *La región más transparente*', *Hispanófila*, 59 (1976), 61–83 (p. 61).

22. For a plot summary of *La región más transparente* see Appendix.

23. The PNR (Partido Nacional Revolucionario) became the PRM (Partido Revolucionario Mexicano) in 1938 and then became the PRI under Alemán in 1946. Donald C. Hodges and Ross Gandy, *Mexico 1910–1976: Reform or Revolution?* (London: Zed Press, 1979), p. 115.

24. Brian Hamnett, *A Concise History of Mexico* (Cambridge: Cambridge University Press, 2000), p. 254.

25. Judith Adler Hellman, *Mexico in Crisis* (London: Holmes and Meier, 1983), p. 57.

26. Donald C. Hodges and Ross Gandy, *Mexico: The End of the Revolution* (Westport, CT: Praeger, 2002), p. 91.

27. Frank Brandenburg, *The Making of Modern Mexico* (Englewood Cliffs, NJ: Prentice Hall, 1964), p. 106.

28. Peter H. Smith, 'Mexico Since 1946: Dynamics of an Authoritarian Regime', in *Mexico Since Independence*, ed. by Leslie Bethell (Cambridge: Cambridge University Press, 1991), pp. 321–96 (p. 347).

29. Montero (p. 61), Robert G. Mead Jr (p. 231) and Lanin Gyurko (pp. 81–82) note that *La región más transparente* condemns the betrayal of the revolution in the post-revolutionary period. Robert G. Mead Jr, 'Carlos Fuentes, airado novelista mexicano', *Hispania*, 50 (1967), 229–35; Lanin A. Gyurko, 'Identity and the Mask in Fuentes' *La región más transparente*', *Hispanófila*, 65 (1979), 75–103.

30. Lanin Gyurko also notes the similarity between the physical description of Robles and Porfirio Díaz. Lanin Gyurko, 'Individual and National Identity in Fuentes' *La región más transparente*', *Kentucky Romance Quarterly*, 25 (1978), 435–57 (p. 437).

31. All references in this chapter are to Carlos Fuentes, *La región más transparente* [first pub. 1958], 7th edn, ed. and intro. by Georgina García Gutiérrez (Madrid: Cátedra, 1999) unless otherwise stated.

32. Jonathan Kandell, 'Mexico's Megalopolis', in *I Saw a City Invincible: Urban Portraits of Latin America*, ed. by Gilbert M. Joseph and Mark D. Szuchman (Wilmington, DE: Scholarly Resources, 1996), pp. 181–201 (p. 184).

33. Anne Rubenstein, *Bad Language, Naked Ladies, and Other Threats to the Nation: A Political History of Comic Books in Mexico* (Durham, NC: Duke University Press, 1998), p. 42.

34. Rubenstein, p. 50; Rafael Hernández Rodríguez, 'Melodrama and Social Comedy in the Cinema of the Golden Age', in *Mexico's Cinema: A Century of Film and Filmmakers*, ed. by Joanne Hershfield and David R. Maciel (Wilmington, DE: Scholarly Resources, 1999), pp. 101–21 (p. 101).

35. Octavio Paz, 'La máscara y la transparencia', in *Homenaje a Carlos Fuentes. Variaciones interpretativas en torno a su obra*, ed. by Helmy F. Giacoman (New York: Las Americas, 1971), pp. 17–22 (p. 18).

36. On the comic strip serial *El viejo nido* see Rubenstein, pp. 50–62.

37. John Brushwood, *Narrative Innovation and Political Change in Mexico* (New York: Peter Lang, 1989), p. 52.

38. Joseph Sommers, 'La búsqueda de la identidad: *La región más transparente* por Carlos Fuentes', in *Homenaje a Carlos Fuentes. Variaciones interpretativas en torno a su obra*, ed. by Helmy F. Giacoman (New York: Las Americas, 1971) pp. 277–326 (p. 324).

39. Steven Boldy, *The Narrative of Carlos Fuentes: Family, Text, Nation* (Durham: Durham University Press, 2002), p. 9; Rosario Castellanos, 'La novela mexicana contemporánea y su valor testimonial', *Hispania*, 47 (1965), 223–30 (p. 226); Gyurko, 'Individual and National Identity', p. 444; Ernest H. Lewald, 'El pensamiento cultural mexicano en *La región más transparente* de Carlos Fuentes', *Revista Hispánica Moderna*, 33 (1967), 216–23 (p. 219); Reeve, 'Octavio Paz and Hiperión', p. 17; Sommers, pp. 308–09.

40. Roger Bartra, *Blood, Ink and Culture: Miseries and Splendors of the Post-Mexican Condition*, trans. by Mark Alan Healey (Durham, NC, and London: Duke University Press, 2002); Claudio Lomnitz-Adler, *Exits from the Labyrinth: Culture and Ideology in the Mexican National Space* (Berkeley: University of California Press, 1992).

CHAPTER 4

La ciudad y el viento:
A Gendered Alternative to
Official Nationalism

Four years after the all-encompassing *La región más transparente* established Mexico City as the preferred new setting for Mexican literature, Dolores Castro published 'una novela corta de la vida provinciana de México en los años inmediatamente posteriores al movimiento revolucionario de 1910' [a short novel about provincial life in Mexico in the years immediately following the revolutionary movement of 1910].[1] This description, which appeared on the back cover of the first and only edition of *La ciudad y el viento*, unashamedly announced that this novel was neither ambitious in scope nor set in Mexico City. In the contemporary literary climate, these statements did not bode well for the reception of the novel.

Nonetheless, the claim that *La ciudad y el viento* was about the immediate aftermath of the revolution seemed to promise the would-be reader a subject matter appropriate to canonical literature, even if the setting was not ideal. Anyone who reads the book, however, is likely to be surprised by the inaccuracy of this statement. The novel is, in fact, set against the backdrop of the second *cristero* rebellions which began in 1934, hardly '*inmediatamente*' [immediately] after the revolution, so why does the back cover not say so? I propose that, when Castro's novel was published, the *cristero* rebellions were still a politically sensitive subject and one which was not suitable for canonical, nation-building literature as it reminded readers of the divisions within the national family. Literature about the path taken by the revolution, on the other hand, remained central to the national canon as demonstrated by the success of Fuentes' *La región más transparente* and *La muerte de Artemio Cruz*, which was published in the same year as *La ciudad y el viento*, in 1962. By this time the old wounds from the *cristero* wars had begun to heal though they were still prone to being re-opened by a misplaced remark or an ill-judged policy. Castro's novel might have been more acceptable had it at least taken the government's side in its representation of the conflict between Church and State, but it remained steadfastly neutral. Three factors, therefore, mitigated against Castro's first and only novel being included in the twentieth-century Mexican literary canon: its provincial setting, its chosen subject matter and its perceived stance in relation to the *cristero* conflict.

La ciudad y el viento is not a well-known text and Dolores Castro has been largely overlooked in Mexican literary history. She is included in only six histories of

Mexican literature, one of which was published before *La ciudad y el viento* and, as a result, only refers to her poetry.[2] In the histories of Mexican literature published after 1962, entries about Castro tend to be brief and focus on her poetry, for which she has achieved growing recognition, particularly since the 1980s. The most detailed entry is in the *Diccionario de escritores mexicanos* which says that the novel is about 'la repercusión que tuvo lo religioso dentro de la vida de un pueblo durante el movimiento cristero' [the repercussions of religion on village life during the *cristero* movement] (Navarrete Maya, 348). The entry is primarily interested in Castro's poetry and her career as a teacher and journalist, but it at least provides a more accurate assessment of the novel's subject matter than that on the novel's back cover.

La ciudad y el viento is Castro's only novel and she has said: 'No escribí otra novela porque la crítica fue muy adversa' [I did not write another novel because the criticism was very unfavourable].[3] The circumstances surrounding the publication of the novel were not altogether unfavourable because Castro had some status in the literary community following the publication of several collections of her poetry: *El corazón transfigurado* (1949), *Nocturnos* (1950), *Siete poemas* (1950), *La tierra está sonando* (1959) and *Cantares de vela* (1960). Castro had been included in José Luis Martínez's *Literatura mexicana siglo XX* and had sent, on request, bibliographical information to the *Departamento de literatura* [Literature Department] of the INBA so that she could be included in the *Anuario de poesía* [Poetry Yearbook] of 1959.[4] Her work had also appeared in an anthology entitled *Ocho poetas mexicanos*.[5] The anthology consisted of work by a group of poets called the *Ocho poetas* [Eight Poets]. The other members of the group were Alejandro Avilés, Roberto Cabral del Hoyo, Rosario Castellanos, Efrén Hernández, Honorato Ignacio Magaloni, Octavio Novaro and Javier Peñalosa (Castro's husband). In a review of Castro's poetry collection *Soles* (1977), Juan Cervera referred to the anthology as 'aquella antología que ha hecho historia' [that anthology which has made history] and expressed regret that it had never been reprinted: 'seguimos inútilmente esperando su reedición, lo que es, sin duda, lamentable por lo valioso de este libro' [we are still helplessly waiting for it to be reprinted, which is a shame given how valuable this book is].[6] Cervera's comments suggest that the anthology had some merit, but never reached a sufficiently wide audience to have a real impact on the careers of its contributors. Nonetheless, group members Novaro and Avilés wrote about Castro's work in the national press, suggesting that being part of this group helped Castro to gain some recognition in her early career.[7] As with Fuentes, contacts within the literary community and being part of a group may have helped Castro, although clearly she did not enjoy the same standing.

Furthermore, Castro's status in the literary community may have been adversely affected by the fact that she was known as a religious poet. In an article published in *Novedades* in February 1948, fellow poets, Vicente Echeverría del Prado and Ramón Gálvez, wrote of Castro's work: 'su influencia principal es la Biblia, sobre todo en sus poemas más recientes' [her principal influence is the Bible, especially in her most recent poems].[8] The collection of poems, *Cantares de vela* (1960) was also published by Editorial Jus, a publishing house which was responsible for publishing much *cristero* literature.[9] Edgar Córdova even suggests that the group to which

Castro belonged was called *Ocho poetas católicos* [Eight Catholic Poets].[10] He is the only critic to use this name but, in view of the religious subject matter of her poetry (and novel), the suggestion is of interest. In his study of *cristero* literature, Alvaro Ruiz Abreu claims that, until very recently, it was difficult to be taken seriously in the intellectual and cultural milieu in Mexico if one was Catholic:

> durante muchas décadas, y hasta fechas muy recientes, declararse católico en el ámbito intelectual en México era una ironía, tenía un claro carácter peyorativo: equivalía a ser un conservador a ultranza, un ser extraño en un país 'revolucionario', colocarse a un lado de la historia, el progreso y lo moderno' (18).

> [for many decades, and until very recently, to say you were Catholic in the intellectual sphere in Mexico was to be ironic, it had a clear pejorative meaning equivalent to being ultra-conservative, an oddity in a 'revolutionary' country, to placing oneself outside history, progress and modernity.]

In the intellectual climate of the time, Castro's supposed beliefs and the apparent expression of them in her work may have led to her being excluded from the canon.

La ciudad y el viento was published by the provincial publishing house Editorial Universidad Veracruzana which, in spite of being relatively small and located outside Mexico City, enjoyed some recognition in this highly centralized industry. A respectable 2000 copies of the first edition of *La ciudad y el viento* were printed as part of the *Ficciones* series and sold for $14.00 pesos each, eleven pesos less than *La región más transparente*. Jesús Arellando commented favourably on the series in *El Día* and Francisco Zendejas in his regular column in *El Excélsior* recommended the collection and Castro's novel to his readers: 'tomen ustedes nota de las últimas ediciones de la Universidad Veracruzana: *Los Segadores*, por J. A. Bardem y *La ciudad y el viento* por Dolores Castro' [take note of the latest books published by Universidad Veracruzana: *Los Segadores* by J. A. Bardem and *La ciudad y el viento* by Dolores Castro].[11] A few days later, a full review of *Los Segadores* appeared in Zendejas' column, 'Multilibros', but he never published a review of *La ciudad y el viento*. Full-page advertisements for the *Ficciones* series appeared in the magazine *El Centavo* and on the back cover of two issues of the magazine *La palabra y el hombre. Revista de la Universidad Veracruzana*.[12] *La ciudad y el viento* was also listed in the *Boletín Bibliográfico Mexicano*.[13] Readers may have been persuaded to read *La ciudad y el viento* because of the publicity and the reputation of the *Ficciones* collection or because they enjoyed other books in the series. Although the Editorial Universidad Veracruzana was not in the same league as the FCE it was, nonetheless, respected and it achieved some recognition for the books it published and especially for the *Ficciones* series of which *La ciudad y el viento* was part. Thus, we must look to other factors to explain why Castro's novel was almost completely ignored by reviewers and excluded from the canon.

The three contemporary reviews of *La ciudad y el viento* I have found provide important clues as to why the novel was not well received. One review was published in *México en la Cultura*, the cultural supplement of *Novedades*, another in *Cuadernos de Bellas Artes*, and a third in *La Cultura en México*, the supplement of *Siempre*.[14] All of these were very respectable publications and the review in *La*

Cultura en México was written by the prominent custodian of literary knowledge, Emmanuel Carballo, who also reviewed *La región más transparente*.

Both Carballo and the anonymous reviewer in *Cuadernos de Bellas Artes* implied that Castro should stick to writing poetry because her attempt to write a novel, they suggested through their use of the verb *intentar* [to try], had not been a success: 'Dolores Castro intenta la "novela corta"' [Dolores Castro tries her hand at the novella] wrote Carballo ('Costumbrismo' xvi) and the *Cuadernos de Bellas Artes* review stated: 'una poetisa: Dolores Castro intentó la novela' [a poetess Dolores Castro tried to write a novel] but 'sigue siendo poetisa' [she remains a poet] ('La ciudad', 89). While acknowledging her as a poet, Castro's reviewers struggled to see her as a novelist. The reviewer in *Cuadernos de Bellas Artes* further criticized the novel for its use of 'procedimientos poéticos' [poetic devices] which dominated 'los propiamente narrativos' [those which were strictly narrative] ('La ciudad', 89). In other words, the style employed was suitable for poetry rather than prose. This comment reinforces the idea that Castro should stick to writing poetry, but it is also noteworthy because the same stylistic criticism could so easily have been levelled at the opening section of *La región más transparente*.

The novel's scope was another feature that was seen as positive in *La región más transparente* but which was criticized in *La ciudad y el viento*. Carballo wrote: 'La historia se fragmenta en varias historias: una para cada personaje' [The story fragments into different stories: one for each character] ('Costumbrismo', xvi). These stories aimed to provide an overview of 'cómo viven, piensan y sienten los habitantes de una reseca ciudad de provincia' [how the inhabitants of a dry provincial town live, think and feel] (xvi). However, Carballo thought that Castro's novel was unsuccessful because 'desgraciadamente, tal síntesis no es factible' [unfortunately, such a synthesis is not feasible] (xvi). In his review of *La región más transparente* Carballo had commented on the vast scope of Fuentes' novel and the 'diversas historias que [...] permiten a Fuentes asomarse a la vida de la ciudad de México y de sus habitantes' [diverse stories which [...] allow Fuentes to look out on the life of Mexico City and its inhabitants], but he refused to believe that the same feat could be achieved in Castro's text ('1958', 11). The fragmented narrative which told the stories of all of the inhabitants of Mexico City was only praiseworthy in a male-authored novel about the nation's capital and was dismissed as impossible in the case of a woman-authored novel set in a provincial town.

Whereas the canonical novels in this study were considered to have a 'modern spirit', Carballo suggested that *La ciudad y el viento* was outdated. Carballo compared Castro's novel to two (male-authored) turn-of-the-century novels and suggested that while these earlier works could be excused for being *costumbrista* novels because this style was in vogue at the time and because of their use of irony, the same could not be said for *La ciudad y el viento* which was 'una novela anacrónica. Vieja por el estilo, la estructura y el tratamiento que da a la anécdota' [an anachronistic novel. Old in style, structure and in its treatment of the story] (Carballo,'Costumbrismo', xvi). Carballo's comments call to mind the criteria established by the *Premio Nacional de Literatura* which required the winning text to possess 'un espíritu moderno, tanto por los problemas en que se inspire, como por la técnica con que los realice' [a modern spirit in the problems which inspire them and in the technique employed].[15] This same standard still appeared to exist in 1962 when reviewers dismissed *La ciudad y el viento* on the basis of its outdated style. It should be noted, however, that such judgements remained highly subjective, and reviewers used comparisons and referenced style as a way of justifying their evaluations which were primarily based on a novel's content. Carballo's comments that Castro's novel was outdated and its style and structure were passé, aim to justify the exclusion of *La ciudad y el viento* from the canon but we should look to the reviewers' assessment of the novel's content to find the real reason for its poor reception.

Ignacio Méndez, author of the review in *México en la Cultura*, claimed that *La ciudad y el viento* was 'de interés actual y permanente' [of current and ongoing interest] (11). Méndez's assertion that *La ciudad y el viento* was of interest to contemporary readers was based on his interpretation of the novel as being about the human condition: 'nos enfrenta a la limitación humana' (11) [it confronts us with the limitations of mankind]. Thus, even though Méndez liked the novel, he did not interpret it as being related to contemporary issues of national concern. On the contrary, he noted that Castro's novel 'desarrolla planes no usuales en nuestra novela contemporánea mexicana' (11) [develops ideas not usually found in the contemporary Mexican novel]. Thus, *La ciudad y el viento* was not seen to have met the requirement that canonical literature should address issues of national concern.

While Méndez's was by far the most favourable of the three reviews of *La ciudad y el viento*, he nevertheless identified two defects: firstly he criticized the novel's uneven style, and secondly he disliked the novel's 'excesiva misericordia hacia algunos personajes, para no entregarlos al lector sin defensa alguna' (11) [excessive compassion for some characters so as not to hand them over defenceless to the reader]. Indeed, a substantial part of his review is taken up with a discussion of the novel's refusal to take sides which, while interesting, could also be 'un poco desconcertante' (11) [a little disconcerting]. According to Méndez, readers expected 'el esclarecimiento simplista que hiciera exclamar al lector: "Estos tienen la razón, y aquellos otros son mendaces"' [a simplistic explanation which makes the reader cry out 'These are right and the others are lying'], but in *La ciudad y el viento* 'no ocurre así, porque la verdad es una especie de elemento químico cuya propiedad peculiar consiste en la dispersión fragmentaria entre cuerpos opuestos. En lugar, pues, de esclarecimientos simplistas, el lector se encuentra con la maraña repartida' (11) [this does not happen because the truth is like a chemical element whose particular property is to disperse itself in pieces among opposite bodies. Instead, therefore, of simplistic explanations the reader finds himself not knowing which way to turn]. Carballo likewise complained of the novel's 'inquebrantable buena fe' [unshakeable good faith] ('Costumbrismo', xvi) and the *Cuadernos de Bellas Artes* review noted the novel's lack of 'malicia' [guile / astuteness] ('La ciudad', 89).

In his analysis of reader reports submitted to the publisher Joaquín Mortiz between 1962 and 1976, Danny J. Anderson notes the frequent occurrence of the term 'malicia', which he defines as 'communicative cunning, or narrative instinct', and asserts that

malicia arises from four interrelated factors: the author's concept of the genre,

the originality of the text's linguistic organization, the effectiveness of the
structure for the reader, and a balanced or appropriate relationship between the
text's formal aspects and the human or vital content of the narrative.[16]

With reference to one report on a woman-authored novel, Anderson notes that 'the
concept of malicia was even applied to the author's choice of subject matter and
narrative strategies', thus raising 'the complex question of gender, of what malicia
might imply when a woman was told that her subject matter was irrelevant' (25).
We may, therefore, deduce that the lack of 'malicia' referred to in the *Cuadernos de
Bellas Artes* review of *La ciudad y el viento* indicates that Castro's novel was deemed to
fall short of the required standard in terms of form and content. The novel's refusal
to totally condemn anyone or to blame one side or another in the Church–State
conflict, around which the plot centres, troubled reviewers who could not even
bring themselves to refer directly to the *cristero* wars. As Anderson's study suggests,
such concerns are likely to have been exacerbated because the novel was written
by a woman. Ultimately, reviewers' reservations about the way in which the novel
represented the Church–State conflict of the 1930s and the author's gender led to
La ciudad y el viento being omitted from the national literary canon.

Although the *cristero* wars had ended more than twenty years prior to the
publication of *La ciudad y el viento* it would still have been incautious for the novel
to adopt a neutral stance with regard to the Church–State conflict. The first *cristero*
wars began in the 1920s under the regime of Plutarco Elías Calles (1924–28). Calles
called for the rigorous enforcement of the anticlerical provisions of the Constitution
requiring the clergy to register with the civil authorities. In response, the clergy
suspended services: this was the final catalyst which drove lay Catholics to war. The
conflict ended in 1929 because the two sides had reached an impasse and it was no
longer in the interest of either side to continue the war.[17] The conditions of the
peace were overwhelmingly favourable to the State and many *cristeros* felt betrayed
by the Church hierarchy which negotiated the peace.[18] In 1934, when Church–State
relations were strained, some veterans of the 1926–29 wars once again took up arms
and 'sporadic warfare broke out [...] accompanied by isolated acts of violence against
schoolteachers, *agraristas*, and all the representatives of the Government' (Meyer, 202).

The second rebellion was principally a protest against the proposed introduction
of socialist education by President Lázaro Cárdenas (1934–40). Although Cárdenas
pursued anticlerical policies in the early part of his presidency, after breaking with
Calles over labour policy, in June 1935, he modified his attitude towards the Church.
As a result, Church–State relations improved and the Church was tolerated as long
as it did not interfere in politics. In subsequent decades, the relationship between the
Church and the State waxed and waned, but according to Roberto Blancarte the
Church consistently avoided outright confrontation with the State.[19] In mid-1961,
however, relations were once again strained because of the introduction of a new
set of compulsory textbooks in all schools, including religious schools. The Church
objected on the grounds that the new textbooks 'negatively portrayed the church
as an obstacle to national development'.[20] The dispute, although it was endorsed by
the church hierarchy, was generally restricted to traditionally strong Catholic areas
and lasted only a year, so that by the end of 1962 the conflict was receding and a

desire to cooperate prevailed (Blancarte, 191, 197). George W. Grayson says that the potential seriousness of the situation should not be underestimated, as it was only as a result of 'secret negotiations at the highest levels of states and church' that a crisis was averted at this time (49).

Writing in 1962, the year in which the textbook controversy ended and *La ciudad y el viento* was published, Howard Cline concludes: 'it could probably be said that at the moment the Church and Church–State relationships in Mexico are not a major preoccupation either of people or of their Government'.[21] However, good Church–State relations depended on an informal truce which was subject to constant renegotiation and could be ended at any time if either side made a wrong move — a fact perfectly illustrated by the textbook controversy. In such a delicate situation, the *cristero* rebellion remained an awkward subject to broach, particularly if you were not seen to side with the State.

Angel Arias Urrutia claims that it is only since President Carlos Salinas de Gortari (1988–94) amended the constitution in 1991 that the *cristero* conflict has ceased to be a taboo subject in Mexico.[22] While the author of *La ciudad y el viento* may have believed that the nuanced portrayal of both sides in *La ciudad y el viento* reflected the prevailing attitude of reconciliation, it seems that she was mistaken. In 1962, no side wanted to discuss or recall the experiences described in the novel as it raised too many questions and risked opening old wounds. The first stage in my following analysis, therefore, aims to reveal the full extent to which the novel can be seen as neutral with respect to the *cristero* conflict which, combined with its choice of a still delicate subject matter, led to *La ciudad y el viento* being excluded from the twentieth-century Mexican literary canon.[23] As a result, I hope to introduce readers to a text that is interesting from an historical-political as well as literary standpoint and so raise the question of whether the nation-building criteria adopted by contemporary reviewers should be replaced, so that novels such as *La ciudad y el viento* will no longer be judged solely according to the political views presented in them.

In his study of *cristero* novels, Arias Urrutia identifies *La ciudad y el viento* as a neutral *novela de la guerra cristera* (92, 94) [novel about the *cristero* conflict]. He claims that the presence of a narrator who is outside the story is a common device in *cristero* literature which is used to create an impression of impartiality and to encourage the reader to be impartial (Arias, 125–26). In addition, making the reader privy to a character's internal thoughts is said to encourage 'una vinculación afectiva entre personaje y lector' [an emotional bond between character and reader], although this tactic can also be used to distance the reader from a character whose thoughts are not in line with the reader's sympathies (Arias, 154, 235). It is through the third-person omniscient narrator, operating outside the story, directing the reader's judgement, describing the character's actions and reporting their words and inner thoughts that *La ciudad y el viento* achieves neutrality. The narrator ensures that none of the characters is seen as being wholly bad or solely to blame, but equally no one is perfect. Even Estela, the least reprehensible character in the novel, could be interpreted as partially responsible for her father's murder because she persuades him to stay in the town to look after her when he really wants to return to the countryside. Although Estela's motives are selfish, the narrator diminishes this characterization by presenting her as vulnerable and as the main victim of events in the town.

Dolores Llamas, the character who stabs Alberto, is also partially defended by the narrator. Dolores' hands are covered in blood and she is holding the murder weapon at the end of the novel. Nonetheless, she is presented as being only one amongst a group of women who attack the caretaker. When Dolores realizes that she is attacking Alberto her reaction highlights the problem of identifying who is to blame. Dolores exclaims: '¡Alberto García de Alba! ¡Tú! ¿Qué he hecho? ¿Qué hemos hecho?' (107) ['Alberto García de Alba! It's you! What have I done? What have we done?']. Dolores first acknowledges her own guilt and then the women's shared responsibility for the murder of the new caretaker. In Dolores' defence she only attacks Alberto because Manuel Berumen, the convent caretaker, lied to her. Berumen led her to believe that the new caretaker was part of an official plot to prevent a religious procession in order to hide the fact that he had been stealing the money entrusted to him by the parade organizers. However, even the objectionable Berumen is given the chance to justify his actions, as the narrator describes how he convinces himself that he lied: 'No precisamente para causar daño, sino para sobrevivir' (89) [not to cause harm but to survive]. The narrator does not suggest that the characters are equally to blame but shows that no one character is solely to blame and nobody is blameless.

The Catholic townspeople share the responsibility for the course of events in the town along with the representatives of the civil authorities. General Suárez orders the death of Juan Garay which ends the uneasy peace in the town. The chief of police, Neftalí González, is partly responsible because he carries out Suárez's order. Of all the representatives of the State the governor, Cuitláhuac Fernández, is portrayed most sympathetically but he is unable to control General Suárez. Faced with the possibility of a revolt by the townspeople, Fernández remains calm and consistently aims to avoid violence. However, he is dependent on the army and so he gives in to Suárez's veiled threat to withdraw the army's support and allows Suárez to have troops and police on stand-by. Washing his hands of all responsibility, he tells Suárez: 'Haga usted lo que crea conveniente, y asuma su responsabilidad' (105) [Do what you think necessary and take responsibility for it]. The governor's decision to allow Suárez to have the troops on stand-by does not affect the outcome of the novel as, unbeknown to the authorities, the townspeople had already decided to attack the new convent caretaker on Monday, before the troops would be in position. Nonetheless, the reader sees that the presence of the police and army in the town would probably have led to an outbreak of violence which the weak governor could have prevented if he had stood up to Suárez and not been afraid of his own power which 'a veces le daba miedo' (53) [sometimes scared him]. Ultimately, the governor is presented by the narrator as well intentioned but unable to do good, and it is only by chance that he is not responsible for the violent unrest in the town.

Every character in *La ciudad y el viento* has a defence and all possess some redemptive characteristic, no matter how small. This feature is not necessarily a shortcoming as the reviewers suggested but part of the novel's refusal to side with either the Church or the State. Of course, it is possible that the reviewers interpreted the novel as intentionally neutral, but knew that such a position was unacceptable and assessed the novel accordingly. Ruiz suggests that pro-*cristero* novels did not live up to the requirements and expectations of official culture exemplified by novels of the Mexican Revolution, and so they were rejected by official culture (22). As a neutral *novela de la guerra cristera* [novel about the *cristero* conflict] *La ciudad y el viento* also failed to meet these standards and so, even if reviewers had interpreted the novel as being deliberately neutral with regards to the Church–State conflict, *La ciudad y el viento* would still not have been included in a canon which was founded on a nation-building agenda.

La ciudad y el viento may also have fallen short of the criteria for canonical literature because it had a female protagonist and can be seen to have a proto-feminist agenda. In the novels of the Mexican Revolution which form the basis of the Mexican canon there is rarely, if ever, a female protagonist or even an important female character. In *cristero* literature, however, as Arias and Guy Thiebaut have observed, women usually have very important roles reflecting the historical role women had in the conflicts.[24] *La ciudad y el viento* follows the example of *cristero* literature in its use of female protagonists and in placing women at the forefront of the novel's action. The important roles accorded to women and the novel's proto-feminist perspective could have presented a problem for reviewers who assessed texts in terms of their perceived national significance and nation-building potential traditionally associated with male protagonists.

The novel's proto-feminist perspective can be seen in the way it represents female characters who are not passive or submissive to men or to the church authorities. Dolores rejects the Bishop's authority when she dismisses his suggestion that churchgoers should obey government orders to close the church and accuses him of being too scared to fight. The women challenge male authority by assuming leadership positions traditionally reserved for men and taking control of the rebellion against the authorities to the extent that the narrator suggests that: 'Quizá [...] los hombres sentían excluidos esta vez del castigo a los ladrones, castigo que las mujeres habían tomado absolutamente por su cuenta' (102) [Perhaps [...] this time the men felt excluded from the punishment of the thieves, punishment which the women had undertaken completely of their own account]. This supplanting of their traditional role is disconcerting for the men, particularly since the women defend their religion in ways which require them to break gendered codes of behaviour. In another sense, however, it can be argued that the women adhere to traditional gender roles, according to which it is their responsibility to safeguard religion in the family and any feminist intention we identify in the novel is likely to be prototypal.

In *La ciudad y el viento* the church is the only place where women can be free and its closure represents a threat to women's liberty. Patience A. Schell has rightly noted that: 'In seeking to regulate the public spaces of the Catholic Church, the State also limited the public spaces of Catholic women' (181–82). The narrator says that it is only inside the church that the women have a voice and some control over their lives: 'Allá sí pueden alzar la voz, unirla a otras, aumentarla en la resonancia de las naves. Allá sí pueden oírse, sentirse poderosas. En canto o plegaria escapa, en voz alta, la represión de días y años vividos en pasivo sometimiento' (7) [There they can raise their voices, join them with others, amplify them with the echoes of the naves. There they can hear themselves and feel powerful. In song or praise said aloud the repression of days and years lived in passive submission escapes]. Thus, the church acts as an escape valve for women's frustrations which cannot be expressed elsewhere. The narrator's description of the role of the Church in women's lives may be disquieting in its suggestion that the church provides a mechanism for controlling women and preventing them from seeking change, but any concerns are offset by the fact that the church also provides women with opportunities for greater freedom than they have elsewhere in their lives. The closure of the limited public meeting spaces open to them angers the female characters, and their protests are portrayed as being as much about women's rights as about religious freedom.

The choice of a female protagonist may have presented an obstacle to reviewers wishing to interpret Castro's novel with reference to national circumstances but, to a greater extent than *Yo también, Adelita*, the action of the novel could be seen to occur in the public sphere and so we might expect it to have been less resistant to dominant interpretive strategies. Nonetheless, a private-national reading highlights the fact that *La ciudad y el viento* presented an alternative vision of the nation to that envisaged by official nationalism. I have suggested that non-canonical novels such as Castro's often benefit from private-national readings as they aim to negotiate a place in the nation for those who have been excluded. Ruiz attributes similar qualities to *cristero* literature, which he says 'afirma los valores de la patria, de su historia, su religión, incluso, y sus héroes con el fin de construir una nación nueva' (20) [affirms the values of the fatherland, of its history, its religion, even, and its heroes with the aim of building a new nation]. *Cristero* literature, he argues, presents an alternative vision of the nation to that of official revolutionary nationalism but, like its revolutionary counterpart, it was marked by 'la huella del nacionalismo de los años treinta' [the footprint of 1930s nationalism] (Ruiz, 20). *La ciudad y el viento* does not, however, employ national allegory. In order to maintain a neutral stance, no one character on either side could be chosen to stand in for the collective or the nation. The case of *La ciudad y el viento* thus suggests that the use of the private to comment on the public sphere is not exclusive to national allegory.

La ciudad y el viento argues for the inclusion of people who, like Estela, were both liberal and Catholic and also those, like Juan Garay, who sought peaceful solutions while still practising his faith. More than any other characters they are presented as the innocent victims caught in the middle of the Church–State conflict. Estela represents a compromise and a way in which the Church–State conflict could be constructively resolved if people were allowed to be both liberal and Catholic. As Matthew Butler has observed, however, this was frequently not an option during the period of the *cristero* conflict, because sending children to the SEP school could result in excommunication, while attending church could cause a village to be denied land rights.[25] Early in the novel, the narrator explains that Estela occupies the middle ground: 'Las dos corrientes de su familia: liberalismo en los hombres, profunda catolicidad en las mujeres, le fluían armónicamente por las venas, y podía tratar con caridad a los creyentes, a los herejes' (23) [The two currents in her family:

liberalism in the men, profound Catholicism in the women, flowed harmoniously through her veins and she treated believers and non-believers with kindness]. Estela's position is, however, untenable as almost every event in the novel affects her in a negative way. At the end of the novel she is forced to retire from society and live in the countryside, representing the impossibility of reconciling the two sides in the public sphere.

A private-national reading of *La ciudad y el viento* also reveals that, through the character of Consolación Lara, the novel presents an alternative approach to the Church–State conflict which is in contrast to the confrontational methods employed by Dolores in her dealings with the civil authorities. In her struggle with the State authorities Dolores over-reacts and eventually resorts to violence. Consolación also stands up to a repressive patriarchal authority figure but, unlike Dolores, she remains calm and uses rational arguments when she confronts her father about his hypocrisy and false pride. Like Dolores, Consolación is ultimately unsuccessful in her attempt to stand up to authority. Nonetheless, her experience illustrates an alternative, less destructive model of behaviour and so the novel uses the private sphere to suggest that Dolores and the *cristeros* were right to stand up for their beliefs, but they should not have resorted to violence.

The private narrative about Jesús Lara can also be seen to shed light on what the novel proposes would be the correct course of action in the Church–State conflict. Jesús is unable to do good because he cannot, or will not, stand up to his father, mirroring the situation between the governor and General Suárez in which the governor is unable to do good because he refuses to stand up to Suárez. Initially, Jesús is portrayed in a very positive manner; he is hard-working, obedient, and sympathetic to the difficulties faced by Estela. However, when his father forbids him to see Estela he does not stand up to him or defend Estela's good name. The parallel drawn between the governor and General Suárez on the one hand, and Jesús and Pascual Lara on the other, would seem to suggest that failing to stand up for what is right can have grave consequences. While the governor's weakness does not have any consequences, the narrative about Jesús demonstrates that weakness can be disastrous, as it means that he fails to look after Estela in her time of greatest need. The situation is, however, complicated by Jesús' dance with Juanita, during which he imagines seducing her; the only reason he does not do so is because he is afraid of his father. It seems that there are in fact two 'lessons' to be drawn from the private situation of Jesús. The first lesson to learn is the importance of standing up for what is right and the second is that weakness can prevent greater harm. The latter 'lesson' may be intended as a justification or defence for the Church which was at times criticized for appearing weak because it was trying to avoid another bloody confrontation.

A private-national reading of *La ciudad y el viento*, according to which parallels are established between the Lara family's private situation and the public events, allows us to appreciate the significance of these characters, who otherwise appear to be unrelated to the 'main action' of the novel. By presenting the Church–State conflict in terms of struggles within a family the novel provides a fresh perspective on contentious issues and presents alternative models of behaviour which could have been used to address the Church–State conflict. None of the novel's reviewers mentioned the Lara family and so completely ignored this aspect of the novel, because of their inability or unwillingness to consider unfamiliar narrative strategies for talking about the public sphere, and because of their reluctance to acknowledge the private sphere as potentially significant.

Even though it does not use national allegory, the non-canonical text *La ciudad y el viento* does lend itself to a private-national reading. Thus, the defining characteristic which distinguishes canonical from non-canonical texts is not the use of national allegory, as Jameson suggested with reference to 'first-' and 'third-world' literature, but the differing relationships between public and private perceived by dominant interpretive strategies in canonical texts compared to non-canonical texts. In the former, the private sphere can be discarded without causing the novel's potential national meaning and significance to be overlooked, whilst the latter benefit from interpretive strategies which are attentive to the relationship between public and private spheres, particularly when trying to uncover their potential national significance. Reviewers of woman-authored novels frequently failed to comprehend the need to consider and apply alternative interpretive strategies. As a result of such ideologically and gender-biased interpretive strategies, many women authors, including Consuelo Delgado and Dolores Castro, were completely excluded from the Mexican literary canon. New interpretive strategies which are attentive to the possibility that women and other marginalized authors addressed the national situation, but did not necessarily share the assumptions or values of official culture, are imperative if we are to reform the canon.

La ciudad y el viento was excluded from the twentieth-century Mexican literary canon because of its choice of location, subject, its neutrality in relation to the Church–State conflict, and its proto-feminist perspective, and not because reviewers failed to read the private in terms of the public and so see its national significance. In this case, even if the reviewers had interpreted the private in terms of the public they would have uncovered — only to an even greater extent — the same unnerving, unacceptable neutrality. Nonetheless, I have again shown that a private-national reading of a woman-authored non-canonical novel provides important new insights into the text. Reading the private in terms of the public in *La ciudad y el viento* enabled us to uncover the richness of a supposedly simple 'novela corta de la vida provinciana' [short novel about provincial life] which challenged the State's understanding of who should be included in the nation. This reading practice may be usefully applied to other woman-authored non-canonical texts, while the rewarding experience of re-interpreting texts such as *Yo también, Adelita* and *La ciudad y el viento* may also lead us to ask on what grounds inclusion in the canon should be based in future, and to suggest that the Mexican canon might be better founded on criteria other than whether or not a novel contributed to post-revolutionary nation-building.

Notes to Chapter 4

1. All references in this chapter are to Dolores Castro, *La ciudad y el viento* (Xalapa: Universidad Veracruzana, 1962) unless otherwise stated. Parts of this chapter were previously published and expand on arguments first presented in Sarah E. L. Bowskill, 'Women, Violence and the Mexican Cristero Wars as represented in *Los recuerdos del porvenir* and *La ciudad y el viento*', *Modern Language Review*, 104.2 (2009), 438–52.

2. Carballo, *Bibliografía de la novela mexicana*, p. 153; Russell M. Cluff and Josefina Lara Valdez, *Diccionario biobibliográfico de escritores de México 1920–1970*, 2nd edn (Mexico: INBA, 1994), pp. 112–13; González Peña, *Historia de la literatura mexicana*, 9th edn, p. 298; José Luis Martínez, *Literatura mexicana siglo XX*, I, 84; II, 30; Millán, pp. 74–75; Laura Navarrete Maya, 'Dolores Castro', in *Diccionario de escritores mexicanos siglo XX*, Tomo I (A-CH), ed. by Aurora M. Ocampo (Mexico: UNAM, 1988), pp. 348–49.

3. 'Hay un verdadero florecimiento de poesía femenina: Dolores Castro', CNIPL/EXP.DC. It should be noted that elsewhere Castro has said that *La ciudad y el viento* 'Fue la única novela que escribí porque en realidad lo que más me interesaba era la poesía' [was the only novel I wrote because what I was really interested in was poetry]. Sandra Avendaño Betanzos, 'Dolores Castro: Lo que uno vive es totalmente fugaz', CNIPL/EXP.DC.

4. Letter from Sr. Antonio Acevedo Escobedo. Jefe del Departamento de Literatura. 25 January 1960. CNIPL/EXP.DC. Letter from Dolores Castro to Acevedo Escobedo. Jefe del Departamento de Literatura. 2 February 1960, CNIPL/EXP.DC.

5. *Ocho poetas mexicanos* (Mexico: Bajo el signo de Ábside, 1955).

6. Juan Cervera, 'Aquí la poesía Dolores Castro, corazón transfigurado', CNIPL/EXP.DC.

7. Alejandro Avilés, 'Dolores Castro y la poesía femenina', *Revista de la Semana*, supl. *El Universal*, 15 February 1953, pp. 17–18; Octavio Novaro, 'Perfiles de Mexico. Dolores Castro', *El Día*, 28 July, 1979, p. 16.

8. Vicente Echeverria del Prado and Ramón Galvez, 'Pausas literarias', *Novedades*, 29 February 1948, FR/DC.

9. Alvaro Ruiz Abreu, *La cristera, una literatura negada (1928–1992)* (Mexico: Universidad Autónoma Metropolitana-Xochimilco, 2003), p. 25.

10. Edgar Córdova, 'Dolores Castro, homenaje a ochenta años en las letras', *Milenio*, 13 April 2003, p. 41.

11. Jesús Arellando, 'Panorámica de las letras', *El Día*, 21 September 1962, p. 9; Francisco Zendejas, 'Multilibros', *El Excélsior*, 5 August 1962, p. 2C.

12. [Advertisement] 'Ediciones de la Universidad Veracruzana Colección — Ficción', *El Centavo*, vol. IV, no. 51 September 1962, unnumbered middle section. The advertisement in *La Palabra y el Hombre* appeared on the back cover of the July–September and October–December issues in 1966.

13. 'Nueva Bibliografía Mexicana', *Boletín Bibliográfico Mexicano*, September–October, 1962, p. 39.

14. Ignacio Méndez, '*La ciudad y el viento*', *México en la Cultura*, supl. *Novedades*, 19 August 1962, p. 11; '*La ciudad y el viento*', *Cuadernos de Bellas Artes*, 1 January 1963, p. 89; Emmanuel Carballo, 'Costumbrismo y mortaja', *La Cultura en México*, supl. *Siempre*, núm 28, 29 August 1962, p. xvi.

15. SEP Archive 1934–1936 Depto. de Bellas Artes Concursos y Certámenes 17-11–218 196. Referencia VII/357.2/3. Concurso de literatura, periodismo, obras científicas, etc. Asunto — Documentación relativa.

16. Danny J. Anderson, 'Creating Cultural Prestige: Editorial Joaquín Mortiz', *Latin American Research Review*, 31 (1996), 3–41 (p. 24, 25).

17. Jean Meyer, *The Cristero Rebellion: The Mexican People between Church and State 1926–1929*, trans. by Richard Southern (Cambridge: Cambridge University Press, 1976), pp. 63–66; James W. Wilkie, 'The Meaning of the Cristero Religious War against the Mexican Revolution', *Journal of Church and State*, 8 (1966), 214–33 (pp. 226–29).

18. Patience A. Schell, *Church and State Education in Revolutionary Mexico City* (Tucson: University of Arizona Press, 2003), p. 194; Wilkie, pp. 230–31.

19. Roberto Blancarte, *Historia de la Iglesia Católica Mexicana* (Mexico: FCE, 1992), pp. 161–65.

20. George W. Grayson, *The Church in Contemporary Mexico* (Washington, DC: Center for Strategic and International Studies, 1992), p. 49.
21. Howard F. Cline, *Mexico: Revolution to Evolution 1940–1960* (London: Oxford University Press, 1962), p. 177.
22. Angel Arias Urrutia, *Cruzados de novela. Las novelas de la guerra cristera* (Pamplona: Ediciones Universidad de Navarra, 2002), p. 10.
23. For a plot summary of the novel see Appendix.
24. Guy Thiebaut, *La Contre-révolution mexicaine à travers sa littérature. L'Exemple du roman cristero de 1926 à nos jours* (Paris: L'Harmattan, 1997), pp. 25, 213; Arias, pp. 112, 234.
25. Matthew Butler, 'God's *Campesinos*? Mexico's Revolutionary Church in the Countryside', *Bulletin of Latin American Research*, 28 (2009), 165–84 (p. 167).

CHAPTER 5

The Exceptional Case of
El desfile del amor

In the last two decades of the twentieth-century Sergio Pitol emerged as a prominent figure on the Mexican literary scene. In this period he won several prestigious national prizes, including the *Premio Nacional de Literatura* in 1993 and the *Premio Juan Rulfo* in 1999. It was only following the publication of *El desfile del amor* in 1984, however, that his work achieved widespread recognition in Mexico. Sergio Pitol has assessed his reputation among Mexican readers prior to the publication of *El desfile del amor* as follows: 'era yo inexistente, una sombra, un excéntrico, alejado de la realidad mexicana y también de la hispanoamericana, enclaustrado en una móvil torre de marfil, fraguando historias bizarras que tenían lugar en Venecia o Samarcanda' [I didn't exist, I was a shadow, an eccentric, distanced from Mexican reality and from the Hispanic American one too, shut away in a mobile marble tower, concocting bizarre stories that took place in Venice or Samarkand].[1] *El desfile del amor* was Pitol's first novel to be set in Mexico and it was this publication which assured him a place at the forefront of Mexican letters, making it a classic example of the need to address contemporary issues of national importance in order to be included in the post-revolutionary canon. The case of *El desfile del amor* is not, however, straightforward, as reviewers readily interpreted events in the private sphere with reference to the public situation whereas they had been unable to do so for woman-authored texts. This chapter shows how reviewers modified their interpretive strategies based on their identification of *El desfile del amor* as a detective novel which, in Latin America, is a genre associated with canonical literature, rather than 'popular fiction'. Thus, I explore the relationship between interpretive strategies, gender, genre and canonicity in the formation of the twentieth-century Mexican novelistic canon.

    El desfile del amor was Pitol's third novel and although his public profile was limited he was an established figure on the Mexican political scene. As Elena Urrutia noted in *La Jornada*, Pitol is part of a long-standing tradition of Mexican intellectuals and writers who have had diplomatic careers.[2] When *El desfile del amor* was published Pitol was the Mexican ambassador to Czechoslovakia and he had worked in the diplomatic service since 1960. He was also a translator and the author of short stories and two novels, *El tañido de una flauta* (1973) and *Juegos Florales* (1982). In the 1980s, Pitol was increasingly productive and received recognition for his work in the form of the *Premio Xavier Villaurrutia* in 1981 for *Nocturno de Bujara* (1981) and the *Premio de Narrativa Colima para Obra Publicada* in 1982 for *Cementerio de tordos* (1982). None of his earlier work, however, enjoyed the same reception as *El desfile del amor*, which reviewers, including Christopher Domínguez Michael, José Joaquín Blanco and Sergio González Rodríguez, claimed was Pitol's best work to date.[3] Furthermore, it is only since the mid-1980s that Pitol has been regularly included in the Mexican canon as it is represented in histories, dictionaries and anthologies of Mexican literature, suggesting that *El desfile del amor* was a landmark publication in Pitol's career.[4]

As the winner of the prestigious *Premio Herralde* awarded by the Spanish publisher Anagrama, *El desfile del amor* aroused the interest of critics and the curiosity of the reading public in his native country.[5] The impact of the Anagrama prize on Pitol's career should not be underestimated as Pitol has since said:

> Mis libros recibieron por años aquí muy escasa atención crítica [...]. El premio español modificó el panorama, mis lectores aumentaron y la crítica ha terminado por situar mi obra en el canon de la literatura mexicana. La noción de tener éxito en Europa me hizo visible en mi país.[6]

> [For years my books received very little critical attention here [in Mexico] [...]. The Spanish prize changed the outlook, my readership increased and criticism has ended up placing my work in the canon of Mexican literature. The fact that I had success in Europe made me visible in my own country.]

Nearly all of the reviews of *El desfile del amor* mentioned the prize confirming its importance for the novel's reception. However, while the examples of *El desfile del amor* and *El indio* clearly suggest that winning literary prizes has a positive impact on a how a novel is received, this cannot be taken as given, as will be seen in the case of *Arráncame la vida*.

The cultural capital accrued as a result of being awarded the *Premio Herralde* was converted into economic capital as Mexican readers were willing to pay a premium price for *El desfile del amor* which cost around $3000 pesos for the first edition and, when that print run sold out, the second edition cost $4000 pesos.[7] Having paid what was a particularly high price for a novel in the context of the Mexican book market, readers were satisfied; Pablo Boullosa Velázquez noted that *El desfile del amor* received 'una calurosa acogida del público lector mexicano' (10) [a warm reception from the Mexican reading public]. Indeed, reviews of *El desfile del amor* were overwhelmingly positive and the fact that the novel was reprinted and published in multiple editions between 1984 and 1993 shows both its importance and popularity; publishers do not reprint books that will not sell. Those reviewers who found shortcomings in Pitol's novel including, for example, Domínguez Michael and Héctor Barrón Soto who disliked the ending, also found much to praise about it.[8] A notable characteristic of the reviews was that they were typically longer than the reviews of *Arráncame la vida* by Ángeles Mastretta, which was published a year later, possibly because they were often magazine articles or articles from newspaper supplements. Only a handful were written by women, revealing that even in the 1980s few women had interpretive authority as custodians of literary knowledge, especially when it came to interpreting a male-authored text.

Reviewers consistently identified Miguel del Solar's investigation into the situation in Mexico in 1942 and into the shooting at the Minerva as the subject of

El desfile del amor. Several commented on the importance of the dates around which the novel centres (1914, 1942 and 1973) which were defining moments in Mexico's past. Elena Urrutia, for example, described them as 'esos años decisivos para el ingreso del país en la modernidad' [those decisive years for the country's entry into modernity].[9] José Felipe Coria likewise highlighted the importance of these years in terms of Mexico's development concluding that '*El desfile del amor*, finalmente, es un sondeo sobre los orígenes de nuestra modernidad' [*El desfile del amor*, in the end, is an enquiry into the origins of our modernity].[10] Selatiel Alatriste, Juan Domingo Argüelles and Ricardo Pohlenz also related events in the novel to the present asking to what extent circumstances had changed.[11] There was, therefore, a consensus among reviewers that the subject matter of *El desfile del amor* was pertinent and even directly relevant to the contemporary context, and consequently the novel was incorporated into the canon.

In addition to identifying the issues of national importance addressed in the novel, reviewers also associated *El desfile del amor* with genres that were considered appropriate for canonical literature. Some reviews, such as the one by Antonio Contreras published in the magazine *Punto*, suggested that *El desfile del amor* was a 'comedia de enredos' [a comedy of intrigue] thus aligning it with a canonical tradition exemplified by the Golden Age Spanish dramatist, Tirso de Molina, who is cited in the novel.[12] There was also a general consensus among reviewers that *El desfile del amor* was either an historical or a detective novel or, most commonly, a combination of these. In Europe and the United States detective fiction is usually considered to be a 'popular' genre and, therefore, not a canonical one. In the Latin American context, however, critics have questioned the 'popular' status of the genre.[13]

Most reviewers believed that *El desfile del amor* was about history but was also a detective novel or drew on this genre. Although there was broad agreement that the novel was related to the detective genre, reviewers disagreed as to whether or not *El desfile del amor* followed the conventions of the genre. Blanco noted that the ending was unconventional for a detective novel as the crimes 'no se resuelven con la nitidez que un lector de novelas policíacas exigiría' ('Pitol', 21) [are not resolved with the neatness that a reader of detective novels would demand]. Blanco did not, however, see this as a shortcoming. Ricardo Pohlenz conceded that Miguel del Solar was atypical of the detective figure but still believed that *El desfile del amor* was a 'novela negra' [hard-boiled detective novel] which possessed one of the defining characteristics of this genre; 'la de evidenciar una situación social' ('El desfile', 2) [that of revealing a social context].

The novel's divergence from the 'classic' model of detective fiction led many reviewers to suggest that *El desfile del amor* used the detective genre, but that it was not limited by it. Humberto Guzmán, for example, claimed: 'sobresale su estructura policíaca sin quedarse nunca en la receta del género' [the use of the structure of a detective novel stands out without it ever sticking to the recipe for the genre].[14] González Rodríguez asserted: 'Si fuera considerada solamente una novela del género detectivesco, *El desfile del amor* sería insuperable comparándola con otras obras mexicanas de esa línea afinidades policíacas y de misterio. Sin embargo, sus alcances son mayores' (2) [if it were only thought of as a detective novel, *El desfile del amor* would be unsurpassable in comparison with other Mexican novels of its kind related to detective work and mystery. However, its achievements are greater]. For some of the reviewers of *El desfile del amor*, the novel was an outstanding example of the detective genre while for others it was more than 'just' a detective novel, it was also an historical novel or a novel which used the detective genre to explore social issues. Thus, the canonical *El desfile del amor* was credited with innovation and thereby elevated to a literary form rather than being perceived as 'popular fiction'.

As well as discussing the genre to which *El desfile del amor* belonged, an important feature of the reviews was the many comparisons they made with other texts. *El desfile del amor* was variously compared to the work of European and US authors whose novels Pitol had translated, to works by Tirso de Molina, Charles Dickens and Ernst Lubitsch which were cited in Pitol's text, and to other authors including Eric Ambler, Henry James, Virginia Woolf and Mario Vargas Llosa.[15] In an emphatic concluding statement to his review in *La Jornada*, José Joaquín Blanco wrote: '*El desfile del amor* sería una novela notable en cualquier momento de cualquier literatura' ('Pitol', 21) [*El desfile del amor* would be a distinguished novel in any period in any literature]. Blanco's statement reveals a recurring concern found in reviews that canonical Mexican novels should also merit a place in other national canons and in the international canon of 'great literature'. The highest praise for a novel, then, is that it would deserve a place in any national canon. Blanco's comments and the numerous comparisons made with canonical European authors confirm that reviewers held Pitol and his work in the highest regard and that they saw his work as worthy of representing Mexico on the world stage.

Another recurring concern in reviews of *El desfile del amor* was style. As we have already seen in previous chapters, comments about style are used by reviewers to praise a novel whose content is of interest or to criticize novels whose content is seen as irrelevant. Many of the reviewers of *El desfile del amor* expressed their appreciation of the novel by praising its 'literary' style. Juan José Reyes, for example, wrote: 'Los diálogos, abundantes, son sin falta eminentemente literarios' [The abundant dialogues are without fail eminently literary].[16] Blanco was similarly enthusiastic about the style employed by *El desfile del amor*. In his review in *La Jornada* he wrote: 'Resulta muy refrescante leer hoy en día una novela *literaria*, esto es, inteligente y rigurosamente compuesta [...]' ('Pitol', 21) [It is very refreshing to read in this day and age a *literary* novel, that is, intelligent and rigorously composed]. The novel's literariness apparently contributed to the reviewers' reading pleasure as Elena Urrutia ('*El desfile del amor*', 23), Boullosa Velázquez (16) Alatriste (48) and Anhalt (2) wrote of their 'entusiasmo' [enthusiasm] on reading *El desfile del amor*. Reviewers of *El desfile del amor* and *Arráncame la vida* placed greater importance on whether or not they enjoyed reading a book than reviewers of the earlier novels but, as will be seen in the next chapter, different kinds of reading pleasure are associated with canonical and non-canonical texts.

In the same way that reviewers of the other canonical novels in this study compared them to murals so too five reviewers described *El desfile del amor* as a 'fresco' or 'mural'.[17] Elena Urrutia wrote:

> Que lo que importa sobre todas las cosas es ese fresco variado y multicolor que Sergio Pitol ha logrado integrar, dentro de la mejor tradición muralista, de un medio compacto que procesa la integración de la familia revolucionaria, en un momento clave para México, en unos años precisamente en los que se define el sentido o la vocación del país ('*El desfile del amor*', 23).

> [What matters above all is this varied and multicoloured fresco that Sergio Pitol has managed to compose, within the best mural tradition, of a closed environment which puts on trial the integration of the revolutionary family, at a key moment for Mexico, in precisely those years in which the direction or purpose of the country was defined.]

Urrutia's comments connect Miguel del Solar's investigation to the legacy of the Mexican revolution which was a favoured topic for national art and literature. Furthermore, as in the cases of *El indio* and *La región más transparente*, the suggestion that *El desfile del amor* was like a fresco or a mural associated the novel with the canonical artistic tradition of public art in Mexico and implied that the novel was suitably broad in scope and addressed contemporary issues of national significance making it worthy of being incorporated into the national literary canon.

The reviews of *El desfile del amor* show a relatively homogeneous response to the novel which would have facilitated consecration; this homogeneity also provides further evidence that interpretive communities share interpretive strategies. Reviewers clearly enjoyed this work, which they saw as a classic example of literary fiction. They were enthusiastic about the chosen subject and setting, and about the novel's perceived use of the detective genre. The reviews also emphasized the international aspect of Pitol's life and writing and it could be argued that there was a tendency in the reviews to see Pitol's literature as worthy of representing Mexico abroad in a way that was an extension of his diplomatic role. Furthermore, as the winner of the *Premio Herralde*, *El desfile del amor* was a shining example of something reviewers were always hoping for, a Mexican novel which addressed national circumstances and was also worthy of international esteem. Unusually in this case the novel had already won acclaim abroad before it was endorsed by Mexican reviewers.

El desfile del amor was widely reviewed, but it has rarely been the subject of academic study suggesting that academic criticism, particularly when produced outside Mexico, does not play a significant role in forming the Mexican canon. Furthermore, whilst reviewers were preoccupied with what the novel had to say about national circumstances, much of the work that has been published on *El desfile del amor* has interpreted the novel with reference to European theory, particularly Bakhtinian theory, and authors, thereby removing the novel from its Mexican context.[18] It is my assertion that inclusion in the Mexican literary canon is based on whether or not a novel is interpreted as having contemporary national significance and so the first stage of the following analysis will focus on the Mexican context that is central to explaining why *El desfile del amor* marked Pitol's entry into the post-revolutionary canon.

Reviewers identified the years 1914, 1942 and 1973 around which *El desfile del amor* was structured as key moments in Mexico's past.[19] These were pivotal years in terms of the country's economic development, periods when the revolutionary project was defined or re-defined, and eventually betrayed. When *El desfile del amor* was published in 1984 these dates held a particular resonance because of the contemporary circumstances: the economy was in crisis and the social pact that had been the bedrock of post-revolutionary politics had collapsed.

In 1914 Venustiano Carranza emerged victorious from the revolution. The *carrancistas* had a 'modern capitalist orientation' and so the seeds were sown for later development models which aggressively pursued a path of rapid economic development and industrialization in the name of progress and modernity (Adler, 16). In the post-revolutionary period the ruling party and the country's development model was founded on the idea of national unity. Presidents Avila Camacho and Alemán invoked national unity in order to discourage 'unpatriotic' opposition and encourage 'collaboration with the government and industry to hasten the economic development of Mexico' (Adler, 41). When the consensus that underpinned Mexican political and economic life collapsed in the late 1960s, however, national unity was revealed to be little more than official rhetoric.

President Luis Echeverría Alvarez (1970–76) tried and failed to re-create the lost consensus within the PRI but, in 1973, following a further deterioration of relations between the State and private sector, the financial boom of the late 1950s and 1960s ended leaving the country in crisis.[20] Temporary relief came when Mexico discovered new oil reserves and an oil boom ensued which lasted until 1982, when oil prices collapsed. Capital flight ensued and, in September 1982, President José López Portillo (1976–82) nationalized the banks, destroying for the foreseeable future the possibility of rebuilding the relationship between the State and the business sector.[21] The split between the State and private sector forced other groups to take sides, causing 'a growing political confrontation' (Newell and Rubio, 263). The consensus which had been the cornerstone of Mexican political and economic life had disappeared and national unity shattered.

The responsibility for repairing the social pact fell to President Miguel de la Madrid Hurtado (1982–88). Undeterred by the current crisis, de la Madrid was convinced 'of having arrived at a turning point in the country' and he introduced drastic reforms (Aguilar Camín, 220–21). Peter Smith notes that 'some observers predicted that the de la Madrid administration, so embattled for so long, would go down as a watershed in Mexican history' (390). In this climate of change and uncertainty, reviewers welcomed *El desfile del amor* because it identified 1914, 1942 and 1973 as the pivotal moments in Mexican history which defined the present and resonated so clearly with contemporary concerns.

The novel's social and political commentary is expressed by means of the detective genre and in the context of del Solar's private investigation. The failure of the revolutionary project is signified by the novel's ending in which the crime is not solved. The solving of the crime, which is the classical ending of a detective novel, reinforces the status quo so that 'there is no doubt, finally, as to the essential stability and moral integrity of society and its institutions' (Simpson, 139). The resolution of the mystery shows that the State has been able, and in the future will be able, to impose order when disorder was/is threatened.[22] An ending whereby the crime is not solved presents an alternative view of society and challenges the ideology of the system.[23] If the closed ending promises that there will be no change, the open ending of *El desfile del amor* indicates the presence of a threat to the status quo, suggesting that change is inevitable because the current PRI regime has lost its ability to rule effectively having lost the consensus.

The detective genre is also employed in *El desfile del amor* to undermine post-revolutionary discourses about modernity. Persephone Braham argues that Latin American detective literature is concerned with the failure of modernity and that in Mexico the failure of modernity was intimately connected to that of the revolutionary project (xii). Furthermore, Braham suggests, the detective genre 'can serve as a fulcrum for exposing the fissures and divergences that characterize the performance of modernity' (x). Thus, not only does the novel identify the key moments which led to the complete collapse of the revolutionary project as envisaged by the PRI, but the characters in the novel are also seen to perform a role rather than reveal their authentic selves, or give a true account of what happened on the night of Erich's death. Progress in any form is presented as being impossible, as del Solar goes round in circles interviewing the same people and not reaching any firm conclusions. Furthermore, at the end of the novel when a car pulls up beside him, just as a car had allegedly pulled up beside Erich before he was shot, there is a suggestion that history is about to repeat itself and del Solar will be killed in the same way as the young man whose death he has been investigating. Were he to be killed in the same way, and presumably by the same people, he would finally see, in the last moments of his life, who had killed Erich and at least have the satisfaction that his investigation was not futile. Even at this moment, however, progress is frustrated; it is just someone pulling over to ask for directions. The dramatic ending which would represent progress and validate del Solar's investigation as something more than a charade is replaced by an anti-climax.

In addition to questioning the path taken by the revolution and undermining the discourses of progress and modernity, *El desfile del amor* can also be said to reveal the emptiness of official discourses which proclaimed a unified national family. Allegory, whereby each character who attends Delfina's party in 1942 represents a different group in society, is used to challenge the view that national unity prevailed despite the presence of groups with opposing interests.[24] At the party, members of the pre- and post-revolutionary elite mingle with famous artists and singers, European Jews, and people who are suspected of having alliances with the Mexican and the German right. Supposedly an allegory of national unity, Delfina's party ends in disaster. The guests misunderstand one another, Erich María Pistauer is killed, Delfina's son is fatally injured and, after the party, two friends, Delfina and Eduviges who represent the post- and pre-revolutionary elite, stop talking to one another. As one of the newspaper reports which del Solar finds in the archive noted: 'el programa unitario no dejaba de ser una ficción' (20) [the unifying programme never ceased to be a fabrication].[25] The tense atmosphere around the Minerva building, the dissolution of Delfina's party and the comments in the newspaper all suggest that, even at its supposed height in the 1940s, national unity was no more than a myth propagated by official discourses to encourage foreign investment and stimulate economic growth.

Furthermore, the novel indicates that this myth was not restricted to the 1940s, as the discourse of national unity was also employed in 1914 and 1973 to create a sense of shared identity and purpose among disparate groups. Delfina remembers attending the wedding of General Aguilar and one of Carranza's daughters where there was an 'infinidad de vivas a la unidad revolucionaria' (219) [an infinite number of hails to revolutionary unity]. However, the unity so enthusiastically proclaimed at the wedding did not last and subsequently fighting broke out between the guests. In 1973, the narrative present, Derny Goenaga, a childhood friend of del Solar, proclaims that the current pact between the State and the economic elite is the 'materialización nueva del concepto de unidad nacional' (165) [new incarnation of the concept of national unity]. Derny, the owner of an advertising company who collects art and regularly travels abroad to eat, to go to the theatre, or to see an exhibition, has a very selective understanding of national unity, one which excludes large sections of Mexican society. Derny's arrogance and his confidence that his prosperity is assured may be ironic for the reader of *El desfile del amor*, who, reading the novel in 1984, would be aware that in 1973 the pact between the political and business elite to which Derny refers was already deteriorating as a result of President Echeverría's policies and that it subsequently collapsed in 1982 when López Portillo nationalized the banks. By drawing attention to the way in which pivotal moments in Mexican history coincided with times when the myth of national unity was propagated, *El desfile del amor* highlights the emptiness of such discourses and the lack of progress made towards establishing genuine social cohesion in the aftermath of the revolution.

Successive post-revolutionary regimes tried to disguise national disunity by creating an official history which emphasized the shared past of all Mexicans and concealed awkward differences, including the fact that not everyone had fought on the same side in the revolution and that not everyone had supported the Allied forces in World War II. The veracity of official history is brought into question by del Solar's investigation because everyone he interviews offers a different interpretation of events, and characters disagree both about what happened and why. As the critic Maricruz Castro Ricalde has observed, this multiplicity of voices belies the idea of official history (167). Newspapers and official documents provide yet more conflicting versions of events which are often implausible or incomplete, suggesting that someone intervened so that the truth could never be discovered. The diverging accounts of the same night undermine the myth of a unified and shared past and, as a single 'true' account is never produced — as it normally is at the end of the classic detective novel — the reader is left questioning whether the truth about the past can ever be uncovered.

As well as departing from the conventions of the detective genre in leaving the case unsolved, *El desfile del amor* also replaced the traditional detective, who is attached to a public institution, with a private detective. Ilan Stavans suggests that the police are replaced by private investigators in Latin American detective fiction because the police are seen as part of the social problem stemming from their involvement with crime and corrupt practices. The choice of a private detective is, therefore, 'an implicit attack upon the governing regimes' (Stavans, 59). This departure, I argue, is also indicative of the different relationship between the public and private spheres in this novel compared to the other canonical male-authored novels studied in this book.

As my reading thus far has suggested, *El desfile del amor* uses the detective genre and, more specifically, del Solar's private investigation to comment on national circumstances. This connection between public and private in the novel is made explicit by del Solar, who intends to use his discoveries about the murder in the Minerva building to shed light on the broader situation in Mexico in 1942. We have seen in previous chapters, however, that reviewers overlooked the private narratives of *El indio* and *La región más transparente* and were unable to read the private in terms of the public in order to uncover the national significance of woman-authored texts such as *Yo también, Adelita*. *El desfile del amor* was the exception to this rule for two reasons. Firstly, having identified *El desfile del amor* as a detective novel it seems that reviewers were aware of the possibility of reading a detective novel as making social comment and adapted their interpretive strategies accordingly. Secondly, like the 'optional' national allegories which Jamseon identifies as being produced in the 'first-world', *El desfile del amor* can be read as bringing the public and private together in order to confirm the separation of the two spheres. In 'optional' allegory 'the allegorical structure tends essentially to separate these levels in some absolute way. We cannot feel its force unless we are convinced of the radical difference between politics and the libidinal: so that its operation reconfirms (rather than annuls) that split between public and private which was attributed to western civilization [...]' (Jameson, 79). I have already identified an allegorical reading of the characters in *El desfile del amor* but the novel does not lend itself to being read as a national allegory; the individual destiny of del Solar does not clearly embody the destiny of Mexico. As noted in the previous chapter, however, it is the different relationship reviewers perceived between the public and private spheres which distinguishes canonical from non-canonical literature, and not the use of national allegory. Initially, it appears that *El desfile del amor*, like *Yo también, Adelita* and *La ciudad y el viento*, blurs the division between public and private. On closer examination, it emerges that although a private-national reading of del Solar's investigation is possible, having brought the public and private together, the novel ultimately reaffirms the split between the two spheres and endorses the primacy of the public.

Del Solar brings public and private together in his investigation because he wants to be part of the history he writes, like the great historians of the past. He is dissatisfied because he believes that his recently published book about Mexico in 1914 could have been written by 'cualquier amanuense poseedor de una mínima instrucción sobre la técnica de evaluar y seleccionar la información dispersa en cartas, documentos públicos y privados y la prensa de una época determinada' (11) [any amanuensis with a basic knowledge of how to evaluate and select the information scattered in letters, public documents, private papers and the press of a given period]. In contrast, his interest in the shooting at the Minerva building has both a personal dimension, in that he was living in the building at the time of Erich's murder and he was distantly related to the victim, and a public significance, as he hopes to use the case as a micro-history to shed light on the broader national and international context of Mexico in 1942.

In the course of his investigation del Solar often fails to differentiate between the public and the private. When he tries to work out when the shooting at the Minerva took place he thinks first about the private and then about the public context: 'No fue difícil precisar la fecha. Cursaba el cuarto año de primaria, de modo que debía ser 1942. La época de los apagones: simulacro de ataques aéreos sobre México' (17) [It wasn't difficult to specify the date. He was in the fourth year of primary school, so it must have been 1942. The time of the blackouts to simulate aerial attacks on Mexico]. The division between public and private is further blurred in del Solar's mind because some of the people he interviews deduce personal motives and others political motives for the crime. After speaking to all of the possible witnesses, del Solar cannot, as he had envisaged, establish a clear connection between the national and international context of 1942 and events at the Minerva.

Unable to reconcile his private experience with national history in order to produce his book, he accepts the primacy of the public over the private narrative. In the end, del Solar dismisses his work on the Minerva case as a 'divertimiento con que se había entretenido' (230, 147) [diversion he had used to entertain himself]. The private dimension that he had hoped to incorporate in his study is described as 'aquellos ángulos enfermizos, vergonzosos casi, de su eventual proyecto' (230) [those unhealthy, almost shameful aspects of his proposed project] which will be forgotten now he has decided to start writing his next book: 'Esa estapa había concluido... En unos días se pondría a trabajar en serio' (230) [That phase was over... In a few days he would set to work in earnest]. Having seen the error of his ways, del Solar separates the private from the public and puts his private interest aside in order to focus on serious national issues using public documents kept in archives instead of interviews with friends and friends of the family.

Frustrated in his efforts to combine an account of public and private events, del Solar chooses to focus on the public issues of national concern in his next book. He is confident that the documents in archives and interviews with public figures will provide him with the clear answers about the situation in Mexico in 1942 that his private investigation had failed to produce. However, the reader may not share his optimism because his experience of consulting the official documents and newspaper articles failed to provide a reliable version of events and he concludes: 'Era evidente la intervención del padre o los hermanos de Delfina para acallar el escándolo. Quizá la importancia de varios de los asistentes a la fiesta dos miembros del Gabinete entre ellos, contribuyera también a ese silencio' (20) [It was clear that Delfina's father or brothers had intervened to silence the scandal. Perhaps the presence of some important guests at the party, among them members of the cabinet, also contributed to the silence]. Likewise, when he consults the judicial records del Solar rejects the version of events they present. The narrator says: 'se oponía radicalmente a aceptar el parte oficial leído hacía poco' (103) [he was completely against accepting the official report he had just read]. The public documents del Solar reads in the course of his investigation are no more (or less) convincing than the private accounts of the witnesses he interviews. In this context, del Solar's willingness to put his faith in public documents for his research into 1942 may be seen as foolish, particularly as all he is likely to achieve by adopting this approach is a repetition of the official version of history. Given the novel's scepticism about official history, such an ending is problematic but suggests that it is only via the public realm that the case can ever be 'proved' and those who are guilty brought to justice. Private investigations and what people say behind closed doors do not matter; it is the public record which must be set straight. Although for much of the novel del Solar tries to connect his own 'private' investigation to national circumstances, the validity of this work is ultimately undermined as the novel reaffirms the split between public and private and prioritizes the public sphere. The public–private divide, which non-canonical novels by Mexican women authors have sought to remove, can, therefore, be seen to be reasserted in Pitol's text and the hierarchy which accords higher status to the public realm is reaffirmed.

The Latin American detective novel which leaves the crime unsolved and replaces the police with a private detective to comment on the fragility of the State and its ideology is like national allegory in that it brings together the public and the private and uses the private sphere to comment on the public situation. However, unlike non-canonical novels where public and private can be seen as being brought together to challenge the division between the spheres, a reading of the public–private relationship in *El desfile del amor* suggests that the spheres are brought together so that the private situation sheds light on the public but, ultimately, the division between the two spheres is affirmed, making it suitable for inclusion in the canon and amenable to dominant interpretive strategies. Nonetheless, a reading which acknowledges the changing relationship of public and private in the text greatly enhances our understanding of the novel.

In terms of my investigation into how the post-revolutionary canon was formed, the key question is why *El desfile del amor* was an exceptional case in which reviewers were able to acknowledge the presence of the private sphere and understand its public significance, when they were unable to do so for the other texts in this study. Firstly, I propose they were able to do so because in the failure of del Solar's investigation they saw confirmation of the primacy of public over private. Secondly, and most importantly, I believe, it is because they were familiar (consciously or unconsciously) with the conventions of the Latin American detective genre, which is a traditionally masculine genre; they understood that a (male-authored) detective novel had to be commenting on society and adapted their interpretive strategies accordingly. As we will now see with Ángeles Mastretta's *Arráncame la vida*, when it came to reviewing an adultery novel by a female author, they misidentified its genre because their interpretive strategies taught them to approach woman-authored novels from certain perspectives and not from others. The cases of *El desfile del amor* and *Arráncame la vida* thus provide strong evidence that the interpretive strategies readers adopt are determined by the perceived genre of a novel and especially by the gender of the author.

Notes to Chapter 5

1. Sergio Pitol quoted in Pedro M. Domene, 'Entrevista. El universo literario y personal de Sergio Pitol (una entrevista que se dilata en el tiempo y en la amistad)', in *Sergio Pitol. El sueño de lo real*, ed. by Pedro M. Domene (Xalapa: Universidad Veracruzana, 2002), pp. 27–39 (p. 30).
2. Elena Urrutia, 'Novela premiada por Anagrama. *El desfile del amor* es una comedia de errores: Pitol', *La Jornada*, 21 December 1984, p. 25.
3. Christopher Domínguez Michael, 'Nueva tristeza mexicana', *Proceso*, 1 April 1985, pp. 60–61 (p. 60); José Joaquín Blanco, 'Pitol: *El desfile del amor*', *La Jornada*, 25 February 1985, p. 21; Sergio González Rodríguez, 'Del regreso: la extrema memoria', *La Jornada*, 13 April 1983, pp. 1–3 (p. 1).
4. Carballo, *Bibliografía de la novela mexicana*, p. 202; Cluff and Valdez, pp. 330–31; Aurora M. Ocampo and Eduardo Serrato Córdova, 'Sergio Pitol', in *Diccionario de escritores mexicanos siglo XX. Desde las generaciones del ateneo y novelistas de la revolución hasta nuestros días*, Tomo VII, ed. by Aurora M. Ocampo (Mexico: UNAM), pp. 528–40; Domínguez Michael and Martínez, pp. 218–19; Josefina Lara Valdez, *Diccionario bio-bibliográfico de escritores contemporáneos de México* (Mexico: INBA, 1988), pp. 173–74. One earlier history of literature to include Pitol was by Millán, pp. 292–93.
5. It should be noted that Pitol submitted the novel for the competition using the pseudonym Rodrigo Torres, so his name did not help him to win the prize.
6. Sergio Pitol, 'Historia de unos premios', in *Sergio Pitol. Los territorios del viajero* by José Balza et al. (Mexico: Ediciones Era, 2000), pp. 9–22 (p. 18).
7. Pablo Boullosa Velázquez, 'Los velos del crimen', *Novedades*, 16 March 1986, pp. 10, 16 (p. 10).
8. Domínguez Michael, 'Nueva tristeza'; Héctor S. Barrón Soto, 'El desfile del amor, de Sergio Pitol', *Sábado*, 22 February 1986, p. 8.
9. Elena Urrutia, '*El desfile del amor*', *La Jornada*, 1 July 1985, p. 23.
10. José Felipe Coria, 'El desfile del amor de Sergio Pitol', *Sábado*, 13 July 1985, p. 11.
11. Selatiel Alatriste, '*El desfile del amor*. Plaza Río de Janeiro (de la historia al refrán)', *Revista UNAM*, February–March 1985, pp. 48–50 (p. 49); Juan Domingo Argüelles, 'Sergio Pitol y Balmorán el empecinado', *El Universal*, 17 November 1989, p. 2; Ricardo Pohlenz, 'El desfile de Pitol', *El Excélsior*, 25 July 1985, p. 2.
12. Antonio Contreras, 'Historia de un crimen', *Punto*, 26 August 1985, p. 20.
13. In the 1940s, Mexican author and critic Alfonso Reyes defended the literary qualities of detective fiction and argued that it could not be categorized as 'low' culture (Simpson, 84). Amelia S. Simpson also argues that detective fiction cannot be termed a 'popular' genre in Latin America because it 'is neither produced nor consumed on the scale that defines popular literature'. Amelia S. Simpson, *Detective Fiction from Latin America* (London: Associated University Presses, 1990), p. 182.
14. Humberto Guzmán, 'Pitol y el sentimiento del carnaval', *El Búho*, 15 November 1992, p. 7.
15. The following compared Pitol and Tirso de Molina or noted the influence of Tirso de Molina in Pitol's work: Federico Campbell, 'Sergio Pitol y su novela *El desfile del* amor', *Proceso*, 24 February 1986, pp. 52–53 (p. 52); Boullosa Velázquez, p. 16; Domínguez Michael, 'Nueva tristeza', pp. 60–61; Margo Glantz, 'El desfile del Pitol. Sergio Pitol, el mismo que canta y baila', *La Jornada*, 13 April 1985, pp. 1–4 (p. 1); Antonio Saborit, 'La comedia de la ignorancia jamás imaginada', *Nexos*, July 1985, pp. 47–51 (p. 50); Serrato, pp. 12–13; 'El desfile del amor', *El Universal*, 17 June 1988, CNIPL/EXP.SP. Articles which compared Pitol and Dickens or noted the influence of Dickens in Pitol's work included: Blanco (21); González Rodríguez (2). Valentín Puig (2) and Omar González (11, 12) referred to both Tirso de Molina and Dickens. Glantz (1) and Monsiváis (26) referred to Lubitsch. Saborit (50) and Hector Orestes Aguilar (2) referred to Eric Ambler. Domínguez Michael ('Nueva tristeza', 61) and González Rodríguez (1–3) compared the novel to the work of Henry James, while Anhalt (10–11) compared it to *Orlando* by Virginia Woolf. Alatriste (49–50) and Mejía (3) compared Pitol's work to that of other Latin American authors: Sergio Fernández (*Los desfiguros de mi corazón*), Sergio Galindo (*Dos Angeles*), Felipe Garrido and Mario Vargas Llosa (*La historia de Mayta* and *Conversación en la Catedral*). Valentín Puig, 'Sergio Pitol. *El desfile del amor*', *El Universal*, 12 December 1986, p. 2; Omar González, '*El desfile del amor*

de Sergio Pitol II', *Sábado*, 16 November 1985, p. 12; Monsiváis, 'Sergio Pitol: Las mitologías'; Hector Orestes Aguilar, 'Cinco ventanas del edificio Minerva', *Novedades*, 6 August 1989, p. 2; Nedda G. de Anhalt, 'El desfile del amor de Sergio Pitol. Historia ahistórica', *Sábado*, 9 March 1985, pp. 10–11; Eduardo Mejía, 'La diestra ironía', *Novedades*, 31 March 1985, p. 3.

16. Juan José Reyes, 'De mujeres y espejismos', *Novedades*, 25 June 1989, CNIPL/EXP.SP.

17. Coria, p. 11; Blanco, p. 21; Urrutia ('*El desfile del amor*', 23); 'Sergio Pitol ganó el Segundo Premio Anagrama de Barcelona con su novela *El desfile del amor*', *El Excélsior*, 17 March 1984, CNIPL/EXP.SP; Francisco Zendejas, 'Narrativa tres en uno', *La Cultura al Día*, supl. *El Excélsior*, 26 February 1983, p. 2.

18. See, for example: Maricruz Castro Ricalde, *Ficción, narración y polifonía. El universo narrativo de Sergio Pitol* (Mexico: Universidad Autónoma del Estado de México, 2000); Luz Fernández de Alba, *Del tañido al arte de la fuga. Una lectura crítica de la fuga* (Mexico: UNAM, 1998); Jesús Salas-Elorza, *La narrativa dialógica de Sergio Pitol* (Providence, RI: Ediciones Inti, 1999). Exceptionally, Juan Villoro considers the Mexican context when he connects the multiplication of versions of the past in the novel to the contemporary situation in Mexico. He writes that the novel is a 'metáfora de México, retrata una sociedad donde la verdad es impronunciable, y toda explicación pública, es un simulacro' [a metaphor of Mexico, it portrays a society where the truth is unspeakable and any public explanation a show] and claims that 'la carga política del libro es evidente: indagar una época de México equivale a abrir expedientes incompatibles' [the political accusation of the book is clear: investigating a period in Mexico's past is equivalent to opening contradictory dossiers] (95, 96). Juan Villoro, 'Los anteojos perdidos', in *Sergio Pitol. Los territorios del viajero*, by José Balza et al. (Mexico: Ediciones Era, 2000), pp. 93–101.

19. For a plot summary of *El desfile del amor* see Appendix.

20. Roberto G. Newell and Luis F. Rubio, *Mexico's Dilemma: The Political Origins of Economic Crisis* (Boulder, CO: Westview Press, 1984), p. 200; P. Smith, p. 368.

21. Héctor Aguilar Camín and Lorenzo Meyer, *In the Shadow of the Mexican Revolution: Contemporary Mexican History, 1910–1989*, trans. by Luis Alberto Fierro (Austin: University of Texas Press, 1993), pp. 216–17; P. Smith, p. 383.

22. Ilan Stavans, *Antiheroes: Mexico and Its Detective Novel*, trans. by Jesse H. Lytle and Jennifer A. Mattson (London: Associated University Presses, 1997), p. 55.

23. Persephone Braham, *Crimes Against the State, Crimes Against Persons: Detective Fiction in Cuba and Mexico* (Minneapolis: University of Minnesota Press, 2004), p. 4; Simpson, p. 139.

24. Several critics have suggested that *El desfile del amor* incorporates an allegory in which the characters are representative of the different social groups in Mexican society in the 1940s. Gerardo Hurtado proposes that the Minerva building 'toma la forma de un microcosmos en cuyo interior se concibe una alegoría del ambiente cosmopolita del México de los cuarenta, así como una irónica versión de la consigna política de aquellos años: la "Unidad Nacional"' [is a microcosm in which an allegory of the cosmopolitan atmosphere of Mexico in the 1940s, like an ironic version of the political slogan of the time 'National Unity' is devised] (95–96). Fernández de Alba claims: 'la fiesta misma [...] es una parodia de la "unidad nacional" en la que estaba empeñado el gobierno ávila-camachista' [the party itself is a parody of 'national unity' on which the Avila-Camacho government was insisiting] (78). María Coira says that the characters interviewed are 'representativos de diferentes sectores sociales (la hija de un revolucionario, los miembros de una familia conservadora, el hombre de negocios, la refugiada europea, etc.)' (175) [representative of different sections of society (the daughter of a revolutionary, the members of a conservative family, the businessman, the European refugee, etc.)]. A similar point is made by Jesús Martínez Gómez (154). Gerardo Hurtado, '*El desfile del amor*, de Sergio Pitol: una tragicomedia policial en tres actos', in *Bang! Bang!: pesquisas sobre narrativa policiaca mexicana*, ed. by Miguel G. Rodríguez Lozano and Enrique Flores (Mexico: UNAM, 2005), pp. 91–113; María Coira, 'Narra una investigación histórica: *El desfile del amor* de Sergio Pitol', *Revista del centro de letras hispanoamericanas*, 5 (1996), 171–81; Jesús Martínez Gómez, 'Parodia, deformación y conocimiento en la narrativa de Sergio Pitol. Tríptico del Carnaval', in *Sergio Pitol. El sueño de lo real*, ed. by Pedro M. Domene (Xalapa: Universidad Veracruzana, 2002), pp. 152–62.

25. All references in this chapter are to Sergio Pitol, *El desfile del amor* [first pub. 1984] (Mexico: Era, 1989) unless otherwise stated.

CHAPTER 6

From Romance to Adultery: Reinterpreting *Arráncame la vida*

Read by millions of people all over the world, *Arráncame la vida* is one of the best-selling Mexican novels and, since it was published, its author Ángeles Mastretta has enjoyed national and international fame. Mastretta is one of a number of women authors who have emerged and had considerable commercial, if not always critical, success since the 1980s as part of what has come to be known as the Mexican *boom femenino*. The success of these authors has been attributed to the fact that there are now more female than male readers in Mexico (Castillo, *Easy Women*, 33). Nonetheless, the mostly male group of custodians of literary knowledge retained interpretive power and the authority to consecrate texts, and so most of these women remain marginalized from the twentieth-century Mexican literary canon.

Arráncame la vida was Mastretta's first novel and it was interpreted and, to a large extent, marketed as 'popular fiction' for entertainment and not as 'literature'. According to the cover of the first edition, *Arráncame la vida* belonged to the popular genre of the *novela de amor* (love story). There are, however, significant differences between the plot of Mastretta's novel and that of the traditional romance novel. While some women authors may be said to experiment with the conventions of the traditional romantic plot, *Arráncame la vida* goes beyond what could be termed experimentation. The novel focuses on what happens after marriage as the protagonist, Catalina, falls in and out of love with her husband, Andrés, and has several adulterous affairs. What is more, Andrés dies in the last chapter, seriously undermining the usual 'happily ever after' ending of a romance novel. Assumptions about women authors and their presumed female readership may have led to the genre of *Arráncame la vida* being misidentified and consequently to the novel being undervalued in the context of the national literary canon. This chapter brings into question the association of *Arráncame la vida* with the popular romance genre by producing a private-national reading which enables me to interpret it as a novel of female adultery. By categorizing *Arráncame la vida* in this way, I aim to alter existing understandings of the novel as a love story and challenge its exclusion from the twentieth-century Mexican novelistic canon.

Five thousand copies of *Arráncame la vida* were published in February 1985 by Editorial Océano and they quickly sold out (Carballo, *Bibliografía de la novela mexicana*, 188). The novel topped the bestseller list, went into a second edition by June 1985, and a tenth edition was printed within two years, by which time fifty thousand copies had been sold.[1] *Arráncame la vida* was soon translated into many languages and became an international bestseller. While international success helped Pitol to consolidate his reputation as a serious author, in Mastretta's case it only served to affirm the perception that she wrote 'popular' and populist fiction that was unworthy of serious attention.

Bourdieu has observed that 'the field of large-scale production [...] is symbolically excluded and discredited' and so those writing literary history do not include 'writers and artists who produced for the market' (39). Although, as Bourdieu acknowledges, the distinction between 'the field of large-scale production' and the 'field of restricted production' to which the canon is connected, is not always clear cut, for Mastretta, being labelled as the author of 'popular fiction' led to her being largely omitted from histories of literature and hence from the canon. Mastretta is infrequently included in histories of Mexican literature and when she is mentioned she receives scant attention.[2] Adolfo Castañón in his *Arbitrario de literatura mexicana* includes only a passing reference to Mastretta and dismisses her work, as well as that of Laura Esquivel, Elena Poniatowska and Carmen Boullosa, as market-oriented entertainment (212). The *Diccionario de escritores mexicanos siglo XX* similarly focuses on the commercial success of Mastretta's first novel, presenting this fact as the novel's most notable achievement (Ortiz, 171). Furthermore, the entry emphasizes the novel's 'feminine perspective': 'Esta obra gira en torno a la percepción femenina del poder en una historia desarrollada en los años treinta y cuarenta, en las ciudades de Puebla y México' [This work revolves around the female perception of power in a story set in the 1930s and 1940s in the towns of Puebla and Mexico City] (Ortiz, 171). The entry does not identify the novel as having national significance and so it is marginalized in the context of canonical Mexican literature.

Mastretta is more often included in histories of literature or in critical studies which focus exclusively on women authors. These publications have emerged alongside, but largely independently of, other, male-dominated accounts of Mexican literature in which the canon is represented. The desirability of separate histories of literature and labels such as 'women's writing' which marginalize, if not exclude, novels by women from the category of 'literature' is questionable. By examining the ways in which we read texts by both men and women authors and adopting a wider range of interpretive strategies, new and better ways to acknowledge women's contributions to literature will emerge which enable us to judge novels by women not solely on the basis of the feminist values expressed in them and novels by men not solely on the basis of their contribution to post-revolutionary nationalism.

As an example of 'women's writing', *Arráncame la vida* is also included on syllabi in US and UK academic institutions and has been the subject of more academic critical attention than any other woman-authored text in this book. Critical attention, much of which comes from outside Mexico, however, seems to have limited impact on canonicity and interpretation, which is established at the review stage, making it difficult for novels that were once rejected to be subsequently incorporated into the canon. As noted earlier, feminist criticism has sometimes been able to argue successfully for the inclusion of authors such as Rosario Castellanos and Elena Garro, but negotiating women's inclusion on a case by case basis is an inefficient and ineffective way to challenge the values which underpin the post-revolutionary canon.

When *Arráncame la vida* was published Mastretta was already a well-known figure within Mexican literary circles; she contributed to newspapers and magazines including *El Excélsior* and *Unomásuno* and had a regular column in the cultural review, *Ovaciones*. Between 1982 and 1985, she was a member 'of the editorial council of the feminist magazine, *FEM*, to which she has also contributed several articles'.[3] Several reviews of *Arráncame la vida* commented that Mastretta was a journalist and Lorenzo León noted that she had connections within the literary community.[4] He told the readers of *El Nacional* that Mastretta and her husband and fellow autor, Héctor Aguilar Camín, were 'enmarcados ellos mismos en un círculo intelectual y académico ligado a importantes instituciones culturales y políticas (*La Jornada*, Cal y Arena (antes Océano), El Colegio de México, etc.) que evidencia una proximidad visual con el poder' [themselves part of an intellectual and academic circle tied to important cultural and political institutions (the newspaper *La Jornada*, the publisher Cal y Arena (previously Océano) and El Colegio de México, etc.) which have clear ties to power] (León, CNIPL/EXP.AM). In addition, Domínguez Michael suggested that Mastretta belonged to an emerging group of authors, including Aguilar Camín, José Joaquín Blanco and José María Pérez Gay, who all published with the increasingly successful and well-respected Océano.[5]

As a woman, however, Mastretta was not an acceptable heir to the canonical literary tradition and her connections were used to cast aspersions on the quality of her work. Laura Guillén claimed that, without her connections, 'la asunción de Mastretta en el ámbito novelístico [...] bien podría pasar inadvertida' [Mastretta's arrival into the world of novel writing [...] could easily go unnoticed].[6] Reviews of *La región más transparente* commented on Fuentes' connections, but they did not do so in a way that suggested that they were the only reason for his novel's success. The findings of this study of six twentieth-century Mexican novels, however, suggests that whereas a male author's connections within the literary community were likely to influence the reception of his work in a positive way, such connections had a negative or no effect in the cases of women authors. Reviewers were more easily able to dismiss *Yo también, Adelita* and *La ciudad y el viento*, but the success of *Arráncame la vida* warranted a more forceful approach and so they attributed her success to her connections and used the novel's bestseller status to discredit it as 'popular fiction'.

Not only did Mastretta not benefit from her connections to Mexico's cultural elite but, as the winner of the 1985 *Premio Mazatlán de Literatura*, she also did not gain as much as Pitol did from winning the *Premio Herralde*. Although she benefited, perhaps to an even greater extent than Pitol, from a commercial perspective, she did not accrue the same amount of cultural capital as a result of the award. Past winners of the *Premio Mazatlán* included Elena Poniatowska (1971), Carlos Fuentes (1972), Luis Spota (1984) and Octavio Paz (1985).[7] Poniatowska was also on the jury that awarded the prize to *Arráncame la vida*.[8] So valued (and valuable to *Arráncame la vida*'s success) were Poniatowska's positive comments that they were quoted in several articles.[9] As women like Poniatowska become established as custodians of literary knowledge, they are in a better position, if they so choose, to help other women to gain access to the closed circle of the Mexican literary community and thence to the literary canon. Poniatowska's presence on the jury and her resounding endorsement of *Arráncame la vida* clearly helped the novel to gain recognition, but neither her support nor the *Premio Mazatlán* were enough to ensure *Arráncame la vida* a place in the canon.

When it was first published, *Arráncame la vida* was reviewed more times than any of the other woman-authored novels in this study, and even more reviews appeared after it was awarded the *Premio Mazatlán*. In the cases of *El indio* and *El desfile del amor*, winning prestigious literary prizes helped to consolidate positive critical responses to these texts but, as Carlos Velázquez Mayoral noted in *El Día*: 'Desde que ganó el 'Premio Mazatlán' [...] la novela ha sido víctima de las opiniones más encontradas. Así, no es raro escuchar que este trabajo es una obscena porquería; o bien, que se trata de una de las obras más importantes de la década' [Since it won the Premio Mazatlan [...] the novel has been the victim of the most conflicting opinions. Thus, it is not unusual to hear that this work is obscene trash; or that it is one of the most important books of the decade].[10] Velázquez Mayoral's comments highlight that there was limited critical consensus when it came to interpreting and evaluating *Arráncame la vida*. Bourdieu has suggested that 'polemics imply a form of recognition; adversaries whom one would prefer to destroy by ignoring them cannot be combated without consecrating them' (42). Following Bourdieu, we may assume that the debates that surrounded *Arráncame la vida* contributed to the novel being recognized as a legitimate object of critical attention. However, we have seen limited evidence that *Arráncame la vida* was effectively consecrated. On the contrary, and as the following discussion of contemporary reviews shows, the novel was so resistant to the dominant interpretive strategies employed by the custodians of literary knowledge that they were unable to produce a common reading of the novel. In spite of their diverging opinions, no reviewer suggested that the novel possessed the requisite scope or national significance needed for it to become canonical literature.

Reviewers variously suggested that *Arráncame la vida* was an historical novel, a political novel, a biography of Catalina's life, a love story, or combinations of the above, but while Pitol was credited with innovatively adapting the detective genre to reflect national circumstances, Mastretta's novel was consistently placed at the margins of canonical genres such as the historical or political novel. In classifying *Arráncame la vida* as an historical novel, reviewers may have been influenced by the fact that they were able to identify the characters with real people as in a *roman-à-clef* (although few used this term).[11] In the 1950s, reviewers of Luis Spota's classic *roman-à-clef Casi el paraíso* (1956) and Fuentes' *La región más transparente* liked being able to identify real people in some or all of the novel's characters (Reeve, 'The Making of *La región*', 46). However, six of the ten reviewers who commented on this device disliked it in *Arráncame la vida*, because they thought that it was too simplistic.[12] Enrique Mercado, for example, wrote: 'como novela histórica o política, *Arráncame la vida* no pasa de representar un juego de equivalencias [...] por lo demás muy fácil de deducir' [as an historical or political novel, *Arráncame la vida* does not go beyond a game of equivalences and a very easy one to deduce at that] (CNIPL/EXP.AM). Although *Arráncame la vida* was associated by some reviewers with the canonical genre of the historical novel, their assessment of the novel on these terms was not favourable.

Furthermore, those reviewers who saw *Arráncame la vida* as an historical novel noted that it was about women's history. Domínguez Michael wrote that *Arráncame la vida* was about 'las historias olvidadas en armarios abandonados por la prisa de la Nación por configurarse en Historia' [stories forgotten in abandoned wardrobes because of the Nation's haste to take its place in History] ('El cuarteto', CNIPL/EXP/AM). In a review in the women's magazine, *Claudia*, Rubén Hernández placed *Arráncame la vida* in the context of novels about 'el movimiento en la Historia de la mujer' [women's position in History] and said that *Arráncame la vida* provided a woman's perspective on history (20, 21). Hernández promoted this subject matter as a positive feature of the novel likely to appeal to his female readership. However, only those novels that are interpreted as being of contemporary national significance are incorporated into the post-revolutionary canon and, as in the case of *Yo también, Adelita*, reviewers who identified *Arráncame la vida* as being about women's history viewed Mastretta's novel as being of only peripheral interest and importance.

Critics who said that *Arráncame la vida* was a political novel also marginalized it by placing it in a sub-category of novels about women in political life. The author Federico Campbell, participating in a round-table discussion, said that *Arráncame la vida* 'tiene el mérito de haber introducido en el campo de la novela mexicana a un personaje escamoteado antes por otros novelistas e incluso por los historiadores: el personaje del consorte del poder' [has the merit of having introduced into the Mexican novel a character previously ignored by other novelists and even by historians: the character of the consort to the powerful].[13] Perhaps reflecting the lack of importance they attached to women's roles in history or political life, several reviewers suggested that the novel was simply about Catalina's life, a life which, for them, had little or no historical or political significance.[14] Although the reviewers who proposed that *Arráncame la vida* was about women's history or women in political life agreed that the novel's new approach was a positive contribution to Mexican literature and history, they nonetheless set Mastretta's novel apart from its mainstream canonical counterparts. Their comments reveal the existence of a hierarchy in which historical and political novels about women are regarded as addressing issues which are of secondary concern and interest.[15]

Somewhat surprisingly, given the description on the dust jacket of the first edition, only seven of twenty-seven reviewers read *Arráncame la vida* as wholly or partially a *novela rosa* or a *novela de amor*.[16] Juan José Reyes and Gilberto Meza rejected such a classification outright. Similar disagreement occurred over the question of whether *Arráncame la vida* was a feminist text. The reviews which addressed this issue can be divided into three categories: those which thought that *Arráncame la vida* was a feminist novel and that this feature was an attribute; those who thought it was not a feminist novel but it should have been; and those who were pleased that it was not a feminist novel. Minerva Margarita Villarreal was particularly strong in her praise of *Arráncame la vida* as a feminist novel. She wrote: 'la visión que impregna esta novela sobre las posibilidades de la mujer es vastísima' [the vision which pervades this novel about women's possibilities is vast] and insisted on the importance of the character of Catalina who, she says was 'el antecedente femenino que todos hubiéramos querido' [the female predecessor we all would have liked] (20). Guillén similarly identified Catalina as a precursor to the feminist movement, but believed that such a representation undermined the novel's credibility (3). María Elvira Bermúdez, Mayling Mendizábal and Enrique Mercado wanted and expected *Arráncame la vida* to be a feminist novel, but were disappointed with what they found.[17] Bermúdez criticized the novel in her review in *El Nacional* because it did not live up to the description on the book's cover which advertised ' "liberación sin arrepentimiento" y la "Venganza" ' ['liberation without remorse' and 'Revenge']. Finally, Gilberto Meza and Alvaro Leyva were pleased that, in their opinion, *Arráncame la vida* was not a feminist novel.[18] The majority of the reviews fell into the first category of welcoming *Arráncame la vida* as a feminist text, but there was much dissent suggesting reviewers had considerable difficulty in reading this woman-authored text because it was resistant to dominant interpretive strategies.

While reviewers disagreed over the genre and subject of *Arráncame la vida*, most appreciated the novel's style. Revealingly, however, reviewers who praised the novel's style did so in ways which associated it with popular rather than canonical literature and with enjoyment rather than the demanding yet satisfying task of reading canonical literature such as *El desfile del amor*. So accessible was *Arráncame la vida* that, according to Carlos Castillo Peraza, 'puede leerse de un tirón' [you can read it in one go].[19] Antonio Haas cautioned against assuming that just because the novel was easy to read it should not be taken seriously, but his warning fell on deaf ears as reviewers associated the novel's subject matter and readable style with entertainment and 'popular fiction' rather than 'literature' ('Ángeles de Puebla').

Novels by and about women are more likely to be excluded from the canon because of prevailing assumptions that women do not write about or have important roles in national life. This problem is exacerbated by dominant interpretive strategies which overlook the ways in which authors who are marginalized from the public sphere can be seen to use the private sphere in order to comment on the public situation if alternative ways of reading are employed. Reviewers of *Arráncame la vida* recognized that the novel included elements from the public (history and politics) and the private (the love story and Catalina's coming-of-age narrative) spheres, but ultimately failed to produce a reading which appreciated the connection between these two elements. The following reading of *Arráncame la vida* as a novel of female adultery and national allegory shows how the public and private can be seen to be inextricably linked. Furthermore, interpreting *Arráncame la vida* in this way reveals how the novel can be seen to address the same contemporary issues of national concern about the PRI that were explored in *El desfile del amor*.

To date, academic criticism has overlooked the significance of Catalina's adultery as did reviewers. Critics have tended to trivialize Catalina's adultery by referring to her 'love affairs',[20] her 'affair',[21] her 'affair with the "true love" of her life',[22] and her 'relaciones extramaritales',[23] instead of using the word adultery. Salvador Oropesa even writes about 'her behaviour' rather than explicitly mentioning adultery.[24]

Indeed, Oropesa denies any relationship between adultery in nineteenth-century novels and *Arráncame la vida*, as does Jane Lavery who says that the novel breaks 'the normal narrative conventions' of the adultery genre (149). However, the following analysis, based on a private-national reading, opens up the possibility of a new interpretation of *Arráncame la vida* as a novel of female adultery and a national allegory which rejects the path taken by post-revolutionary governments.

I follow Bill Overton in using the term 'novel of female adultery' which, he suggests, is more accurate than 'adultery novel' as the novels almost always deal exclusively with female adultery.[25] Male adultery may be present in these novels, as it is in *Arráncame la vida*, but it is not regarded as important or worthy of censure because of the existence of a double standard (Overton, vi). The novel of female adultery emerged in nineteenth-century Europe, most were male-authored and centred on the experiences of a middle- or upper-class married woman (Overton, vi). However, the tradition soon expanded beyond its original context and although, as far as I am aware, there is no Mexican tradition of novels of female adultery, there is evidence that the author of *Arráncame la vida* was aware of the genre because, in her second novel, *Mal de amores*, she refers to Ana Ozores, the adulteress protagonist in the most famous example of adultery fiction in the Spanish language, *La Regenta* by Leopoldo Alas (Clarín).[26] While Mastretta referred to the most famous adulteress in Spanish literature in her second novel, in her first she wrote her own novel of female adultery centred on the experiences of the upwardly mobile Catalina.[27]

For a novel to be considered a novel of female adultery it is not sufficient for it to contain an act of adultery by a woman. Rather, Overton suggests, it must use the theme of adultery as a vehicle through which to criticize society, or to make political comment (5, 224). Tony Tanner concurs, arguing that the central concept of adultery novels is their use of a woman's adultery to represent a threat to bourgeois society.[28] Readers of nineteenth-century female adultery, therefore, habitually interpreted the private with reference to the public situation, as did the readers of the nineteenth-century national romances in Latin America identified by Sommer. In post-revolutionary Mexico, however, this practice was no longer the norm, suggesting that dominant interpretive strategies can and do alter over time. The emergence of a new interpretive strategy which assumed a separation of the public and private spheres may be linked to changes in the nature of bourgeois marriage as it came to have less of a public role in joining families together for political reasons. Even though the dominant interpretive strategy had changed, I show how a private-national reading of Mastretta's late twentieth-century novel enables Catalina's adultery to be viewed as a critique of the PRI regime which is represented by her husband, Andrés.

Lou Charnon-Deutsch notes that the nineteenth-century novels of female adultery were written in response to a perceived crisis in society and in the institution of marriage which resulted in concerns about the 'stability and continuity of bourgeois society'.[29] Marriage underpinned contemporary bourgeois society and, according to Tanner, in a society in which marriage is so closely connected to the 'System', a wife's adultery is a threat to society itself and an 'assault' on the social structure (17). In the Mexico of the 1930s represented in *Arráncame la vida*, the established order is similarly presented as being underpinned by bourgeois marriage and the family unit. Just as in nineteenth-century Europe, marriage in *Arráncame la vida* is 'linked very closely to the transmission of property, the idea of the family, and to the role of motherhood' (Overton, 4). Thus, Andrés brings his illegitimate children to live with him and Catalina in order to maintain an illusion of family, he emphasizes the importance of family in his election speeches, and is preoccupied with writing his will on his deathbed to ensure the continuation of his legacy. Catalina's infidelity threatens the unity of this bourgeois family and Andrés' legacy signifying a threat to the national family and to the legacy of the PRI.

Only by the woman's death, as happened in most novels of female adultery, could the bourgeois, patriarchal order be secured because 'by punishing its offenders, society's institutions reaffirm themselves' (Charnon-Deutsch, 159). The woman's death also affirmed the 'double standard of conduct in sexual relations' (Charnon-Deutsch, 159). At the end of *Arráncame la vida*, however, it is the husband who dies and the young and still attractive Catalina is not punished but rather is rewarded with her freedom. In charge of her own destiny, she says she is 'casi feliz' (182) [almost happy].[30] In this unconventional ending, the established order, represented by Andrés, is not only threatened but overthrown and so, by extension, is the PRI regime for which he stands.

A private-national reading of *Arráncame la vida* reveals that, as well as being a novel of female adultery, Mastretta's novel can also be seen to utilize national allegory. In keeping with Jameson's definition of national allegory, Catalina's story and destiny represent the embattled situation of the collective, the private sphere is used to comment on the public situation and libidinal investment is particularly significant. Allegorically, Catalina stands in for the Mexican *pueblo* and her lovers and husband represent different potential leaders of the *pueblo*. Andrés represents the 'military men who came to power in Mexico following the revolution' and were in the ascendancy under President Calles (1924–28) (Knights, 69).[31] Andrés presents himself as a revolutionary hero to win over Catalina and her parents. By reading Andrés' actions as representative of those of the post-revolutionary elite the reader is led to understand that the latter constructed a glorious revolutionary past in order to win over the *pueblo*, represented by Catalina, which chose its leader because of his (supposed) achievements during the revolution. Even when Catalina uncovers Andrés' lies and misdeeds she still stands by her husband because she wants to be the governor's wife, suggesting that the *pueblo* was willing to ignore the dubious past of its leaders because it was seduced by their promises. On the one hand, therefore, the *pueblo* could be viewed as an accomplice to the military men in power in the immediate post-revolutionary period just as Catalina realizes that she is perceived as 'la cómplice oficial' (91) [the official accomplice]. On the other hand, Catalina is completely dependent on her husband even though he pays her little attention, in the same way, perhaps, that the *pueblo* relied on the post-revolutionary leaders who were similarly neglectful of their responsibilities.

Despite having ignored his wife for some time, when Andrés begins his campaign to become governor of Puebla he is once again attentive to Catalina and she reports: 'Andrés me cortejó como si lo necesitara' (76) [Andrés courted me as if he needed to]. This change in Andrés' attitude highlights the way in which post-revolutionary military leaders paid attention to the *pueblo* only when it was politically expedient for them to do so at election time. Following the election, Catalina and Andrés' relationship deteriorates as Catalina learns more and more about her husband's corruption. As a result, she refuses to have sex with him and begins to consider alternative partners, signifying the *pueblo*'s search for a new leader. Catalina first develops an interest in Fernando Arizmendi who, unbeknownst to her, is homosexual. This relationship is unsuccessful, but is illustrative of the power Andrés still has over Catalina, as he is able to control the path the relationship takes. Over time, Andrés' power wanes and Catalina is able to have adulterous affairs. Thus, *Arráncame la vida* plots the process whereby the military leaders which Andrés represents were removed from power to be replaced by the technocrats including Manuel Avila Camacho (1940–46), represented in the novel by Rodolfo, and Miguel Alemán Valdés (1946–52), represented by Martín Cienfuegos.[32] These men were responsible for the institutionalization of the PRI and the introduction of the model for economic development which catastrophically failed forty years later but, the novel suggests, they did not have the endorsement of the *pueblo*.

Andrés becomes part of the ruling party under Aguirre, who represents President Lázaro Cárdenas.[33] During his time in office Cárdenas aimed to bring the army under civilian control and to this end, he incorporated military men into the ruling PRM (Adler, 47). When Avila Camacho came to power, Cárdenas' programme had successfully reduced the army's influence and ability to intervene (Adler, 47). Andrés' influence is thus reduced under Rodolfo, and Cienfuegos is chosen ahead of Andrés as the official candidate to succeed Rodolfo reflecting the way in which the military were subsequently eliminated from the PRI by Mexico's first civilian president Miguel Alemán Valdés. Andrés' death at the end of the novel symbolizes that the process of removing the military elite from power is complete. Nonetheless, Rodolfo and Cienfuegos are both linked to Andrés as both are 'adopted' by his mother suggesting that, although the men who succeed in becoming president are not the same type of military leader as Andrés, they are 'related' to the old regime; they are part of the same family.

The new established order which replaces Andrés was not, however, chosen or approved by Catalina, the representative of the *pueblo*, who explicitly rejects Rodolfo's advances; firstly when he is going around the country as a presidential candidate and secondly on Independence Day when he is President. Catalina's rejection of Rodolfo is absolute to the extent that not even his power can seduce her: 'Fito no se me antojaba ni un poco. Ni aunque lo hubiera hecho presidente del mundo me hubiera gustado tocarlo' (152) [Not even if he had been made president of the world would I have liked to touch him]. With Rodolfo in power Catalina begins her most significant adulterous affair with Carlos Vives.

Allegorically, Catalina's choice of Vives over Andrés and Rodolfo suggests that the Mexican *pueblo* would have chosen a leader like Vives, but they were denied this option. Schaefer identifies Vives with 'civilian popular governments, insurgent workers' movements, independent trade unions and plural political parties' (99–100). The alternative Vives offers is also cosmopolitan. When Catalina meets Vives he has just returned from studying in London, he has visited New York, and his ambition is to conduct in Vienna. As a conductor of the *Orquesta Sinfónica Nacional* (National Symphony Orchestra), Vives is associated with high culture, but, as Knights has noted, he 'crosses the divide between high and popular culture' (74) and he plays music which Catalina describes as 'algo que se podía tararear como si la hubiera pedido mi papá' (222) [something you could hum as if my father had requested it]. Significantly, the music Vives plays reminds Catalina that she misses her father suggesting that she is still looking for a replacement father figure and that Vives is a potential candidate. Vives, however, is unable to permanently replace Andrés or the established order that he represents.

For a time, Andrés encourages Vives, the son of an old friend, to embark on a political career in the hope that he will be his successor. Whereas his 'adopted' brothers, Rodolfo and Martín, are rivals, Andrés hopes that Vives will be his adopted son (270). A fatherly relationship between the two men is suggested by Andrés' description of how he used to play with Vives when he was a child. When it becomes apparent that Vives' politics are different to Andrés', however, Andrés warns Vives to stay out of politics. Despite these warnings, Vives continues to support Andrés' political enemies and Andrés has him killed, possibly because of his politics but equally possibly because of his relationship with Catalina.

It is unclear whether Andrés knows about Catalina's adultery as Catalina is the narrator and she could never be sure if Andrés believed her when she told him that she was faithful. Consequently, neither the reader nor she knows whether Vives was killed because of their relationship or because of his politics. When Vives goes missing she blames his political activities; she asks herself: '¿Por qué se metía en política?... ¿Por qué la fiebre idiota de la política?' (283) [Why did he get involved in politics?... Why the idiotic fever of politics?]. The fact that Vives is taken to a clandestine prison for political enemies at the same time as the trade union leader Medina is killed also suggests political motives. On the other hand, while Vives is being kidnapped, Andrés talks to Catalina about her fidelity, which may indicate that he knows about her adultery. Ultimately, it is impossible to separate the personal and political motives for Vives' murder and even if we accept that Andrés had Vives killed because of his affair with Catalina, a private-national reading of *Arráncame la vida* still leads us to understand this murder as being politically motivated.

After Vives' death and Rodolfo's election to the presidency Andrés no longer exerts the same power or influence in the political life of Mexico and his loss of status is reflected in his relationship with Catalina who embarks on a further adulterous affair with the cinema director, Alonso Quijano. Andrés' waning influence is highlighted by the fact that, even when faced by a lesser rival than Vives had been, he is unable to control Catalina who says: 'No me apenó verlo perder fuerza. Salía con Alonso como si fuéramos novios' (350) [I wasn't sad to see him lose strength. I went out with Alonso as if we were boyfriend and girlfriend]. After Andrés dies Catalina is free and her closing words are: 'estaba sola, nadie me mandaba' (382) [I was alone, with no one to order me around]. At the wake she is warned not to remarry too quickly, suggesting that there is no suitable leader for the *pueblo* to endorse; this can be read as a clear indictment of the rule of the PRI which

Arráncame la vida suggests had ruled Mexico without the people's endorsement since 1940 and whose time, the novel anticipates, was coming to an end.

As has been seen with reference to *El desfile del amor*, in the mid-1980s the PRI was in crisis. My reading of *Arráncame la vida* as a novel of female adultery and national allegory has suggested that Catalina's adultery represents a threat to the established order and that the trajectory of her marriage to Andrés and her rejection of Rodolfo reflects the gradual collapse of the social pact between the *pueblo* and the ruling elite which culminated at the time of the country's political and economic crisis in the 1980s. The men with whom Catalina has adulterous affairs represent potential leaders of the nation. At the end of the novel, however, no suitable alternative candidate has survived and so the *pueblo* is left without a leader, only a ruler who does not have the *pueblo*'s endorsement but is still able to rule, while the *pueblo* can only offer passive resistance and is, therefore, only 'casi feliz' (182) [almost happy]. In this way, I have shown that Mastretta's novel could have been seen to capture the mood of the times and address contemporary issues of national concern. Had reviewers identified *Arráncame la vida* as a novel of female adultery they may have adopted, as they did for *El desfile del amor*, interpretive strategies which enabled them to read the private sphere in terms of the public situation. However, reviewers did not read *Arráncame la vida* in this way because dominant interpretive strategies did not understand the private as commenting on the public situation apart from in exceptional cases, and the fact that the novel of female adultery has traditionally been considered the preserve of male authors may have led reviewers to assume that Mastretta could or would not produce a novel of female adultery, potentially costing *Arráncame la vida* a place in the post-revolutionary literary canon.

According to Overton, 'there is no canonical novel of female adultery written by a woman' (viii). That is not to say, however, that adultery does not occur in woman-authored texts but woman-authored novels which deal with adultery have received less critical attention than their male-authored counterparts. These novels by women typically use adultery to challenge women's subordination and the double sexual standard, making these novels 'a striking illustration of how powerfully the social and literary establishment has worked to exclude writing which has challenged dominant perspectives and values' (Overton, 119). The marginalization of woman-authored novels which deal with adultery, including *Arráncame la vida*, provides further evidence that assumptions about genre and appropriate subject matter are connected to an author's gender and have an important role in determining whether or not a novel can become canonical.

Arráncame la vida features several instances of female adultery and, as Overton suggests was the case in nineteenth-century woman-authored novels which featured female adultery, it is used to critique women's unequal position in marriage and society and the sexual double standard. Mastretta's novel can thus be seen to draw on the non-canonical tradition of woman-authored novels featuring adultery, as well as on the more canonical, male-authored tradition of the novel of female adultery. *Arráncame la vida* calls into question women's unequal status by highlighting the double standard governing men and women's behaviour in marriage. Thus, Catalina cannot prevent Andrés from having affairs whereas he can hit her for being indiscreet by flirting with Arizmendi at a dinner party. When Catalina asks why he does not have to be discreet, Andrés justifies his actions with reference to the different rules governing men and women's behaviour: 'Yo no tengo por qué disimular, yo soy un señor, tú eres una mujer y las mujeres cuando andan de cabras locas queriéndose coger a todo el que les pone a temblar el ombligo se llaman putas' (129) [I don't have to be discreet, I am a man, you're a woman and when women go round wanting to fuck anyone who makes them tremble they call them whore]. As in the woman-authored, post-war British fiction analysed by Niamh Baker in which adultery is a 'challenge to the husband's ownership of the wife's body', Catalina's adultery is also associated with her challenging Andrés' control over her body: she masturbates thinking of Arizmendi after Andrés hits her for flirting and she withholds her body from him before choosing to give it to Vives.[34] Catalina does not accept her unequal status or leave her husband's authority unquestioned, but her success in resisting is limited.

All of Catalina's friends also commit adultery, which is presented in each case as representing a challenge to their husband's authority. Pepa's husband keeps her confined to the house but she still manages to commit adultery with the doctor while maintaining the appearance of obedience and subservience to her husband, thus subverting his authority. Mónica's husband is ill and she works to support the family, yet it is still expected that she will be subject to her husband's wishes, so when she stays out late one night to be with her lover her husband is said to be so angry that he was about to 'perder la parálisis para levantarse a golpearla' (145) [recover from his paralysis so that he could get up and hit her]. Her absence represents a challenge to his authority so great that he is almost able to walk again in his effort to punish his wife's transgression. Catalina's other friend, Bibi, has an affair with a young bullfighter who is only interested in her because of her husband's position as the owner of a chain of newspapers. Bibi's experience serves to highlight that, while Catalina and her friends may challenge their husband's authority to an extent, ultimately their husbands are more powerful than they are. There is, however, a glimmer of hope that women's situation may be improving; although Catalina's step-daughter, Lilia, has an unfaithful and unloved husband there is a suggestion that she will be able to challenge her husband's authority more effectively than Catalina and her friends because she possesses more confidence and some financial independence. Lilia is not an equal partner in her marriage, but she is in a better position than the older women in the novel, suggesting the gradual progress made by women from one generation to the next and particularly between Catalina and Lilia's generation, as a result of the growing women's movement in Mexico.

In conclusion, *Arráncame la vida* combined both the male- and female-authored traditions of the novel of female adultery. As part of the (once) canonical tradition of the novel of female adultery, *Arráncame la vida* can be interpreted as fulfilling all of the conditions of a canonical text: it addressed contemporary issues of national concern and captured the spirit of the time in criticizing, and reflecting on the failure of, the PRI regime. In addition, however, *Arráncame la vida* can also be seen to use the marginalized, non-canonical genre of woman-authored novels which feature adultery to reflect on the progress and origins of the women's movement, and to suggest that women still suffered unequal treatment in marriage because of society's attitudes and the persistence of a sexual double standard. The combination of the canonical novel of female adultery with the non-canonical use of adultery to denounce the unequal position of women in marriage may have damaged *Arráncame la vida*'s chances of being incorporated into the canon. The fact remains, however, that in the mid 1980s, after the feminist movement had made the personal political and vice versa, reviewers were still unable to see the public situation reflected through the private sphere in a woman-authored text. This failure is all the more striking because in the case of *El desfile del amor* they had been able to do so. The only explanation is that there is a connection between perceived genre and the interpretive strategy used, and assumptions about genre are linked to the gender of the author.

In the case of *Arráncame la vida* a private-national reading produces a new interpretation which enables us to see the novel as commenting on contemporary issues of national concern. The fact that this reading was so different to that produced by contemporary reviewers should alert us to the importance of reading actively in a way that is attentive to the possibility of using multiple and different interpretive strategies. By adopting new interpretive strategies, groundbreaking new readings of woman-authored novels can emerge; these novels can be re-evaluated and potentially incorporated into a new twentieth-century Mexican literary canon in which the value of the text is neither determined by an author's gender nor, ideally, based on the values expressed in the work.

Notes to Chapter 6

1. Perla Schwartz, 'Una hojeada a la novela de Mastretta', CNIPL/EXP.AM; Braulio Peralta, 'Deseo narrar sucesos para sacármelos del alma. Mi novela es una historia, no un ensayo feminista: Ángeles Mastretta', *La Jornada*, 11 June 1985, p. 25; Javier Aranda Luna, 'Editan *Arráncame* en 4 países europeos. El periodismo esclaviza aún más que la literatura: Ángeles Mastretta', *La Jornada*, 1 April 1987, p. 33.

2. Mastretta appears in the following histories of literature published in Mexico: Carballo, *Bibliografía de la novela mexicana*, p. 188; Cluff and Valdez, p. 268; Adolfo Castañón, *Arbitrario de literatura mexicana paseos I*, 2nd edn (Mexico: Vuelta, 1995), p. 212; Martínez and Domínguez Michael; Patricia Ortiz Flores, 'Ángeles Mastretta', in *Diccionario de escritores mexicanos siglo XX. Desde las generaciones del ateneo y novelistas de la revolución hasta nuestros días*, Tomo V, ed. by Aurora M. Ocampo (Mexico: UNAM, 2000), pp. 171–75; Valdez, p. 135.

3. Jane Lavery, *Ángeles Mastretta: Textual Multiplicity* (Suffolk: Tamesis, 2005), p. 1.

4. Lorenzo León, 'La pareja Aguilar-Mastretta: su dualidad artística', CNIPL/EXP.AM.

5. Christopher Domínguez Michael, 'El cuarteto del nuevo realismo', *La Jornada*, 10 March 1986, pp. 3–4, CNIPL/EXP.AM.

6. Laura Guillén, 'Ficción Irrupción Desangelada', *El Semanario Cultural*, supl. *Novedades*, 12 May 1985, p. 3.

7. 'Premio Mazatlán de Literatura' <http://www.carnavalmazatlan.net/premiomztlit.php> [accessed 8 February 2010].

8. Patricia Vega, 'Ángeles Mastretta, Premio Mazatlán de Literatura 1985, por su novela', *La Jornada*, 6 January 1986, p. 25. The other members of the jury were Antonio Haas, one of the founders of the prize, Margarita Michelena and Héctor Azar. Haas and Michelena subsequently wrote four reviews and articles about the prize-winning novel: Antonio Haas, 'El Premio a *Arráncame la vida*. Ángeles de Puebla', *La Cultura al Día*, supl. *El Excélsior*, 29 January 1986, pp. 1, 2, 3; Antonio Haas, 'Ángeles Mastretta Premio Mazatlán 1986', *El Excélsior*, 15 February 1986, pp. 7A,

8A; Margarita Michelena, '¿Qué pasa allí? El Premio Villarrutia', *El Excélsior*, 10 February 1986, p. 7A; Margarita Michelena, '¡Estas sí! Palabras de mujer', *Siempre*, 19 February 1986, pp. 20–21.

9. See especially Patricia Vega's article in *La Jornada*, 'Ángeles Mastretta, Premio Mazatlán de Literatura 1985, por su novela', which is almost entirely made up of quotations from Poniatowska.

10. Carlos Velázquez Mayoral, 'Ángeles Mastretta, *Arráncame la vida*, México, Océano, 1986 2ª ed.', *El Día*, 26 May 1986, p. 10.

11. The following identified the characters in the novel with historical figures: Dolores Campos, 'She's (Not) The Boss', *Mexico en la Cultura*, supl. *Novedades*, 24 July 1985, p. 47; Rafael Luviano Delgado, 'Ángeles Mastretta, escribir es angustiante, pero no hacerlo más', 6 February 1986, CNIPL/EXP.AM; Haas, 'Ángeles de Puebla'; Rubén Hernández, '*Arráncame la vida*', *Claudia*, July 1987, pp. 20–21; Guillermo J. Fadanelli, and Naief Yehya, 'La literatura a la que estamos condenados'. *Sábado*, 7 October 1989, p. 6 and 14 October 1989, pp. 5–7; Víctor Magdaleno, 'Entre la literatura y el chisme', *El Día*, 1 April 1985, p. 10; Enrique Mercado, 'Arráncame el sosiego', 1 June 1985, CNIPL/EXP.AM; Gilberto Meza, 'El poder y el celofán', *La Jornada*, 22 June 1985, pp. 1, 4; Michelena, '¡Estas sí!'.

12. Fadanelli, Haas ('Ángeles de Puebla...'), V. Magdaleno, Mercado, Meza, Michelena ('¡Estas sí!...') all disliked the fictionalized representation of real people in the novel.

13. Quoted in Javier Molina, 'En *Arráncame la vida*, la consorte del poder: Campbell (mesa redonda sobre la novela política)', *La Jornada*, 28 August 1988, p. 23.

14. The following suggested that the novel was about Catalina's life: Anamari Gomís, 'Ella encarnaba boleros', *Nexos*, July 1985, pp. 51–52; V. Magdaleno, p. 10; Mayling Mendizábal, 'El complejo laberinto femenino *Arráncame la vida*', 3 April 1986, CNIPL EXP/AM; Juan José Reyes, 'Riesgos ante la historia', *Semanario Cultural*, supl. *Novedades*, 2 June 1985, p. 3; Velázquez Mayoral, p. 10.

15. The perception that narratives about women's lives are unsuitable in canonical literature is not peculiar to Mexico. Elaine Showalter, for example, has made similar observations with reference to nineteenth and twentieth-century English literature: 'Feminine, feminist, or female, the woman's novel has always had to struggle against the cultural and historical forces that relegated women's experience to the second rank' (p. 36). Elaine Showalter, *A Literature of Their Own from Charlotte Bronte to Doris Lessing* (London: Virago, 1999). See also: Sandra M. Gilbert and Susan Gubar, *The Madwoman in the Attic: The Woman Writer and the Nineteenth-Century Literary Imagination* (New Haven, CT: Yale University Press, 1979), pp. 67–68.

16. The following identified the novel with the romance tradition: Campos (A7), Juan Coronado, 'Arráncame la vida de Ángeles Mastretta', *Sábado*, supl. *Unomásuno*, 4 May 1985, p. 12; Héctor Gaitán Rojo, '*Arráncame la vida*' 20 April 1985, CNIPL EXP/AM; Guillén (3); Michelena, 'Que pasa' (7A); Peralta (125); Minerva Margarita Villarreal, '*Arráncame la vida* novela rosa mexicana', *Punto*, 19 May 1986, pp. 19–20.

17. María Elvira Bermúdez, 'Plegadera', *El Nacional*, 26 May 1985, p. 10.

18. Alvaro Leyva, 'El desfile del vacío', *Casa del Tiempo*, August–September 1985, pp. 60–62.

19. Carlos Castillo Peraza, 'No fornicaras (en hamaca)', *La Jornada*, 4 June 1985, CNIPL/EXP.AM.

20. Niamh Thornton, *Women and the War Story in Mexico. La Novela de la Revolución* (Lampeter: Edwin Mellen Press, 2006), p. 186.

21. Vanessa Knights, '(De)constructing Gender: The Bolero in Ángeles Mastretta's *Arráncame la vida*', *Journal of Romance Studies*, 1 (2001), 69–84 (p. 74); Schaefer, p. 97.

22. Danny J. Anderson, 'Displacement: Strategies of Transformation in *Arráncame la vida*', in *The Other Mirror: Women's Narrative in Mexico, 1980–1995*, ed. by Kristine Ibsen (Westport, CT: Greenwood Press, 1997), pp. 13–27, p. 15.

23. Edelmira Ramírez Leyva, 'Mastretta y las mujeres de su ficción', in *Mujeres latinoamericanas del siglo XX. Historia y cultura. Tomo I*, ed. by Luisa Campuzano (Mexico: Universidad Autónoma and Casa de las Americas, 1998), pp. 247–54 (p. 248).

24. Salvador A. Oropesa, 'Popular Culture and Gender/Genre Construction in Mexican Bolero by Ángeles Mastretta', in *Bodies and Biases: Sexualities in Hispanic Cultures and Literature*, ed. by David William Foster and Roberto Reis (Minneapolis: University of Minnesota Press, 1996), pp. 137–64 (p. 147).

25. Bill Overton, *The Novel of Female Adultery: Love and Gender in Continental European Fiction, 1830–1900* (London: Macmillan, 1996), p. vii.
26. Ángeles Mastretta, *Mal de amores* [first pub. 1996], 8th edn (Madrid: Punto de Lectura, 2004), p. 28. Leopoldo Alas, *La Regenta* (first published 1884, 1885).
27. For a plot summary of the novel see Appendix.
28. Tony Tanner, *Adultery in the Novel: Contract and Transgression* (Baltimore, MD: Johns Hopkins University Press, 1979).
29. Lou Charnon-Deutsch, *Gender and Representation: Women in Spanish Realist Fiction* (Amsterdam: John Benjamins, 1990), p. 20.
30. All references in this chapter are to Ángeles Mastretta, *Arráncame la vida* [first publ. 1985] (Madrid: Suma de Letras, 2001) unless otherwise stated.
31. See also: Schaefer, p. 99. Lavery (53), Fornet, Anderson ('Displacement', 13), and Lemaitre León have specifically suggested that Andrés represents the governor of Puebla, Maximino Avila Camacho. Jorge Fornet, *Reescrituras de la memoria. Novela femenina y Revolución en México* (Havana: Editorial Letras Cubanas, 1994), p. 62; Monique J. Lemaitre León, 'La historia oficial frente al discurso de la 'ficción' femenina en *Arráncame la vida* de Ángeles Mastretta', *Texto Crítico*, 3 (1996), 99–114 (p. 103).
32. Lemaitre (103), Fornet (62) and Oropesa (150) also interpret Rodolfo as representing Avila Camacho. Fornet (62) and Knights (70) interpret Cienfuegos as representing Alemán. As noted in note 11 some reviewers also interpreted the characters in the novel as historical figures.
33. Lemaitre (109) and Fornet (121) also interpret Aguirre as representing Cárdenas as did some reviewers (cf. note 11).
34. Niamh Baker, *Happily Ever After: Women's Fiction in Postwar Britain 1945–1960* (New York: St Martin's Press, 1989), pp. 92–93.

CONCLUSION

Towards a Twenty-First-Century Literary Canon

In 1934 the Mexican State established the *Premio Nacional de Literatura* and thereby took a decisive step towards creating a new literary canon. It was hoped that the prize would foster a literature which, following the example of revolutionary public mural art, would contribute to building the post-revolutionary nation. The prize promoted literature that was 'modern' and possessed 'social purpose'. Gregorio López y Fuentes' novel *El indio* was the first to be deemed to meet the new standard for Mexican literature. In the decades that followed, the need for literature to be interpreted as having social value in order to become canonical persisted. While *El indio* combined nation-building with State-building by incorporating what amounted to a literary rendering of *cardenista* policy and official discourses, later texts, including *La región más transparente* and *El desfile del amor*, were able to take advantage of the prevailing mood of the times and produced nation-building literature which was not so enmeshed in State-building. These novels were able to address issues of national concern in a way that included a cautious questioning of the path taken by post-revolutionary regimes. At key moments of crisis when the legitimacy of the State came into question, *La región más transparente and El desfile del amor* could be said to have provided platforms from which to begin the process of re-imagining the nation.

Following the end of one-party PRI rule in Mexico in the year 2000, this may be an opportune moment to undertake further research into the shifting relationship between State- and nation-building literature, which I have suggested was diluted over the course of the twentieth-century. The nature and extent of State involvement in the development of literary cultures through, for example, national prizes for literature, literary festivals and State-sponsorship and subsidy of the publishing industry, likewise warrant further study. The Mexican case may also be usefully compared to other national contexts.

In order to be incorporated into the post-revolutionary Mexican national canon, novels had to be well received by reviewers in the national press. These custodians of literary knowledge formed an interpretive community of privileged readers who shared interpretive strategies, had the authority to consecrate texts and access to the institutional means to do so. Reviews of the canonical male-authored texts in this study consistently identified these novels as having national significance and reinforced their praise with reference to the texts' likeness to mural art which aimed to be all-encompassing and to educate viewers in the values of post-revolutionary society. Reviews of novels which were to become canonical made favourable comparisons with Mexican authors and literary traditions, illustrating the way in which they viewed the canon as an imagined tradition that was not unlike a family tree in the way in which new generations were added. The comparisons they made to renowned foreign authors also highlight the way in which, throughout the twentieth-century, the custodians of literary knowledge continued to be preoccupied, as they had been in the 1920s, with producing a national literature which would help to confirm Mexico's position as an independent, civilized nation on the world stage. Reviewers were, however, less than consistent in their aesthetic judgements, demonstrating that there is no identifiable canonical aesthetic underpinning the twentieth-century Mexican novelistic canon and that content is of primary importance in determining inclusion in the canon. An examination of more reviews of other canonical and non-canonical novels may enable us to further refine our understanding of the dominant interpretive strategy in post-revolutionary Mexico. One approach, which was adopted in this study, involves looking at all of the reviews of a particular text. Alternatively, we may look at all of the reviews written by a particular reviewer, such as those written by Francisco Zendejas for his column 'Multilibros' in *El Excélsior* or Jacobo Dalevuelta for his 'Libros nuevos' column for *El Universal*. In this way, we would not only learn more about dominant interpretive strategies and their evolution but also about the custodians of literary knowledge.

Following Bourdieu's recommendation that cultural products should be under-stood with reference to the literary field in which they were produced and circulated, and in addition to recognizing the role reviewers played in establishing a novel's meaning and assessing its value, this book has highlighted the other mechanisms and complex institutional processes which worked to form the post-revolutionary Mexican novelistic canon. *El indio*, *La región más transparente* and *El desfile del amor* exemplify the circumstances in which certain novels became canonical. An examination of the contexts in which *Yo también*, *Adelita*, *La ciudad y el viento* and *Arráncame la vida* were produced has revealed factors that contributed to the exclusion of these novels from the Mexican canon. The author's status in the literary community, the publisher, publicity, the awarding of literary prizes and the way in which a novel was received abroad all had an impact on the process of consecration. One of the most significant findings of this study, however, is that the gender of the author is the overriding factor which impacted on canonicity. At the most fundamental level, reviewers made interpretive assumptions about novels simply because they were written by a man or a woman.

Faced with a woman's name on the cover, reviewers interpreted the novel's content as private and domestic and not as a contribution to post-revolutionary nation-building. For much of the twentieth-century, such judgements meant that woman-authored novels reached a very limited audience. As the publishing industry grew in the latter decades of the century, books became more affordable, literacy in Mexico improved, and so woman-authored novels such as, for example, Ángeles Mastretta's *Arráncame la vida*, found a larger and more receptive (female) readership. The custodians of literary knowledge and other stakeholders in the literary field reacted by decrying the influence of the 'general public' who, in their view, were ill-equipped to evaluate literature. In Mastretta's case, the external factors which helped the male authors in this study to become canonical, including connections with the literary community, commercial success and winning a literary prize, became hindrances. Fuentes' connections helped him to become the heir to a canonical literary tradition while Mastretta's success was dismissed as being solely as a result of her connections. Commercial success and literary prizes in Mexico and abroad for Fuentes and Pitol were markers of prestige, for Mastretta, it was further evidence that she wrote 'popular fiction' unsuitable for incorporation into the canon. It is hoped that this study has gone some way towards showing that the artificial opposition between 'popular' or 'commercial literature' and canonical literature is heavily gendered and that this distinction operates in a way which excludes women from the Mexican canon and even from the literary field. Nonetheless, there is still scope for work, for example comparing the Mexican *boom femenino* to the original *boom*, to further challenge the marginalization of literature by women authors.[1]

As a result of the almost unanimous and often ubiquitous praise written by prominent custodians of literary knowledge and published in the national press, the male authors in this study were assured of their place in the Mexican canon. Their repeated inclusion in histories of Mexican literature meant that their work would be remembered, re-read, and reprinted and that the interpretation of them as nation-building narratives would be fixed and perpetuated for successive generations of future readers. Reviewers thus set the tone for subsequent criticism and we can conclude that, in Mexico at least, consecration is not dependent on a place in the curriculum, rather, the process by which a novel is incorporated into or omitted from the canon begins at a very early stage in a book's life. The role of the reviewer in canon formation must not, therefore, be underestimated and we may wish to examine the validity of the commonly held belief, expressed by Bourdieu and Guillory, for example, that canons are reliant on schools and universities for their effectiveness, and consider the other processes and mechanisms by which canons may be formed outside the educational system.[2] In relation to the time it takes for a novel to become canonical, Bourdieu suggests that ' "the process of canonization" culminating in consecration, appears to vary in proportion to the degree that their [agents of preservation and consecration] authority is widely recognized and can be durably imposed' (123). In the Mexican case we can conclude that the accelerated process of consecration is the result of authority being concentrated in the hands of a tight-knit community of custodians of literary knowledge and a few institutions which act as agents of legitimation. The fact that histories of literature can be, were, and continue to be readily re-printed and regularly updated over the course of the twentieth-century has served to establish an enduring canon of post-revolutionary literature.

As new histories of literature continue to be published each year there is a pressing need to reconsider not only who we include and why but also whether we should organize the entries in such volumes alphabetically, chronologically, thematically or otherwise. Some of the most recent histories of literature, including Christopher Domínguez Michael's *Diccionario crítico de la literatura mexicana (1955–2005)* and José Joaquín Blanco's *Crónica literaria. Un siglo de escritores mexicanos*, are based on and often reprint reviews which their authors have written in national newspapers and magazines.[3] These histories of literature confirm the still important role played by reviews and custodians of literary knowledge in contemporary Mexican literary culture. They may also suggest to us one way in which we might produce a new kind of literary history in which reviews are included to show how a text was read when it was first published. Clearly, however, it would be important to recognize the limitations of such a perspective, for example by highlighting subsequent or alternative ways of reading the novel. In addition, this new literary history could aim to locate texts in the literary field in which they were produced and received. Technological advances which enable us to produce, store and make available ever larger archives mean that in future we will be able to recognize a wider range of authors, texts and interpretations, because literary history will no longer be bound by the limitations of a physical book.

Academic criticism has been shown to have little impact on national canon formation beyond arguing for the inclusion of individual women and thereby negotiating inclusion on a one by one basis. As stated, Nellie Campobello, Rosario Castellanos, Elena Garro and Elena Poniatowska all benefited from such efforts but it remains difficult, although not impossible, for feminist critics to argue successfully for the inclusion of women authors. Not even Mastretta, about whom much criticism has been produced, has benefited from sufficient academic attention or vociferous support to gain access to the canon by this means. Ultimately, creating a separate canon of women novelists or arguing for the merits of a particular author on an individual basis is an ineffective means by which to challenge the underlying mechanisms of canon formation, which has been one of the fundamental aims of this study.

I have shown that novels became canonical because of the way they were read and so in order to challenge women's exclusion from the canon we must address the role played by interpretive strategies. Too often, reviewers in twentieth-century Mexico made assumptions about texts based on the gender of the author and took it for granted that novels by and about women would not address issues of national significance. Consequently, they overlooked the ways in which women authors could be seen to use the private sphere to comment on the national situation. In the same way that Jameson suggests that 'third-world' texts are 'resistant to our conventional western habits of reading', I have shown that non-canonical Mexican novels were similarly resistant to the dominant interpretive strategies that were adopted in post-revolutionary Mexico. In both cases, dominant interpretive strategies were ill equipped to understand the marginalized voices which tried to connect the private sphere to which they were restricted with the public sphere in order to negotiate their own inclusion into the nation. Alternative interpretive strategies, such as the private-national reading used in this study, are needed if we are to recognize these marginalized perspectives. Private-national readings of woman-authored novels produced new interpretations which meant that they could be read on the same basis as their male-authored counterparts. The private-national reading is only one possible interpretive strategy among many but one which has proved particularly fruitful in the case of women authors in post-revolutionary

Mexico. It is hoped that the approach taken in this study may be usefully adopted, applied and tested with reference to Mexican and other literatures and that other interpretive strategies will be developed and deployed in ways that enhance our understanding and appreciation of different texts.

Private-national readings of male-authored texts also provided new insights. In the case of *El indio* it was possible to identify the hitherto overlooked significance of the private narrative relating to the guide and his fiancée and *La región más transparente* was shown to have more in common with Paz's 'The Labyrinth of Solitude' than had previously been recognized. Perhaps the most revealing case was *El desfile del amor*, in which the boundaries between public and private were not clear-cut. What emerged was a connection between gender, perceived genre and interpretive strategies. The perceived genre of the novel clearly influenced the reviewers' chosen interpretive strategy. For this piece of detective fiction, reviewers were able to read the private in terms of the public situation, as they had been able to in nineteenth-century novels of female adultery and the national romances identified by Sommer. Further research into historical ways of reading may help us to uncover forgotten interpretive strategies which could enhance our appreciation of contemporary texts.

By producing private-national readings I have been able to challenge the widespread misconception that woman-authored novels were excluded from the canon because they were not 'good enough'. The new interpretations showed that some of the woman-authored novels were as 'good' as the male-authored novels when assessed according to whether or not they contributed to post-revolutionary nation-building i.e. according to the same standard as their male-authored counterparts. However, some of the new readings also show that while canonical male-authored texts were consistently interpreted as being in keeping with the mood of the time the same was not always true of the woman-authored texts. Even if reviewers had been able to interpret *Yo también, Adelita, La ciudad y el viento* and *Arráncame la vida* as addressing national circumstances, these novels may still have been excluded from the Mexican national canon because they challenged the hegemonic view of who should be included in the public sphere by writing women and, in the case of *La ciudad y el viento*, Catholics, into the nation.

Failure to measure up to the standard set for post-revolutionary national literature meant almost certain oblivion for many novels, but by disregarding this standard and judging each text afresh I would venture that we are likely to find many more accounts that are interesting and informative from an historical and literary perspective. These novels provide us with the opportunity to connect with wide-ranging experiences and perspectives in a way that a history book or a canonical text can often fail to do. They are also of particular interest for our efforts to understand the limits of national discourses and how they were contested by marginal subjects as they provide evidence of the specific counter-discourses that were produced in post-revolutionary Mexico. Finally, these novels must lead us to question the criteria that should be used to form literary canons.

This study has outlined two approaches to challenging existing gender-biased mechanisms of canon formation. The first involved uncovering the circumstances and readings which produced a male-dominated Mexican canon of nation-building literature. The second approach questioned women's exclusion from the canon by developing and adopting alternative interpretive strategies which, when applied to canonical male-authored novels, also yielded new insights. The potential benefits of applying different interpretive strategies are well illustrated by the six Mexican novels studied here. Interpretive strategies are at the heart of canon formation; they should not be determined by the author's gender and do not have to be tied to nation-building. It is now time for a novel's inclusion in the canon to be based on multiple, openly-acknowledged interpretive strategies.

Notes to the Conclusion

1. For a comparison of the reception of some of the authors of the Mexican *boom femenino* with that of those of the original *boom* see Bowskill, 'The Origins of the *boom femenino mexicano*'.
2. Bourdieu associates canon formation with the education system (p. 32) as does Guillory who equates the school syllabus with the canon (p. 6).
3. Christopher Domínguez Michael, *Diccionario crítico de la literatura mexicana (1955–2005)*, (Mexico: FCE, 2007); José Joaquín Blanco, *Crónica literaria. Un siglo de escritores mexicanos* (Mexico: Cal y Arena, 1996). See also: Huberto Batis, *Crítica bajo presión. Prosa Mexicana 1964–1985. Selección del autor* (Mexico: UNAM, 2004).

APPENDIX: PLOT SUMMARIES

Appendix 1: Plot Summary of *El indio* by Gregorio López y Fuentes

El indio is about the experiences of an indigenous community which lives on a *ranchería* [rural settlement] cut off from the rest of the population in an unspecified part of Mexico. The novel begins before the revolution and ends after it, but no specific dates are mentioned in the text. Nor are names used in the novel; instead characters are identified according to their function. The main characters are the guide, the fiancée, the hunter/rival and the teacher-leader. The guide is appointed by the community elders to assist a group of white men from the town who visit the *ranchería*. Once away from the village, the men ask the guide to show them where his ancestor's gold is hidden. The guide refuses and so they attack him and leave him for dead. When the men return to the village without the guide, the community realizes its mistake and kills one of the men. Another group of white men, including the municipal president, his secretary and the local teacher, sets out from the town to exact revenge, but turn back on the recommendation of the teacher. The guide, who survived the attack, returns to the village but he is crippled and so the elders, at the request of the girl's father, break off his engagement to his fiancée. The elders also give permission for the fiancée to marry the hunter because he will be able to provide for her. This decision marks the beginning of a feud between the two families, during which the hunter will be killed.

When the revolution begins, it has little impact on the indigenous community until they are asked to provide food for troops in the neighbourhood and also twenty conscripts, nineteen of whom never return. The remaining conscript is briefly reunited with his family but he has changed and adapted to the *mestizo* way of life and no longer wishes to return to the *ranchería* where his help is needed. Nonetheless, his experience highlights the opportunities available to those who can adapt and the value of the knowledge they could bring to their communities.

In the aftermath of the revolution, a school inspector realizes that the indigenous community would benefit from a teacher who is bilingual and indigenous but has had contact with white / *mestizo* culture, and so he appoints the teacher-leader. As well as educating the children the teacher-leader helps the indigenous community to claim some of their rights. Although he is soon co-opted by government officials and leaves the *ranchería* for a better job in the town, the reader has seen how successful this approach could be if it were continued.

After the revolution, the indigenous community suffers from a smallpox epidemic in which the guide's former fiancée and her child die; the guide buries them. When the epidemic has cleared, a local politician visits the *ranchería* promising revolutionary progress in the form of roads which the community is engaged to help to build. At the same time as the road is being built the priest asks them to build a church and to go on a pilgrimage to thank God for sparing them from smallpox. These tasks place a heavy burden on the community and they derive no benefit from them. This failure was not inevitable and the project to build the road, if properly implemented, would have significantly improved community life. At the end of the novel, the guide is left alone, fearing future contact with the outside world, but the outcome could so easily have been different.

Appendix 2: Plot Summary of *Yo también, Adelita* by Consuelo Delgado

Yo también, Adelita spans the period from the 1908 Viesca uprising, which was one of the earliest demonstrations against the regime of Porfirio Díaz, until 1917, when Venustiano Carranza confirmed his hold on power with the signing of the new Constitution. Narrated in the third person by an omniscient narrator, the novel charts the journey of Rosina González from childhood to adulthood against the backdrop of the revolution. Rosina's educational career and her romantic relationships feature prominently in the novel. The main characters are all members of Rosina's middle-class family: her old and wise grandfather, Estanislao, her mother, María, her sporadically employed father, Juan, and her strict, Catholic aunt, Herlinda, who has joined the upper class by means of a socially advantageous marriage. Her grandfather's brother, Pedro, who participates in the Viesca uprising, his wife, Concha, and his sons José, Pablo, and Alberto, who fight in the revolution, all have important roles in the novel.

At the beginning of the novel, Pedro is captured and imprisoned for his role in the Viesca uprising. Concha buys his freedom, but Pedro dies soon afterwards, leaving his family in difficult economic circumstances. Estanislao senses that there will be further unrest and moves the family away from the countryside to nearby Torreón, where Rosina starts school. She performs well, despite being bullied by a rich girl called Sara Romero, and is offered a scholarship to a local teacher training college, but her grandfather insists that she should attend the *Escuela Normal para Maestras* in Mexico City. At the national teacher training college Rosina is again confronted by an upper-class girl, called Elodia, who ridicules the poorer students, but Rosina has one close friend, Aurora. A relationship develops between Aurora and Rosina's second cousin, Pablo, who has moved to Mexico City to work for the new President, Francisco Madero. When Madero is betrayed by the former head of his army, Victoriano Huerta, in February 1913, Pablo is forced to decide between following Huerta and defecting to fight with the *Maderistas*. Pablo refuses to betray the *Maderista* cause and is killed fighting against Huerta. Rosina then develops a romantic interest in the boy next door, Enrique, but she is too scared to act on her feelings.

In spite of the difficulties and risks of travelling at this time, Rosina and her grandfather still visit one another. During one trip to Torreón, Rosina is reunited with Alberto and a relationship soon develops, much to the annoyance of Herlinda. The rest of the family is also concerned, but Rosina and Alberto ignore their family's reservations and get married in Mexico City. The couple live together although periodically Alberto goes to fight for the *convencionistas* against Carranza.[1] On one such occasion, he goes missing for a long time and eventually Rosina receives a letter saying that he was killed in battle. In the midst of her grief, Rosina realises that she is pregnant with Alberto's child and the novel ends with the narrator echoing the words of Alberto, promising a better future thanks to the sacrifices made by men and women during the revolution.

Appendix 3: Plot summary of *La región más transparente* by Carlos Fuentes

La región más transparente is divided into three parts; parts one and two are set in 1951 while part three is set in 1954 and reflects on the lack of change in the intervening three years. The novel centres around the inhabitants of post-revolutionary Mexico City: the ex-revolutionary turned businessman, Federico Robles, his wife, the social-climber Norma Larragoiti, and his mistress, Hortensia Chacón. Other characters include the would-be writer Rodrigo Pola, the intellectual Manuel Zamacona, Pimpinela de Ovando, a member of the Porfirian aristocracy, and Gabriel who has just returned from participating in the *bracero* programme in the United States. The mysterious Ixca Cienfuegos questions each character about their past because he has been sent by his mother, Teódula Moctezuma, to find a suitable sacrifice to her gods. When Norma dies in a domestic fire Teódula believes that this is the sacrifice that her son had promised her. By the end of the novel Manuel, Gabriel, Rodrigo's mother, Rosenda Pola, and the taxi driver, Juan Morales, are also dead and Ixca's poor advice has caused Robles to lose his business empire. The apparent success stories are those of Rodrigo, who has become a famous screen-writer, and Pimpinela who has married Rodrigo and recovered her family's lost fortune, but the only character who has truly found happiness is Robles, who has abandoned his old life to live in the countryside with Hortensia and his new born child.

Appendix 4: Plot Summary of *La ciudad y el viento* by Dolores Castro

La ciudad y el viento is about the impact that the *cristero* conflicts (1926–29 and 1934–36) had on an unnamed, provincial Mexican town. Set in 1934, the novel focuses on the escalation of tensions between the Catholic citizens and the secular, civil authorities which lead to the murders of Juan Garay and Alberto García de Alba. The Catholic townspeople include the elderly spinster, Dolores Llamas, the convent caretaker, Manuel Berumen, Garay and the Lara family. The State authorities are represented by the governor, Cuitláhuac Fernández, the leader of the army in the area, General Suárez, and the chief of police, Neftalí González. The García de Alba family also lives in the town; they do not belong to either group but are caught up in the middle of the dispute.

The problems in the town begin with the closure of the church. The already tense situation is aggravated when the chief of police, under orders from General Suárez, has Juan Garay killed for being a *cristero*. Garay is not a *cristero*, as he opposes violence in defence of one's religion, but he does lead a group of Catholics who meet illegally to pray and worship in their homes. In response to the kidnapping and murder of Garay, the townspeople, led by Dolores Llamas, plan to parade a statue of the virgin through the streets. The parade would be in breach of Article 24 of the 1917 Constitution which forbade public displays of religion. Dolores charges Berumen with looking after the money raised for the parade, but he spends it. Berumen is sacked by General Suárez in order to give Alberto a job and so he is unable to repay the stolen money. Rather than admit his guilt, he lies to Dolores telling her that the authorities sacked him so that they could appoint a replacement caretaker who would help them to steal the pedestal belonging to the statue of the virgin and so prevent the parade from taking place. As a result of Berumen's lies, Dolores mobilizes the religious community, and particularly the women, in the town to attack the new caretaker of the convent who, unbeknownst to her, is her friend Alberto, who recently returned to the town to look after his daughter, Estela. Alberto's murder at the hands of Dolores is the culmination of the conflict between the religious and civil authorities. The novel ends announcing Estela's departure as she asks herself '¿Cómo juzgar a los asesinos? ¿Quiénes fueron los asesinos de su padre?' (D. Castro, 111) [How should the killers be judged? Who were her father's killers?]. The reader is also encouraged to ask these questions although the answers are far from clear, because the novel shows that both sides share responsibility for events in the town but refuses to support one side over the other.

Appendix 5: Plot Summary of *El desfile del amor* by Sergio Pitol

El desfile del amor is set in Mexico City in 1973. The novel is about an investigation carried out by the historian Miguel del Solar, who has returned to Mexico following the death of his wife. He has recently completed a history of 1914 and now plans to write about Mexico's international relations at the time when the oil companies were expropriated, in March 1938. However, when a friend of his gives him a government dossier about the illegal activities of German agents in Mexico he changes his mind. The dossier refers to two assassinations which took place in the Minerva building where he had lived for a short time as a boy, with his aunt and uncle. The victim was the stepson of his aunt's brother. Del Solar hopes that events in the Minerva will shed light on, or be illustrative of, the wider national and international context in 1942, the year Mexico entered World War II and he opts to pursue this line of enquiry.

Del Solar interviews the people who had lived in the building at the time of the shooting and attended the party that was held there that night. These people are, or were, friends or friends of the family and together represent a cross-section of Mexican society in the 1940s. He talks to his aunt, Eduviges, whose family had been wealthy and well established in society, but they lost everything during the revolution. He interviews society lady Delfina Uribe, daughter of a *carrancista* ideologue and hostess of the party. Delfina's son was wounded in the shooting and later died from his injuries. Other guests del Solar interviews include Emma Werfel, who had attended the party with her mother, Ida, who was a prominent Jewish Hispanist. Ida and her daughter came to Mexico having fled Nazi Germany. The famous painter Julio Escobedo, his wife Ruth, and Minerva resident Pedro

Balmorán are also questioned. Balmorán is an aspiring writer who was injured in the shooting and still lives in the Minerva building. Finally, del Solar talks to a childhood friend, Derny Goenaga, who is now the head of a marketing firm and part of the jet-setting elite. Despite conducting all of these interviews, often speaking to each person on more than one occasion, del Solar fails to discover what happened on the night Erich María Pistauer was killed and reaches no firm conclusion about the motive for the shooting. At the end of the novel, del Solar is unconvinced that further investigation of events at the Minerva will help him to produce the book about 1942 and so ends that aspect of his study to focus on the international context, using information taken from public archives. Del Solar also decides to stay in Mexico with his children instead of going back to England and there is a hint that a romantic relationship will develop with his friend Amparo.

Appendix 6: Plot Summary of *Arráncame la vida* by Ángeles Mastretta

Arráncame la vida is set in Puebla and Mexico City. The first-person narrative of the narrator-protagonist, Catalina, spans the period from approximately 1933 to 1946. At the beginning of the novel, sixteen-year-old Catalina escapes her poor background by marrying General Andrés Ascencio, who presents himself as a revolutionary hero who fought in the revolution for Madero before supporting Obregón and Carranza. Later, however, Catalina discovers that Andrés in fact fought with Huerta against Madero in the 1913 coup of the *decena trágica*.[2]

After a few years of marriage, Catalina gets pregnant and, following a difficult pregnancy during which she has her first adulterous affair with Pablo, Catalina gives birth to Verania. At this time, Andrés brings two children from his first marriage and four children whom he fathered with his mistresses to live with them. Among them is Lilia, with whom Catalina develops a good relationship. When Andrés becomes the candidate for the governorship of Puebla the whole family accompanies him on an election tour and he is duly elected Governor in a rigged election. As the governor's wife, Catalina becomes ever more aware of her husband's corruption. When Catalina finds out that Andrés ordered a massacre because some landowners would not sell their land to him she refuses to have sex with her husband. Subsequently, she flirts with a minor government official, Fernando Arizmendi. When Andrés notices he punishes her but then allows her to continue seeing Arizmendi because he learns, as Catalina later discovers, that Arizmendi is homosexual. In the meantime, Catalina discovers that her friend, Pepa, is having an adulterous affair. Another friend, Mónica, also embarks on an adulterous relationship and a third friend, Bibi, goes from being the mistress of newspaper tycoon Gómez Soto to being his second wife. When Bibi later has an affair with a bullfighter, who is using her to get publicity in her husband's newspaper, Catalina helps Bibi resolve the situation with her husband so she does not lose everything she has.

In the late 1930s, Andrés' friend, Rodolfo (Fito) Campos, becomes the official candidate for the presidency. When Rodolfo wins the election, Andrés and Catalina move to Mexico City. Andrés is too involved in politics to pay much attention to

Catalina, who meets Carlos Vives. Vives is an orchestra conductor and the son of a general with whom Andrés was good friends. Vives is also involved with the trade union the *Confederación de Trabajadores Mexicanos* (CTM) [Confederation of Mexican Workers] and is friends with the leader, Alvaro Cordera, whom Andrés is trying to have removed. Andrés starts to show more interest in his wife, but Catalina has fallen in love with Vives and begins a second adulterous relationship. It is never clear whether Andrés knows about the affair, but he has Cordera and Vives killed; Cordera at least, for political reasons.

The relationship between Catalina and Vives is paralleled in that between Lilia and Javier Uriarte. Andrés organizes an arranged marriage for Lilia which will be politically advantageous for him; Lilia resists because she does not love her would-be husband Emilio. She is in love with Javier, who dies mysteriously in a motorbike accident, probably arranged by Andrés. Subsequently, Lilia appears to give in to her father's wishes and marries Emilio, but she shows her new husband up at the wedding by leaving separately. At Lilia's wedding, Catalina meets the man with whom she will have her third adulterous relationship, the cinema director, Alonso Quijano. Also at the wedding Catalina meets the wife of one of the men who Andrés had killed in a dispute over land. This woman gives her a special type of tea which 'daba fuerzas pero hacía costumbre, y había que tenerle cuidado porque tomado todos los días curaba de momento pero a la larga mataba' (Mastretta, *Arráncame*, 322) [gave strength but was addictive and you had to be careful because if drunk everyday it would cure you in the short term but kill you in the long run]. By this stage in the novel, Andrés is getting old and is starting to lose his political power and he begins to drink the tea which Catalina gives him to make him feel better or, perhaps, to kill him. Catalina spends much of her time in Acapulco with Quijano but when Andrés arrives unannounced Quijano leaves. Catalina's relationship with Quijano ends and she is reconciled with her husband. Having learned that his mother has 'adopted' Martín Cienfuegos, just as she previously 'adopted' Campos, Andrés drinks increasing amounts of the special tea. Cienfuegos is now in line to be the next president and when his 'adopted' brother is assured of the presidency, Andrés dies leaving everything to a still young and attractive Catalina, who is advised at the wake that she should not rush to remarry because widowhood is the ideal state for women. She closes her narrative saying that she is 'divertida con mi futuro, casi feliz' (Mastretta, *Arráncame*, 182) [entertained with my future, almost happy].

Notes to the Appendix

1. The supporters of Zapata and Villa who joined forces following the Convention of Aguascalientes were known as *convencionistas*.
2. The *decena trágica* was the period of uprising which led to the overthrow of the Madero government in February 1913.

BIBLIOGRAPHY

Mexico City Archives

Archivo Hemerográfico de Escritores. Centro Nacional de Información y Promoción de la Literatura

Biblioteca Nacional. Fondo Reservado. Fondo Silvino M. González

Archivo General de la Nación. Galería 3, Presidentes: Fondo Lázaro Cárdenas

Archivo de la Secretaría de Educación Pública (SEP).1934–1936. Depto. de Bellas Artes Concursos y Certámenes 17-11-218 196

Works cited

[Advertisement], *La Palabra y el Hombre. Revista de la Universidad Veracruzana*, July–September, 1966, back page

[Advertisement], *Letras. Publicación Literaria y Bibliografía*, June 1935, p. 12

[Advertisement] 'Andres Botas Librería y Papelería', *Letras*, October 1936, p. 13

[Advertisement] 'Ediciones de la Universidad Veracruzana Colección — Ficción', *El Centavo*, vol. IV, no. 51, September 1962, unnumbered middle section

'El desfile del amor', *El Universal*, 17 June 1988. CNIPL/EXP.SP

'En busca de la identidad perdida', *El Excélsior*, 24 June 1983. CNIPL/ EXP.s. XIX/1

'Estados Unidos aclama la novela de Carlos Fuentes como una de las mejores de 1960', *México en la Cultura*, supl. *Novedades*, 19 December 1960, p. 3

'Gran Exito de la Obra de Carlos Fuentes', *El Excélsior*, 9 April 1958, 1st section, p. 7. FR/ CF

'Hay un verdadero florecimiento de poesía femenina: Dolores Castro', CNIPL/EXP.DC

'La ciudad y el viento', *Cuadernos de Bellas Artes*, 1 January 1963, p. 89

'Libros', *Cuadernos Americanos*, July–October, 1958, pp. 581–83

'No lo olvide. Los premios nacionales sobre literatura, teatro, contribución científica y labor periodística', *El Universal Gráfico*, 9 July 1935

'Nueva bibliografía Mexicana. Ultimas novedades', *Boletín Bibliográfico Mexicano*, May–June 1958, p. 28

'Nueva Bibliografía Mexicana', *Boletín Bibliográfico Mexicano*, September–October 1962, p. 39

Ocho poetas mexicanos (Mexico: Bajo el signo de Ábside, 1955)

'Premio Mazatlán de Literatura' <http://www.carnavalmazatlan.net/premiomztlit.php> [accessed 8 February 10]

'Presentación', *Yo también, Adelita* by Consuelo Delgado (Mexico: Ediciones del Grupo en Marcha, 1936), pp. 7–9

'Sergio Pitol ganó el Segundo Premio Anagrama de Barcelona con su novela *El desfile del amor*', *El Excélsior*, 17 March 1984. CNIPL/EXP.SP

'Su mesa de redacción. Uno de los buenos éxitos', *Diorama de la Cultura*, supl. *El Excélsior*, 13 April 1958, p. 2

[Untitled review of *El indio*], *Revista de México de Cultura*, supl. *El Nacional*, 7 August 1955, pp. 8–9

ADLER HELLMAN, JUDITH, *Mexico in Crisis* (London: Holmes and Meier, 1983)

AGUILAR CAMÍN, HÉCTOR, and LORENZO MEYER, *In the Shadow of the Mexican Revolution: Contemporary Mexican History, 1910–1989*, trans. by Luis Alberto Fierro (Austin: University of Texas Press, 1993)

AGUILAR, HECTOR ORESTES, 'Cinco ventanas del edificio Minerva', *Novedades*, 6 August 1989, p. 2.

AHMAD, AIJAZ, 'Jameson's Rhetoric of Otherness and the "National Allegory"', *Social Text*, 17 (1987), 3–25

ALATRISTE, SEALTIEL, '*El desfile del amor*. Plaza Río de Janeiro (de la historia al refrán)', *Revista UNAM*, February–March 1985, pp. 48–50

ALEGRÍA, FERNANDO, 'López y Fuentes: trayectoria y temas', in *Recopilación de textos sobre la novela de la Revolución Mexicana*, ed. by Rogelio Rodríguez Coronel (Havana: Casa de las Ameritas, 1975), pp. 288–94

ALVARADO, JOSÉ, 'Correo menor', *Diorama de la Cultura*, supl. *El Excélsior*, 22 June 1958, p. 2

ALVAREZ Z., MARÍA EDMÉE, *Literatura mexicana e hispanoamericana. Manual para uso de los alumnos de las escuelas preparatorias*, 6th edn (Mexico: Porrúa, 1966)

ANDA, JOSEPH DE, 'The Indian in the Works of Gregorio López y Fuentes' (unpublished doctoral thesis, University of Southern California, 1969)

ANDERSON, DANNY J., 'Creating Cultural Prestige: Editorial Joaquín Mortiz', *Latin American Research Review*, 31 (1996), 3–41

——'Displacement: Strategies of Transformation in *Arráncame la vida*', in *The Other Mirror: Women's Narrative in Mexico, 1980–1995*, ed. by Kristine Ibsen (Westport, CT: Greenwood Press, 1997), pp. 13–27; first publ. in *Journal of the Midwest Modern Language Association*, 21 (1988), 15–27

ANHALT, NEDDA G. DE, 'El desfile del amor de Sergio Pitol. Historia ahistórica', *Sábado*, 9 March 1985, pp. 10–11

ARANDA LUNA, JAVIER, 'Editan *Arráncame la vida* en 4 países europeos. El periodismo esclaviza aún más que la literatura: Ángeles Mastretta', *La Jornada*, 1 April 1987, p. 33

ARELLANDO, JESÚS, 'Panoramica de las letras', *El Día*, 21 September 1962, p. 9

ARIAS URRUTIA, ANGEL, *Cruzados de novela. Las novelas de la guerra cristera* (Pamplona: Ediciones Universidad de Navarra, 2002)

AVENDAÑO BETANZOS, SANDRA, 'Dolores Castro: Lo que uno vive es totalmente fugaz', CNIPL/EXP.DC

AVILÉS, ALEJANDRO, 'Dolores Castro y la poesía femenina del ...', *Revista de la Semana*, supl. *El Universal*, 15 February 1953, pp. 17–18

BAKER, NIAMH, *Happily Ever After: Women's Fiction in Postwar Britain 1945–1960* (New York: St Martin's Press, 1989)

BARTRA, ROGER, *Blood, Ink and Culture: Miseries and Splendors of the Post-Mexican Condition*, trans. by Mark Alan Healey (Durham, NC, and London: Duke University Press, 2002)

BASNETT, SUSAN, *Knives and Angels: Women Writers in Latin America* (London: Zed Books, 1990)

BATIS, HUBERTO, *Crítica bajo presión. Prosa Mexicana 1964–1985. Selección del autor* (Mexico: UNAM, 2004)

BARRÓN SOTO, HÉCTOR S., 'El desfile del amor, de Sergio Pitol', *Sábado*, 22 February 1986, p. 8

BENJAMIN, THOMAS, *La Revolución: Mexico's Great Revolution as Memory, Myth and History* (Austin: University of Texas Press, 2000)

BERMÚDEZ, MARÍA ELVIRA, 'Plegadera', *El Nacional*, 26 May 1985, p. 10

BIRON, REBECCA E., '*Un hogar insólito*: Elena Garro and Mexican literary culture', in *The Effects of the Nation: Mexican Art in an Age of Globalization*, ed. by Carl Good and John V. Waldron (Philadelphia: Temple University Press, 2001), pp. 138–59

BLANCARTE, ROBERTO, *Historia de la Iglesia Católica Mexicana* (Mexico: FCE, 1992)

BLANCO, JOSÉ JOAQUÍN, 'Pitol: *El desfile del amor*', *La Jornada*, 25 February 1985, p. 21

——*Crónica literaria. Un siglo de escritores mexicanos* (Mexico: Cal y Arena, 1996)

BOLDY, STEVEN, *The Narrative of Carlos Fuentes: Family, Text, Nation* (Durham: Durham University Press, 2002)

BOULLOSA VELÁZQUEZ, PABLO 'Los velos del crimen', *Novedades*, 16 March 1986, pp. 10, 16

BOURDIEU, PIERRE, *The Field of Cultural Production*, ed. and intro. by Randal Johnson (Cambridge: Polity Press, 1993)

BOWSKILL, SARAH E. L, '*Yo también, Adelita*: A National Allegory of the Mexican Revolution and a Call for Women's Suffrage', in *Revolucionarias: Conflict and Gender in Latin American Narratives by Women*, ed. by Par Kumaraswami and Niamh Thornton (Oxford: Peter Lang, 2007), pp. 139–64

——'Women, Violence and the Mexican Cristero Wars as represented in *Los recuerdos del porvenir* and *La ciudad y el viento*', *Modern Language Review*, 104.2 (2009), 438–52

——'The Origins of the *boom femenino mexicano*' in *The boom femenino in Mexico: Reading Contemporary Women's Writing*, ed. by Nuala Finnegan and Jane Lavery (Newcastle: Cambridge Scholars, 2010), pp. 73–89

BRADU, FABIENNE, *Señas particulares: Escritora. Ensayos sobre escritoras mexicanas del siglo XX* (Mexico: FCE, 1987)

BRAHAM, PERSEPHONE, *Crimes Against the State, Crimes Against Persons: Detective Fiction in Cuba and Mexico* (Minneapolos: University of Minnesota Press, 2004)

BRANDENBURG, FRANK, *The Making of Modern Mexico* (Englewood Cliffs, NJ: Prentice Hall, 1964)

BROOKSBANK JONES, ANNY, and CATHERINE DAVIES, *Latin American Women's Writing: Feminist Readings in Theory and Crisis* (Oxford: Clarendon Press, 1996)

BRUCE-NOVOA, JUAN, 'La novela de la Revolución Mexicana: la topología del final', *Hispania*, 74 (1991), 36–44

BRUSHWOOD, JOHN, *Narrative Innovation and Political Change in Mexico* (New York: Peter Lang, 1989)

BUTLER, MATTHEW, 'God's *Campesinos*? Mexico's Revolutionary Church in the Countryside', *Bulletin of Latin American Research*, 28 (2009), 165–84

CALLEROS, MARIO, 'Enjuicia el México de los últimos años', *La Gaceta*, March 1958, p. 1

CAMP, RODERIC A., *Intellectuals and the State in Twentieth Century Mexico* (Austin: University of Texas Press, 1985)

CAMPBELL, FEDERICO, 'Sergio Pitol y su novela *El desfile del amor*', *Proceso*, 24 February 1986, pp. 52–53

CAMPO, XORGE DEL, *Cuentistas y novelistas de la Revolución Mexicana, tomo VI*, 2nd edn (Mexico: Ediciones Luzbel, 1985)

CAMPOS, DOLORES, 'She's (Not) The Boss', *México en la Cultura*, supl. *Novedades*, 24 July 1985, p. 47

CARBALLO, EMMANUEL, '1958: el año de la novela', *México en la Cultura*, supl. *Novedades*, 28 December 1958, pp. 1, 11

——'Costumbrismo y mortaja', *La Cultura en México*, supl. *Siempre*, núm. 28, 29 August 1962, p. xvi

——*Diecinueve protagonistas de la literatura mexicana del siglo XX* (Mexico: Empresas Editoriales, 1965)

——*Protagonistas de la literatura mexicana*, 2nd edn (Mexico: Ediciones del Ermitaño/SEP, 1985)

——*Bibliografía de la novela mexicana del siglo XX* (Mexico: UNAM, 1988)

——*Historia de las letras mexicanas en el siglo XIX* (Mexico: Reloj de Sol, 1991)

——*Protagonistas de la literatura mexicana*, 4th rev. edn (Mexico: Editorial Porrúa, 1994)

——*Diccionario crítico de las letras mexicanas en el siglo XIX* (Mexico: Editorial Océano & CONACULTA, 2001)

CARDOZA Y ARAGON, LUIS, 'El pro y el contra de una escandalosa novela. El pro', *México en la Cultura*, supl. *Novedades*, 11 May 1958, pp. 1, 2

CARRIÓN, BENJAMÍN, 'El escritor ecuatoriano Benjamín Carrión le entra al juega-jueguito de los críticos y juzga como una gran novela *La región más transparente*', *México en la Cultura*, supl. *Novedades*, 25 May 1958, pp. 2, 7

CASTAÑÓN, ADOLFO, *Arbitrario de literatura mexicana paseos I*, 2nd edn (Mexico: Vuelta, 1995)

CASTELLANOS, ROSARIO, 'La novela mexicana contemporánea y su valor testimonial', *Hispania*, 47 (1965), 223–30

CASTILLO PERAZA, CARLOS, 'No fornicaras (en hamaca)', *La Jornada*, 4 June 1985, CNIPL/EXP.AM

CASTILLO, DEBRA A., *Talking Back: Toward a Latin American Feminist Literary Criticism* (Ithaca, NY: Cornell University Press, 1992)

——*Easy Women: Sex and Gender in Modern Mexican Fiction* (Minneapolis: University of Minneosta Press, 1998)

CASTRO, DOLORES, *La ciudad y el viento* (Xalapa: Universidad Veracruzana, 1962)

CASTRO RICALDE, MARICRUZ, *Ficción, narración y polifonía. El universo narrativo de Sergio Pitol* (Mexico: Universidad Autónoma del Estado de México, 2000)

CERVANTES, EULOGIO, 'Carlos Fuentes y el plagiarismo', *El Excélsior*, FR/CF

CERVERA, JUAN, 'Aquí la poesía Dolores Castro, corazón transfigurado', CNIPL/EXP.DC

CHARNON-DEUTSCH, LOU, *Gender and Representation: Women in Spanish Realist Fiction* (Amsterdam: John Benjamins, 1990)

CHUMACERO, ALI, 'Primera novela de Carlos Fuentes', FR/CF

——'La revolución y sus descendientes', FR/CF

CLINE, HOWARD F., *Mexico: Revolution to Evolution 1940–1960* (London: Oxford University Press, 1962)

CLUFF, RUSSELL M., and JOSEFINA LARA VALDEZ, *Diccionario biobibliográfico de escritores de México 1920–1970*, 2nd edn (Mexico: INBA, 1994)

COCKCROFT, JAMES D., *Intellectual Precursors of the Mexican Revolution (1900–1913)* (Austin: University of Texas Press, 1968)

COHN, DEBORAH, 'The Mexican Intelligentsia, 1950–1968: Cosmopolitanism, National Identity, and the State', *Mexican Studies/ Estudios Mexicanos*, 21.1 (2005), 141–92

COIRA, MARÍA, 'Narra una investigación histórica: *El desfile del amor* de Sergio Pitol', *Revista del centro de letras hispanoamericanas*, 5 (1996), 171–81

CONTRERAS, ANTONIO, 'Historia de un crimen', *Punto*, 26 August 1985, p. 20

CORDERO, SALVADOR, 'Un libro y un escritor', *Letras*, May 1936, p. 2

CÓRDOVA, EDGAR, 'Dolores Castro, homenaje a ochenta años en las letras', *Milenio*, 13 April 2003, p. 41

CORIA, JOSÉ FELIPE, 'El desfile del amor de Sergio Pitol', *Sábado*, 13 July 1985, p. 11

CORONADO, JUAN, 'Arráncame la vida de Ángeles Mastretta', *Sábado*, supl. *Unomásuno*, 4 May 1985, p. 12

DALEVUELTA, JACOBO, 'Libros Nuevos', *El Universal*, 27 June 1935, p. 3

——'Libros nuevos', *El Universal*, 27 December 1935, 1st section, p. 3

——'Libros Nuevos', *El Universal*, 7 August 1936, 1st section, p. 3

DELGADO, CONSUELO, *Yo también, Adelita* (Mexico: Ediciones del Grupo en Marcha, 1936)

DOMENE, PEDRO M., 'Entrevista. El universo literario y personal de Sergio Pitol (una entrevista que se dilata en el tiempo y en la amistad)', in *Sergio Pitol. El sueño de lo real*, ed. by Pedro M. Domene (Xalapa: Universidad Veracruzana, 2002), pp. 27–39

DOMECQ, BRIANDA, *Mujer que publica...Mujer pública. Ensayos sobre literatura femenina* (Mexico: Editorial Diana, 1994)

DOMINGO ARGÜELLES, JUAN, 'Sergio Pitol y Balmorán el empecinado', *El Universal*, 17 November 1989, p. 2

DOMÍNGUEZ MICHAEL, CHRISTOPHER, 'Nueva tristeza mexicana', *Proceso*, 1 April 1985, pp. 60–61

——'El cuarteto del nuevo realismo', *La Jornada*, 10 March 1986, pp. 3–4. CNIPL/EXP. AM

——*Diccionario crítico de la literatura mexicana (1955–2005)* (Mexico: FCE, 2007)

DUEÑAS, DANIEL, 'Repertorio', *El Sol de México en la Cultura*, supl. *El sol de México*, 14 August 1977, p. 2

ECHEVERRIA DEL PRADO, VICENTE, and RAMÓN GÁLVEZ, 'Pausas literarias', *Novedades*, 29 February 1948, FR/DC

ENGLEKIRK, JOHN, '*El indio*. Novela mexicana, por Gregorio López y Fuentes, *Letras*, December 1937, p. 8

——'The "Discovery" of *Los de abajo*', *Hispania*, 18 (1935), 53–62

FADANELLI, GUILLERMO J. and NAIEF YEHYA, 'La literatura a la que estamos condenados I'. *Sábado*, 7 October 1989, p. 6

——'La literatura a la que estamos condenados II', *Sábado*, 14 October 1989, pp. 5–7

FERNÁNDEZ DE ALBA, LUZ, *Del tañido al arte de la fuga. Una lectura crítica de la fuga* (Mexico: UNAM, 1998)

FINNEGAN, NUALA, and JANE LAVERY, eds, *The boom femenino in Mexico: Reading Contemporary Women's Writing* (Newcastle: Cambridge Scholars, 2010)

FISH, STANLEY, *Is there a text in this class? The Authority of Interpretive Communities* (Cambridge, MA: Harvard University Press, 1980)

FISHER, LILLIAN ESTELLE, 'The Influence of the Present Mexican Revolution upon the Status of Mexican Women', *Hispanic American Historical Review*, 22 (1942), 211–28

FORNET, JORGE, *Reescrituras de la memoria. Novela femenina y Revolución en México* (Havana: Editorial Letras Cubanas, 1994)

FRANCO, JEAN, *Plotting Women: Gender and Representation in Mexico* (London: Verso, 1989)

FUENTES, CARLOS, *La región más transparente*, 7th edn, ed. and intro. by Georgina García Gutiérrez (Madrid: Cátedra, 1999); first pub. 1958

GAITÁN ROJO, HÉCTOR, '*Arráncame la vida*', 20 April 1985, CNIPL/EXP.AM

GARCÍA, KAY S., *Broken Bars: New Perspectives from Mexican Women Writers* (Albuquerque: University of New Mexico Press, 1994)

GARCÍA ASCOT, J. M., '*La región más transparente*: un libro de gran importancia que crece con la ferocidad de ciertas oposiciones', *México en la Cultura*, supl. *Novedades*, 11 May 1958, pp. 2, 10

GARRO, ELENA, 'El pro y el contra de una escandalosa novela. El contra', *México en la Cultura*, supl. *Novedades*, 11 May 1958, pp. 1, 10

GILBERT, PATRICIO, 'Carlos Fuentes. En la ruta de la buena novela', FR/CF

GILBERT, SANDRA M. and SUSAN GUBAR, *The Madwoman in the Attic: The Woman Writer and the Nineteenth-Century Literary Imagination* (New Haven, CT: Yale University Press, 1979)

GLANTZ, MARGO, 'El desfile del Pitol. Sergio Pitol, el mismo que canta y baila', *La Jornada*, 13 April 1985, pp. 1–4

GOMÍS, ANAMARI, 'Ella encarnaba boleros', *Nexos*, July 1985, pp. 51–52

GONZÁLEZ GUERRERO, F., 'Enciclopedia Mínima. Aguila que cae', *El Universal Gráfico*, 14 June 1935, pp. 7, 13

——'Enciclopedia Mínima. El volador', *El Universal Gráfico*, 17 July 1935, p. 6

——'Enciclopedia Mínima. El Nahual', *El Universal Gráfico*, 22 August 1935, pp. 7, 11

——'Enciclopedia Mínima. Superstición', *El Universal Gráfico*, 23 August 1935, pp. 7, 11

GONZÁLEZ PEÑA, CARLOS, *Historia de la literatura mexicana. Desde los orígenes hasta nuestros días*, 5th edn (Mexico: Editorial Porrúa, 1954); first publ. 1928

——*Historia de la literatura mexicana. Desde los orígenes hasta nuestros días*, 8th–10th and 12th edns, with an appendix by the Centro de Estudios Literarios de la UNAM (Mexico: Editorial Porrúa, 1963, 1966, 1969, 1975)

GONZÁLEZ RODRÍGUEZ, SERGIO, 'Del regreso: la extrema memoria', *La Jornada*, 13 April 1983, pp. 1–3.

GONZÁLEZ-STEPHAN, BEATRIZ, *Fundaciones: canon, historia y cultura nacional. La historiografía literaria del liberalismo hispanoamericano del siglo* XIX (Madrid: Iberoamericana, 2002)

GONZÁLEZ, OMAR, '*El desfile del amor* de Sergio Pitol II', *Sábado*, 16 November 1985, p. 12

GRANT, CATHERINE, 'Preface', in *Monstrous Projections of Femininity in the Fictions of Mexican Writer Rosario Castellanos*, by Nuala Finnegan (Lewiston, NY: Edwin Mellen Press, 2000), pp. xvii–xviii

GRAYSON, GEORGE W., *The Church in Contemporary Mexico* (Washington, DC: Center for Strategic and International Studies, 1992)

GRINGOIRE, PEDRO, 'Por el mundo de los libros', *El Excélsior*, 16 August 1936, 3rd section, p. 2

GUILLÉN, LAURA, 'Ficción Irrupción Desangelada', *El Semanario Cultural*, supl. *Novedades*, 12 May 1985, p. 3

GUILLORY, JOHN, *Cultural Capital: The Problem of Literary Canon Formation* (Chicago: University of Chicago Press, 1993)

GUZMÁN, HUMBERTO, 'Pitol y el sentimiento del carnaval', *El Búho*, 15 November 1992, p. 7

GYURKO, LANIN A., 'Identity and the Mask in Fuentes' *La región más transparente*', *Hispanófila*, 65 (1979), 75–103.

——'Individual and National Identity in Fuentes' *La región más transparente*', *Kentucky Romance Quarterly*, 25 (1978), 435–57

HAAS, ANTONIO, 'Ángeles Mastretta Premio Mazatlán 1986', *El Excélsior*, 15 February 1986, pp. 7A, 8A

——'El Premio a *Arráncame la vida*. Ángeles de Puebla', *La Cultura al Día*, supl. *El Excélsior*, 29 January 1986, pp. 1, 2, 3

HAMNETT, BRIAN R., *A Concise History of Mexico* (Cambridge: Cambridge University Press, 2000)

HERNÁNDEZ, RUBÉN, '*Arráncame la vida*', *Claudia*, July 1987, pp. 20–21

HERNÁNDEZ RODRÍGUEZ, RAFAEL, 'Melodrama and Social Comedy in the Cinema of the Golden Age', in *Mexico's Cinema: A Century of Film and Filmmakers*, ed. by Joanne Hershfield and David R. Maciel (Wilmington, DE: Scholarly Resources, 1999), pp. 101–21

HERRERA FRIMONT, CELESTINO, 'Gregorio López y Fuentes y el premio nacional de literatura', *El Nacional*, 9 August 1936, Suplemento, p. 3

HERRNSTEIN SMITH, BARBARA, *Contingencies of Value: Alternative Perspectives for Critical Theory* (Cambridge, MA: Harvard University Press, 1988)

HIGUERA, ERNESTO, 'Una novela social de Gregorio López y Fuentes', *Cuadrante Rojo*, 1939, pp. 149–52

HODGES, DONALD C., and ROSS GANDY, *Mexico 1910–1976: Reform or Revolution?* (London: Zed Press, 1979)

——*Mexico: The End of the Revolution* (Westport, CT: Praeger, 2002)

HOWLAND BUSTAMENTE, SERGIO, *Historia de la literatura mexicana. Con algunas notas sobre literatura de Hispanoamérica* (Mexico: Editorial F. Trillas, 1961)

HUGGAN, GRAHAM, *The Post-colonial Exotic: Marketing the Margins* (London: Routledge, 2001)

HURTADO, GERARDO, '*El desfile del amor*, de Sergio Pitol: una tragicomedia policial en tres actos', in *Bang! Bang!: pesquisas sobre narrativa policiaca mexicana*, ed. by Miguel G. Rodríguez Lozano and Enrique Flores (Mexico: UNAM, 2005), pp. 91–113

IBSEN, KRISTINE, 'The Other Mirror: Introduction', in *The Other Mirror: Women's Narrative in Mexico, 1980–1995*, ed. by Kristine Ibsen (Westport, CT: Greenwood Press, 1997)

JAMESON, FREDRIC, 'Third-World Literature in the Era of Multinational Capitalism', *Social Text*, 15 (1986), 65–88

JIMÉNEZ RUEDA, JULIO, *Historia de la literatura mexicana* (Mexico: Editorial Cultura, 1928)

—— *Historia de la literatura mexicana*, 2nd–7th edns (Mexico: Ediciones Botas,1934, 1942, 1946, 1953, 1957, 1960)

KAMINSKY, AMY K., *Reading the Body Politic: Feminist Criticism and Latin American Women Writers* (Minneapolis: University of Minnesota Press, 1993)

KANDELL, JONATHAN, 'Mexico's Megalopolis', in *I Saw a City Invincible: Urban Portraits of Latin America*, ed. by Gilbert M. Joseph and Mark D. Szuchman (Wilmington, DE: Scholarly Resources, 1996), pp. 181–201

KATTAR, JEANNETTE,'Gregorio López y Fuentes et son roman: *El indio*' (unpublished doctoral thesis Centre de Hautes Etudes Afro-Ibero-Americaines de l'Université de Dakar, 1969)

KNIGHT, ALAN, *The Mexican Revolution: Porfirians, Liberals and Peasants*, 2 vols (Lincoln: University of Nebraska Press, 1990)

—— 'Racism, Revolution, and Indigensimo: Mexico, 1910–1940', in *The Idea of Race in Latin America, 1870–1940*, ed. by Richard Graham (Austin: University of Texas Press, 1990), pp. 71–113

KNIGHTS, VANESSA, '(De)constructing Gender: The Bolero in Ángeles Mastretta's *Arráncame la vida*', *Journal of Romance Studies*, 1 (2001), 69–84

LAVERY, JANE, *Ángeles Mastretta: Textual Multiplicity* (Suffolk: Tamesis, 2005)

LEMAITRE LEÓN, MONIQUE J., 'La historia oficial frente al discurso de la 'ficción' femenina en *Arráncame la vida* de Ángeles Mastretta', *Texto Crítico*, 3 (1996), 99–114

LEÓN, LORENZO, 'La pareja Aguilar-Mastreta: su dualidad artística', CNIPL/EXP.AM

LERÍN, MANUEL, 'Una novela sobre el destino urbano', *Revista de México de Cultura*, supl. *El Nacional*, 4 May 1958, p. 11

LEWALD, ERNEST H., 'El pensamiento cultural mexicano en *La región más transparente* de Carlos Fuentes', *Revista Hispánica Moderna*, 33 (1967), 216–23

LEWIS, STEPHEN E., 'The Nation, Education and the "Indian Problem" in Mexico, 1920–1940', in *The Eagle and the Virgin: Nation and Cultural Revolution in Mexico, 1920–1940*, ed. by Mary K. Vaughan and Stephen E. Lewis (Durham, NC: Duke University Press, 2006), pp. 176–95

LEYVA, ALVARO, 'El desfile del vacío', *Casa del Tiempo*, August–September 1985, pp. 60–62

LOMNITZ-ADLER, CLAUDIO, *Exits from the Labyrinth: Culture and Ideology in the Mexican National Space* (Berkeley: University of California Press, 1992)

LÓPEZ, RICK A.,'The Noche Mexicana and the Exhibition of Popular Arts: Two Ways of Exalting Indianness', in *The Eagle and the Virgin: Nation and Cultural Revolution in Mexico, 1920–1940*, ed. by Mary K. Vaughan and Stephen E. Lewis (Durham, NC, and London: Duke University Press, 2006), pp. 23–42

LÓPEZ Y FUENTES, GREGORIO, *El indio*, 5th edn (Mexico: Editorial Porrúa, 1972); first pub. 1935

—— *El indio*, trans. by Anita Brenner (New York: Frederick Ungar, 1937; repr. 1961)

LUVIANO DELGADO, RAFAEL, 'Ángeles Mastretta, escribir es angustiante, pero no hacerlo más', 6 February 1986, CNIPL/EXP.AM

MAGDALENO, MAURICIO, 'Escaparate', *El Nacional*, 30 June 1935, 2nd section, p. 1

MAGDALENO, VÍCTOR, 'Entre la literatura y el chisme', *El Día*, 1 April 1985, p. 10

MARTÍNEZ CACERES, ARTURO, 'Carlos Fuentes escándolo y literatura', *Revista de México de Cultura*, supl. *El Nacional*, 5 October 1958, p. 2

MARTÍNEZ GÓMEZ, JESÚS, 'Parodia, deformación y conocimiento en la narrativa de Sergio Pitol. Tríptico del Carnaval', in *Sergio Pitol. El sueño de lo real*, ed. by Pedro M. Domene (Xalapa: Universidad Veracruzana, 2002), pp. 152–62

MARTÍNEZ, JOSÉ LUIS, *Literatura mexicana siglo XX 1910–1949. Primera parte* (Mexico: Antigua Librería Robredo, 1949)

——*Literatura mexicana siglo XX 1910–1949. Guías bibliográficas. Segunda Parte* (Mexico: Antigua Librería Robredo, 1950)

——*La expresión nacional. Letras mexicanas del siglo XIX* (Mexico: Imprenta Universitaria, 1955)

——AND CHRISTOPHER DOMÍNGUEZ MICHAEL, *La literatura mexicana del siglo XX* (Mexico: CONACULTA, 1995)

MASTRETTA, ÁNGELES, *Arráncame la vida* (Madrid: Suma de Letras, 2001); first pub. 1985

——*Mal de amores*, 8th edn, (Madrid: Punto de Lectura, 2004); first pub. 1996

McCLINTOCK, ANNE, *Imperial Leather: Race, Gender and Sexuality in the Colonial Contest* (London: Routledge, 1995)

MEAD JR, ROBERT G., 'Carlos Fuentes, airado novelista mexicano', *Hispania*, 50 (1967), 229–35

MEJÍA, EDUARDO, 'La diestra ironía', *Novedades*, 31 March 1985, p. 3

MÉNDEZ, IGNACIO, '*La ciudad y el viento*', *México en la Cultura*, supl. *Novedades*, 19 August 1962, p. 11

MENDIZÁBAL, MAYLING, 'El complejo laberinto femenino *Arráncame la vida*', CNIPL/EXP. AM

MENDOZA, MARÍA LUISA, 'Carlos Fuentes. El Mexicano', *El Excélsior*, 6 December 1959, FR/CF

MEOUCHI, EDMUNDO, 'Buñuelosis galopante...', FR/CF

MERCADO ENRIQUE, 'Arráncame el sosiego', CNIPL/EXP.AM

MEYER, JEAN, *The Cristero Rebellion: The Mexican People between Church and State, 1926–1929*, trans. by Richard Southern (Cambridge: Cambridge University Press, 1976)

MEZA, GILBERTO, 'El poder y el celofán', *La Jornada*, 22 June 1985, pp. 1, 4

MICHELENA, MARGARITA, '¡Estas sí! Palabras de mujer', *Siempre*, 19 February 1986, pp. 20–21

——'¿Qué pasa allí? El Premio Villarrutia', *El Excélsior*, 10 February 1986, p. 7A

MILLÁN, MARÍA DEL CARMEN, *Diccionario de escritores mexicanos* (Mexico: UNAM, 1967)

MILLER, BETH, *Women in Hispanic Literature: Icons and Fallen Idols* (Berkeley: University of California Press, 1983)

MOLINA, JAVIER, 'En *Arráncame la vida*, la consorte del poder: Campbell (mesa redonda sobre la novela política)', *La Jornada*, 28 August 1988, p. 23

MONSIVÁIS, CARLOS, 'Carlos Fuentes visto por Carlos Monsiváis', FR/CF

——'Sergio Pitol: Las mitologías del rencor y del humor', *La Jornada Semanal*, 16 July 1989, pp. 23–29; repr. in *Tiempo cerrado, tiempo abierto. Sergio Pitol ante la crítica*, ed. by Eduardo Serrato (México: Ediciones Era, 1994), pp. 40–52; and in *Sergio Pitol. El sueño de lo real*, ed. by Pedro Domene (Veracruz: Universidad Veracruzana, 2002), pp. 168–80

MONTAÑO GARFIAS, ERICKA, 'Confieren a Carlos Monsiváis el premio literario Juan Rulfo', *La Jornada*, 5 September 2006, <http://www.jornada.unam.mx/2006/09/05/index.php?section=cultura&article=a04n1cul> [accessed 11 February 2010]

MONTERO, OSCAR J., 'The Role of Ixca Cienfuegos in the Thematic Fabric of *La región más transparente*', *Hispanófila*, 59 (1976), 61–83

MOORE, ERNEST, *Bibliografía de novelistas de la Revolución Mexicana* (New York: Burt Franklin, 1972); first pub. 1941

MUDROVCIC, MARÍA EUGENIA, 'Reading Latin American Literature Abroad: Agency and Canon Formation in the Sixties and Seventies', in *Voice-Overs: Translation and Latin American Literature*, ed. by Daniel Balderston and Mary Schwartz (New York: State University of New York Press, 2002), pp. 129–43

NAVARRETE MAYA, LAURA, 'Dolores Castro', in *Diccionario de escritores mexicanos siglo XX. Desde las generaciones del ateneo y novelistas de la revolución hasta nuestros días*, Tomo I (A-CH), ed. by Aurora M. Ocampo (Mexico: UNAM, 1988), pp. 348–49

NEWELL, ROBERTO G., and LUIS F. RUBIO, *Mexico's Dilemma: The Political Origins of Economic Crisis* (Boulder, CO: Westview Press, 1984)

NOVARO, OCTAVIO, 'Perfiles de Mexico. Dolores Castro', *El Día*, 28 July 1979, p. 16

NOVO, SALVADOR, 'Carlos Fuentes, una revelación', *El Sol de México en la Cultura*, supl. *El sol de México*, 14 August 1977, p. 2

OCAMPO, AURORA M., 'Gregorio López y Fuentes', in *Diccionario de escritores mexicanos siglo XX. Desde las generaciones del ateneo y novelistas de la revolución hasta nuestros días*, Tomo IV (H-LL), ed. by Aurora M. Ocampo (Mexico: UNAM, 1997), pp. 462–65

——AND EDUARDO SERRATO CÓRDOVA, 'Sergio Pitol', in *Diccionario de escritores mexicanos siglo XX. Desde las generaciones del ateneo y novelistas de la revolución hasta nuestros días*, Tomo VII, ed. by Aurora M. Ocampo (Mexico: UNAM), pp. 528–40

OLCOTT, JOCELYN, *Revolutionary Women in Postrevolutionary Mexico* (Durham, NC: Duke University Press, 2006)

OROPESA, SALVADOR A., 'Popular Culture and Gender/Genre Construction in Mexican Bolero by Ángeles Mastretta', in *Bodies and Biases: Sexualities in Hispanic Cultures and Literature*, ed. by David William Foster and Roberto Reis (Minneapolis: University of Minnesota Press, 1996), pp. 137–64

ORTIZ FLORES, PATRICIA, 'Ángeles Mastretta' in *Diccionario de escritores mexicanos siglo XX. Desde las generaciones del ateneo y novelistas de la revolución hasta nuestros días*, Tomo V, ed. by Aurora M. Ocampo (Mexico: UNAM, 2000), pp. 171–75

OVERTON, BILL, *The Novel of Female Adultery: Love and Gender in Continental European Fiction, 1830–1900* (London: Macmillan, 1996)

PACHECO, JOSÉ EMILIO, 'Notas bibliográficas', *Estaciones. Revista Literaria de México*, summer 1958, no. 10, pp. 193–96

PARODI, ENRIQUETA DE, 'Yo también... Adelita por Consuelo Salgado', *El Nacional*, 25 August 1936, 2nd section, p. 6

PAZ, OCTAVIO 'La máscara y la transparencia', in *Homenaje a Carlos Fuentes. Variaciones interpretativas en torno a su obra*, ed. by Helmy F. Giacoman (New York: Las Americas, 1971), pp. 17–22

——'The Labyrinth of Solitude', in *The Labyrinth of Solitude*, trans. by Lysander Kemp, Yara Milos, Rachel Phillips Belash (London: Penguin, 1990)

PERALTA, BRAULIO, 'Deseo narrar sucesos para sacarmelos del alma. Mi novela es una historia, no un ensayo feminista: Ángeles Mastretta', *La Jornada*, 11 June 1985, p. 25

PEREIRA ALVES, A., '*El indio*. Novela de Gregorio López y Fuentes', *Letras*, June 1938, p. 4

PERKINS, DAVID, *Is Literary History Possible?* (Baltimore, MD: Johns Hopkins University Press, 1992)

PITOL, SERGIO, *El desfile del amor* (Mexico: Era, 1989); first pub. 1984

——'Historia de unos premios', in *Sergio Pitol. Los territorios del viajero*, ed. by José Balza et al. (Mexico: Ediciones Era, 2000), pp. 9–22

POHLENZ, RICARDO, 'El desfile de Pitol', *El Excélsior*, 25 July 1985, p. 2

PONIATOWSKA, ELENA, 'Carlos Fuentes, un tropel de caballos desbocados', *Novedades*, April 1958, pp. 1–2

——*Las siete cabritas* (Mexico: Era, 2000)

PORRA, GONZALO DE LA, 'Puntos de Vista. Los "Premios Nacionales"', *El Universal*, 27 March 1936 1st section, p. 3

PORTUONDO, JOSÉ ANTONIO,'La concreción de un mito', in *Recopilación de textos sobre la novela de la Revolución Mexicana*, ed. by Rogelio Rodríguez Coronel (Havana: Casa de las Américas, 1975), pp. 283–87

PUIG, VALENTÍN, 'Sergio Pitol. *El desfile del amor*', *El Universal*, 12 December 1986, p. 2

RADWAY, JANICE A., *Reading the Romance: Women, Patriarchy and Popular Literature* (Chapel Hill: University of North Carolina Press, 1991)

RAMÍREZ LEYVA, EDELMIRA, 'Mastretta y las mujeres de su ficción', in *Mujeres latinoamericanas del siglo XX. Historia y cultura. Tomo I*, ed. by Luisa Campuzano (Mexico: Universidad Autónoma and Casa de las Americas, 1998), pp. 247–54

RAMÍREZ, LUIS ENRIQUE, *La ingobernable. Encuentros y desencuentros con Elena Garro* (Mexico: Hoja Casa Editorial, 2000)

RANGEL GUERRA, ALFONSO, 'La novela de Carlos Fuentes', *Armas y Letras*, 1958, pp. 76–80

REEVE, RICHARD M., 'Octavio Paz and Hiperión in *La región más transparente*: Plagiarism, Caricature Or...?', *Chasqui*, 3 (1974), 13–25

——'The Making of *La región más transparente*: 1949–1974', in *Carlos Fuentes: A Critical View*, ed. by Robert Brody and Charles Rossman (Austin: University of Texas Press, 1982), pp. 34–63

REYES, ALFONSO, and HÉCTOR PÉREZ MARTÍNEZ, *A vuelta de correo. Una polémica sobre la literatura nacional*, ed. by Silvia Molina (Mexico: UNAM and Universidad de Colima, 1988)

REYES, JUAN JOSÉ, 'Riesgos ante la historia', *Semanario Cultural*, supl. *Novedades*, 2 June 1985, p. 3

——'De mujeres y espejismos', *Novedades*, 25 June 1989, CNIPL/EXP.SP

ROBLES, MARTHA, *La sombra fugitiva. Escritoras en la cultura nacional* (Mexico: UNAM, 1985)

RUBENSTEIN, ANNE, *Bad Language, Naked Ladies, and Other Threats to the Nation: A Political History of Comic Books in Mexico* (Durham, NC: Duke University Press, 1998)

RUIZ ABREU, ALVARO, *La cristera, una literatura negada (1928–1992)* (Mexico: Universidad Autónoma Metropolitana-Xochimilco, 2003)

SABORIT, ANTONIO, 'La comedia de la ignorancia jamás imaginada', *Nexos*, July 1985, pp. 47–51

SALAS-ELORZA, JESÚS, *La narrativa dialogica de Sergio Pitol* (Providence, RI: Ediciones Inti, 1999)

SALAZAR MALLÉN, RUBÉN, 'En torno a la novela. *El indio*, de Gregorio López y Fuentes', *El Universal*, 19 December 1935, 1st section, p. 3

SCHAEFER, CLAUDIA, *Textured Lives: Women, Art and Representation in Modern Mexico* (Tucson: University of Arizona Press, 1992)

SCHELL, PATIENCE A., *Church and State Education in Revolutionary Mexico City* (Tucson: University of Arizona Press, 2003)

SCHWARTZ, PERLA, 'Una hojeada a la novela de Mastretta', CNIPL/EXP.AM

SEGRE, ERICA, *Intersected Identities: Strategies of Visualization in Nineteenth and Twentieth-Century Mexican Culture* (New York: Berghahn Books, 2007)

SELVA, SALOMÓN DE LA, 'Un gran libro mexicano. *El indio* de Gregorio López y Fuentes', *El Universal*, 24 October 1935, 1st section, pp. 3, 10

SERRATO, EDUARDO C., 'Pitol: la nueva picaresca', *El Nacional*, 8 June 1991, pp. 12–13

SHOWALTER, ELAINE, *A Literature of Their Own from Charlotte Bronte to Doris Lessing* (London: Virago, 1999)

SIMPSON, AMELIA S., *Detective Fiction from Latin America* (London: Associated University Presses, 1990)

SMITH, PETER H., 'Mexico Since 1946: Dynamics of an Authoritarian Regime', in *Mexico Since Independence*, ed. by Leslie Bethell (Cambridge: Cambridge University Press, 1991), pp. 321–96

SMITH, VERITY, 'Canon. The Literary Canon in Spanish America', in *The Encyclopedia of Latin American Literature*, ed. by Verity Smith (London: Fitzroy Dearborn Publishers, 1997), pp. 163–64

SOLANA, RAFAEL, [UNTITLED], *El Universal*, 14 September 1958, FR/CF

SOMMER, DORIS, *Foundational Fictions: The National Romances of Latin America* (Berkeley: University of California Press, 1991)

SOMMERS, JOSEPH, 'La búsqueda de la identidad: *La región más transparente* por Carlos Fuentes', in *Homenaje a Carlos Fuentes. Variaciones interpretativas en torno a su obra*, ed. by Helmy F. Giacoman (New York: Las Americas, 1971) pp. 277–326

SPERATTI PIÑERO, E. S., 'Carta abierta a Carlos Fuentes a propósito de su primera novela', *Universidad de Mexico*, April 1958, p. 28

STAVANS, ILAN, *Antiheroes: Mexico and Its Detective Novel*, trans. by Jesse H. Lytle and Jennifer A. Mattson (London: Associated University Presses, 1997)

STEELE, CYNTHIA, *Narrativa indigenista en los Estados Unidos y México*, trans. by Manuel Fernández Perera (Mexico: Instituto Nacional Indigenista, 1985)

——*Politics, Gender and the Mexican Novel, 1968–1988: Beyond the Pyramid* (Austin: University of Texas Press, 1992)

TANNER, TONY, *Adultery in the Novel: Contract and Transgression* (Baltimore, MD: Johns Hopkins University Press, 1979)

THIEBAUT, GUY, *La Contre-révolution mexicaine à travers sa littérature. L'Exemple du roman cristero de 1926 à nos jours* (Paris : L'Harmattan, 1997)

THORNTON, NIAMH, *Women and the War Story in Mexico: La Novela de la Revolución* (Lampeter: Edwin Mellen Press, 2006)

TORRIENTE, LOLÓ DE LA, '*El indio* y Huasteca en su tiempo', in *Recopilación de textos sobre la novela de la Revolución Mexicana*, ed. by Rogelio Rodríguez Coronel (Havana: Casa de las Américas, 1975), pp. 308–15

URRUTIA, ELENA, '*El desfile del amor*', *La Jornada*, 1 July 1985, p. 23

——'Novela premiada por Anagrama. *El desfile del amor* es una comedia de errores: Pitol', *La Jornada*, 21 December 1984, p. 25

VALDÉS, MARÍA ELENA DE, *The Shattered Mirror: Representations of Women in Mexican Literature* (Austin: University of Texas Press, 1998)

VALDEZ, JOSEFINA LARA, *Diccionario bio-bibliográfico de escritores contemporáneos de México* (Mexico: INBA, 1988)

VALENZUELA RODARTE, ALBERTO, *Historia de la literatura en México* (Mexico: Editorial Jus, 1961)

VAUGHAN, MARY K., *Cultural Politics in Revolution: Teachers, Peasants, and Schools in Mexico, 1930–1940* (Tucson: University of Arizona Press, 1997)

VEGA, PATRICIA, 'Ángeles Mastretta, Premio Mazatlán de Literatura 1985, por su novela', *La Jornada*, 6 January 1986, p. 25.

VELÁZQUEZ MAYORAL, CARLOS, 'Ángeles Mastretta, *Arráncame la vida*, México, Océano, 1986 2ª ed.', *El Día*, 26 May 1986, p. 10

VILLARREAL, MINERVA MARGARITA, '*Arráncame la vida* novela rosa mexicana', *Punto*, 19 May 1986, pp. 19–20

VILLORO, JUAN, 'Los anteojos perdidos', in *Sergio Pitol. Los territorios del viajero*, ed. by José Balza et al. (Mexico: Ediciones Era, 2000), pp. 93–101

WATERS, WENDY, 'Remapping Identities: Road Construction and Nation Building in Postrevolutionary Mexico', in *The Eagle and the Virgin: Nation and Cultural Revolution in Mexico, 1920–1940*, ed. by Mary K. Vaughan and Stephen E. Lewis (Durham, NC: Duke University Press, 2006), pp. 221–42

WEST, ANTHONY, 'El New Yorker comenta la obra de Carlos Fuentes', *México en la Cultura* supl. *Novedades*, 12 March 1961, p. 4

WILKIE, JAMES W. 'The Meaning of the Cristero Religious War Against the Mexican Revolution', *Journal of Church and State*, 8 (1966), 214–33

YUVAL-DAVIS, NIRA, *Gender and Nation* (London: Sage Publications, 1997)

ZENDEJAS, FRANCISCO, 'Multilibros', *El Excélsior*, 4 April, 1958 section B, pp. 1, 3

——'Multilibros' *El Excélsior*, 9 April 1958, 1st section, p. 5

——'Multilibros', *El Excélsior*, 5 August 1962, p. 2C

——'Multilibros', *El Excélsior* 1 October 1962, pp. 1B, 3B

——'Narrativa tres en uno', *La Cultura al Día*, supl. *El Excélsior*, 26 February 1983, p. 2

INDEX

*For Product Safety Concerns and Information please contact
our EU representative GPSR@taylorandfrancis.com Taylor & Francis
Verlag GmbH, Kaufingerstraße 24, 80331 München, Germany*

T - #0097 - 090625 - C0 - 247/170/7 [9] - CB - 9781907975059 - Matt Lamination